TULIPS

TULIPS

Species and Hybrids
for the Gardener

RICHARD WILFORD

TIMBER PRESS

Frontispiece: *Tulipa kaufmanniana* 'Giuseppe Verdi'
Page 6: *Tulipa clusiana* 'Cynthia'
Page 8: *Tulipa kaufmanniana*

Published in 2006 by
Timber Press, Inc.
The Haseltine Building
133 S.W. Second Avenue, Suite 450
Portland, Oregon 97204-3527, U.S.A.
www.timberpress.com
For contact information regarding editorial, marketing, sales, and
distribution in the United Kingdom, see www.timberpress.co.uk.

Printed in Hong Kong

Library of Congress Cataloging-in-Publication Data

Wilford, Richard, 1964–
    Tulips : species and hybrids for the gardener / Richard Wilford.
        p. cm.
    Includes bibliographical references and index.
    ISBN-13: 978-0-88192-763-4 (hardback)
    ISBN-10: 0-88192-763-5
    1. Tulips. 2. Tulips—Varieties. I. Title.
    SB413.T9W55 2006
    635.9'3432—dc22
                                                            2005014685

A catalog record for this book is also available from the British Library.

CONTENTS

Acknowledgements 7
1 Introduction 9
2 Geography 13
3 The Tulip Plant 21
4 Cultivation 33
5 History & Classification 51
6 Species Descriptions 74
7 The Genus *Amana* 173
8 Garden Hybrid Tulips 176
Conversion Table 197
Where to Buy Tulip Species 198
Glossary 200
Bibliography 202
Index 206

ACKNOWLEDGEMENTS

This book is an amalgamation of past and present knowledge about tulips. My aim is to bring together in one volume the findings of botanists and horticulturists from the last two hundred and fifty years and combine them with my own observations and experience of growing these wonderful plants. I have had support from a number of people, and their help with this book is greatly appreciated.

Firstly, I would like to thank the Royal Botanic Gardens, Kew, for allowing me use of the magnificent library and outstanding living collections during the preparation of this book. In particular I would like to thank Nigel Taylor, Mike Fay, Stewart Henchie, and Mike Sinnott for their help, advice, and support.

When I started work at Kew at the beginning of 1989, I was given the bulb collection to look after, under the watchful eye of Tony Hall. Tulips were part of that collection and one of the few genera I recognized straight away. Little did I know that fifteen years later I would be writing a book about them. I would like to thank Tony Hall not only for showing me how to grow bulbs properly but also for making me realize how fascinating these plants are.

Brian Mathew was a botanist in the herbarium when I started at Kew and his knowledge of bulbs is legendary. He has patiently answered my questions and has always been an inspiration through his writing.

From Timber Press I would like to thank Anna Mumford for giving me the opportunity to write this book.

Last but not least I must thank my wife, Kate, and sons, Tom and Matthew, for putting up with me when I appeared to live in another world, a world far removed from the realities of everyday life. I filled their garden, greenhouse, and cold frame with tulips. Without my family's support and understanding, this book would not have been possible.

1

INTRODUCTION

A tulip must be one of the most recognizable flowers in the garden. Even someone without the slightest interest in plants or gardening should be able to tell you what a tulip looks like. Asked to conjure up a picture in their mind's eye and most people will probably see a simple-looking plant with two or three leaves emerging from the ground and a tall, straight stem holding a brightly coloured (probably red) cup-shaped flower. However, ask a number of people where tulips come from, and the answers will not be so clear.

The tulips in parks and gardens today are far removed from their wild ancestors. Growers have selected, hybridized, modified, and developed their plants to produce the remarkable number of cultivars on offer. Most of the tulip bulbs available commercially come from Holland, where growers have been cultivating them for hundreds of years and producing millions each year to sell around the world. Fly to Amsterdam in spring and, as the plane descends, you can see the remarkable strips of colour from the orderly rows of flowering bulbs covering the seemingly endless flat fields. The soil here is ideal for growing bulbs, but tulips are not native to this part of the world. So where do tulips grow wild?

Turkey is a common answer, but the tulips that grow wild there represent only a fraction of the total number of known tulip species. The reason Turkey is so strongly linked to the tulip is that the first tulips to arrive in Europe came from Turkey in the sixteenth century, where their beauty was appreciated long before the bulbs became popular in Europe. To find the ancestral home of the tulip you have to look further east, to the steppes, hills, and mountains of central Asia.

Tulip species are less widely grown than the garden hybrids, and they are unlikely to ever outsell them or even approach their level of popularity, but more and more are becoming available. Today even the casual gardener is aware of their existence. The various species available are frequently listed under the heading 'botanical tulips', which makes them sound a bit dull or specialized—only for enthusiasts and probably difficult to grow. Tulip species are not difficult to grow and they are certainly not dull.

Plant enthusiasts and specialists often disregard hybrids in favour of species, and tulips have not escaped this peculiar brand of horticultural snobbery. However, a new audience is emerging, drawn to tulip species by their more subtle beauty and their longevity in the garden, providing they are given the right conditions.

You do not have to buy species tulips new every year to guarantee flowers. Plant your bulbs in the right place and they will reward you with colourful blooms year after year, and may even increase by themselves to form sizeable colonies in time. As the number of commercially available species increases, so does the desire for gardeners to understand them, learn how to grow them, and find out how they differ from each other and where they come from.

The last botanical monograph on the genus *Tulipa* was published in 1940. It was written by Sir Daniel Hall, director of the John Innes Horticultural Institution, where a large number of the species were grown. Part of this collection was later passed on to Cambridge Botanic Garden, England, where the National Collection of tulip species is now held. More recently, Anna Pavord wrote *The Tulip* (1999), a wonderful book on the history of the tulip. Pavord included a review of the species, but the heart of her book is the story of the garden tulip, from its cultivation in Persian and Turkish gardens in the fifteenth and sixteenth centuries, to the modern cultivars still being produced in Holland. I have not attempted to cover the story of the garden tulip, as I could not hope to improve on Anna Pavord's work and it is pointless covering ground that has already been written about so beautifully. What I have done is to take a closer look at the species.

To fully appreciate the variability of tulips and understand how they differ from each other, you have to get to know the wild species. Many countries in the tulip homelands of western and central Asia are now becoming more accessible to Western botanists. In the second half of the twentieth century, new floras such as *Flora Iranica* and *Flora of Turkey and the East Aegean Islands* (hereafter *Flora of Turkey*) have been researched and published, helping us to understand the genus *Tulipa* better. However, classifying wild tulips is a complicated business. You can study the flora of a region and grow representatives in your garden, but neither activity can prepare you for the bewildering variety of forms of tulips that you will encounter in the wild.

This book is a gardener's guide so I have concentrated on species that are in general cultivation, with some lesser-known species thrown in to give an

Tulipa saxatilis in the Kedros Mountains of Crete

idea of the variation found in the genus. Some of these more obscure plants can be seen in specialist collections and botanic gardens, and it is likely that at least a few will become more widely available in the future. Commercially available tulip species tend to be quite uniform, and often only one clone of each is grown. This means that the species you can buy are distinct, with a few exceptions, which makes them easier to identify than tulips in the wild.

It can be difficult to pick out distinct species and put a name to them when you are standing in a meadow or on a rocky hillside, surrounded by wild tulips in a range of colours, shapes, and sizes. If you are lucky enough to find yourself in this situation, it may be better to give up on the names and just enjoy the tulips for what they are.

Tulip species are the starting point in the long story of the garden tulip and they are still out there, growing in the wild. They may be smaller and less bold than the garden hybrids, and a little extra care may be needed to grow some of them successfully, but they can amaze you with the intensity of their colour and surprise you with the size of their flowers. Growing in distant mountain ranges, hidden gorges, and remote meadows are plants that wouldn't look out of place in the brightest, most flamboyant garden. They are beautiful, they are infinitely variable, and they can be grown in your own backyard. How can you resist?

2
GEOGRAPHY

The best way to grow a healthy, thriving plant in cultivation is to find out where it comes from and try and mimic the conditions it grows under in the wild. Looking at a plant's geography can indicate how much light or shade the plant needs, the type of soil it prefers, the temperatures it can survive, and, most importantly, when to water and how much water to give. Tulips grow from a bulb, which immediately tells you that for part of the year they survive with little or no water. The formation of a bulb is an adaptation to a prolonged period of drought. Tulips grow in areas where summers are dry. How dry and for how long depends on the climate where they grow. Looking at a tulip's geography provides important information on its preferred environment.

Mapping out the natural range of a genus and highlighting where variation among the plants is most concentrated can provide clues to how the species have spread. A large number of distinct species in one area suggests that the genus has occupied this area for a long time. A great deal of variation, with many forms differing only slightly from one another, indicates an area where the species are still developing. This latter situation is especially true of the genus *Tulipa*, in which the species are still evolving and advancing, colonizing new areas, sometimes with the help of man.

Another reason for looking at geography is to find out where to see the plants growing wild. Pictures and books can be helpful and informative, but nothing matches finding a plant growing in its natural habitat. There you experience the conditions firsthand, the strength of the wind in your hair, the intensity of the sun on your back, and the texture of the soil between your fingers. You can see whole plant communities, not just isolated plants in pots. Only then can you really begin to appreciate the environment in which a plant grows.

Tulips grow wild in Europe, North Africa, and Asia. This is where the plants you can buy and grow originally came from, where the range of forms is far greater than is found in commercial stocks, and, most intriguing of all, where tulips yet to be seen in cultivation may be hiding, waiting to be discovered. The range of the genus extends in a broad sweep from the Iberian Peninsula of south-western Europe, along the northern and southern coasts of the Mediterranean, through Turkey, the Middle East and Iran, to central Asia, western China, and the western Himalaya. In the north the range reaches southern Siberia before the climate becomes too cold for tulips to survive. To the south, progress is halted by the hot, dry deserts of the Arabian Peninsula and south-eastern Pakistan, and the Sahara of Africa.

When the number and variety of species across the range of the genus are studied, two centres of diversity can be identified. These are regions where the most variation and highest number of species are found. The main centre of diversity is in central Asia, in an area covering the Tien Shan and Pamir Alai mountain ranges. The second is the Caucasus Mountains, between the Black Sea and the Caspian Sea.

Tulips are usually found in hills and mountains, where the winter may be cold and icy but the spring brings moisture, allowing them to grow and flower before the onset of the hot, dry summer, when they retreat underground. It is in central Asia, in countries like Uzbekistan, Kyrgyzstan, and

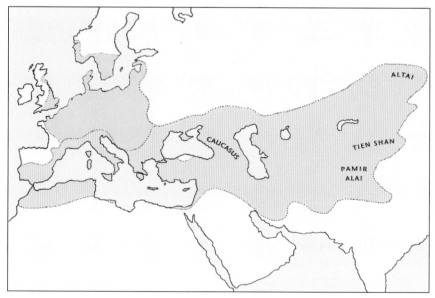

The natural range of the genus *Tulipa*, shown in red, stretches from south-western Europe and North Africa to north-western China and the western Himalaya. The range is extended north in Europe, shown in green, by naturalized plants, primarily *T. sylvestris*.

Tajikistan, that the genus *Tulipa* originated. From here it has spread west, as far as the Atlantic Ocean.

In the wild, tulips frequently grow on grassy or stony slopes, in an open situation, where they are not crowded out or shaded by trees and large shrubs. They can grow on rocky ground or in gorges, emerging between stones or in crevices, or clinging to ledges. Some species, such as *Tulipa borszczowii* and *T. lehmanniana*, have crept away from the mountains and grow in sandy soils, in the steppes of central Asia, while others, like *T. dasystemonoides* and *T. tschimganica*, have explored higher elevations and become established in subalpine regions. The majority are confined to the middle ground, in hills or on lower slopes of high mountains.

The range of tulips from the Tien Shan is huge. More than twenty of the species described in this book are native to these mountains. The Tien Shan is made up of many mountain ranges, some reaching over 5000 m (16,400 ft.), that run along the border of Kyrgyzstan and Kazakhstan, and into the Chinese autonomous region of Xinjiang. Most of these ranges, such as the Kirghiz, the Talas Ala Tau, and the Chatkal Range, are south of the city of Almaty and east of Tashkent. To the north-east of Almaty is the Dzungarian Ala Tau and to the north of Tashkent, stretching like a finger pointing towards the Aral Sea, is the Karatau (Qarataū) Range. Many tulips in the Tien Shan are widespread, their populations overlapping and giving rise to hybrids. They include the well-known species *Tulipa greigii* and *T. kaufmanniana*. *Tulipa kolpakowskiana* and its close relatives, such as *T. ostrowskiana*, *T. tetraphylla*, and *T. iliensis*, are found in these ranges, as is another group of closely related species that includes *T. albertii* and *T. vvedenskyi*. The Tien Shan is also home to several of the species classified in section *Biflores*, including *T. turkestanica*, *T. bifloriformis*, *T. dasystemon*, and *T. tarda*.

To the south-east of Tashkent is the Fergana Basin, with the Fergana Range in the east, home to the beautiful *Tulipa ferganica*. To the south of Fergana are the Turkestan and Zeravshan Ranges, the latter home to *T. orithyioides* and the dazzling red *T. ingens*. These mountains are part of the Pamir Alai, which, like the Tien Shan, is a group of ranges, reaching nearly 7500 m (24,600 ft.) high. They form a western extension of the Himalaya and to the south they merge with the Hindu Kush of Afghanistan. Widely cultivated tulips from this region include *T. linifolia*, *T. praestans*, and the magnificent *T. fosteriana*. Some species from the Tien Shan, such as *T. dasystemon*, *T. turkestanica*, and *T. neustruevae*, are also found in the Pamir Alai.

The Altai Mountains rise up in north-eastern Kazakhstan, continuing into north-western China, Mongolia, and southern Siberia. The climate here is severely continental, with long, freezing winters. Summers can be hot, reaching 40°C (104°F) on the lower slopes, but they are fairly short. This region is the northern limit for the natural range of the genus *Tulipa* and the few species that grow here include *T. uniflora*, *T. heteropetala*, and *T. patens*. These tulips are used to dry winters because all water is frozen in their natural home. They need to be grown more like alpine plants and are difficult to keep in the open garden in areas where winters are wet and temperatures fluctuate above and below freezing point. *Tulipa altaica* and *T. kolpakowskiana* also reach this far north, the former taking its name from these mountains.

To the south-east of the Pamir Alai, the genus *Tulipa* reaches the western Himalaya, in Kashmir and northern India. Here grows *T. clusiana*, the lady tulip, sometimes reaching altitudes of 3350 m (11,000 ft.). This variable species produces flowers in shades of yellow and white, often with red or pink staining on the outside. It is not confined to this part of the world but is also found much further west, in Afghanistan and Iran. It has even become naturalized in southern Europe and western Turkey.

To the west of the Tien Shan and Pamir Alai are the steppes of the Kyzylkum and Karakum Deserts in southern Kazakhstan, Uzbekistan, and Turkmenistan. Between these two desert regions, the Amu Dar'ya River flows from the Pamir Alai to the Aral Sea. To the north of the Kyzylkum is the Syr Dar'ya River, flowing out of the Fergana Basin, also to the Aral Sea. Few tulips have penetrated this region and those that have, such as *Tulipa bifloriformis*, *T. greigii*, and *T. korolkowii*, usually follow mountain ranges, such as the Karatau Range and the Nuratau Range north of Samarkand, Uzbekistan. *Tulipa borszczowii* and *T. lehmanniana* survive in this dry, inhospitable place, growing in sandy soil and stony desert. Tulips that grow here need careful watering in cultivation and need to be grown in a bulb frame or glasshouse, to keep off excess moisture.

Along the border of Turkmenistan and Iran is the Kopet–Dag Range, home to several species including *Tulipa hoogiana* and *T. montana*. The latter is also found in other parts of Iran, such as the Elburz Mountains, north of Tehran. *Tulipa systola*, *T. ulophylla*, *T. biflora*, *T. sylvestris*, and *T. aucheriana* are among the species found in Iran. Hot, dry summers are common in this part of the world, and tulips from here will also need some protection from rain in cultivation.

In north-western Iran, around Tabriz, and over the border into Azerbaijan and Turkey are more species that can be grown in the open garden, including the various forms of *Tulipa humilis*. A brick-red form of this species, named *T. kurdica*, is found in Iraq, as are *T. biflora* and *T. systola*. From this region northwards the number of species begins to increase as the Caucasus Mountains, the second centre of diversity for the genus *Tulipa*, are reached.

The Caucasus Mountains stretch 1200 km (750 miles) from the Black Sea to the Caspian Sea, through Georgia, Armenia, and Azerbaijan. There are two main ranges, the Greater and Lesser Caucasus, and the highest mountain, Mount Elbrus, reaches 5642 m (18,510 ft.). Tulip species found growing in this region include *Tulipa eichleri, T. julia, T. humilis, T. schrenkii*, and *T. sosnovskyi*. The range of the Turkish species *T. armena* extends into the Caucasus, and *T. biflora* passes through these mountains on its way to south-eastern Europe.

To the north and east of the Black Sea are found *Tulipa biflora, T. bieber-steiniana*, and *T. schrenkii*. This region is also at the western edge of the range of *T. patens*.

Many of the Turkish species, such as *Tulipa agenensis, T. clusiana, T. sin-tenisii*, and *T. undulatifolia*, are plants of cultivated ground and have most likely been introduced from further east. Truly wild species include *T. armena, T. julia, T. biflora*, and *T. humilis*. Despite the extensive study of the Turkish flora, new species are still being discovered, such as *T. cinnabarina* from the Taurus Mountains in the south of the country.

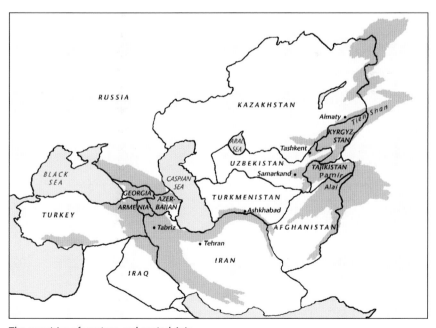

The countries of western and central Asia.

In western Turkey are species that are also found on the Balkan Penin-sula and Greek islands. *Tulipa orphanidea* is a variable species that grows in the mountains of Greece, Bulgaria, and Turkey. Variations of this tulip have been named individually, including the Greek *T. hageri*, the Cretan *T. goulimyi* and *T. doerfleri*, and the Turkish *T. whittallii*. *Tulipa saxatilis* grows in south-western Turkey and on the islands of Rhodes and Crete. *Tulipa sylvestris* is also found in Turkey, as well as a large part of Europe, and a form of *T. undulatifolia*, named *T. boeotica*, is found in the Balkans.

The natural range of the genus *Tulipa* is extended west by *T. sylvestris* in its various guises. Individually named variants of this species from Europe and North Africa include *T. australis*, *T. primulina*, and *T. celsiana*. With this group of tulips, the range of the genus reaches the mountains of Spain and Portugal, and the Atlas Mountains of Morocco.

Other tulips found growing in Europe include *Tulipa agenensis*, *T. prae-cox*, and *T. clusiana*, which are introduced species from Asia. *Tulip cypria* is endemic to Cyprus, and *T. bakeri* and *T. cretica* are endemic to Crete.

In Europe, the range of the genus has expanded north through natural-ization. Like all bulbs, tulips form a storage organ to survive the dry sum-mer, making them easy to transport and sell. In their dormant state, bulbs can travel long distances without any attention, other than keeping them dry and cool. They can sit on the shelves of shops and garden centres for weeks or can be posted around the world without any detrimental effect. Man has undoubtedly helped the spread of tulips and once in their new home some have made the most of their new surroundings. They become naturalized, often spreading by stolons to form small populations in fields, meadows, or-chards, and on waste ground. In this way, the yellow-flowered *Tulipa sylvestris* has reached as far north as Scotland and southern Scandinavia.

It can be difficult to see tulips in the wild. An organized tour to Iran or the Tien Shan is a wonderful experience but can be costly. Visiting other ar-eas within the range of the genus may be problematic due to frequent polit-ical unrest or even war. Turkey is a vast and beautiful country, and well worth a visit, but to see a range of species in a small area, a trip to the Greek island of Crete is ideal.

Crete is home to five species of tulip and with a little searching you should be able to come across them all. *Tulipa goulimyi* is the hardest to find as it grows in only a small area on the western coast of the island, near Falas-sarna. It has attractive, wavy-edged leaves and a red flower that peers from between stones and low shrubs. Closely related is *T. doerfleri*, which grows in larger numbers, in fields in the Kedros Mountains of west-central Crete.

Tulipa goulimyi growing wild in Crete

Tulipa bakeri on the Omalos plain, Crete

On rocky ground and in gorges across the island you can find the tiny, pale pink *Tulipa cretica* and the larger-flowered, pink to lilac-purple *T. saxatilis*. The latter can often be seen high up on gorge walls or cliffs, where the flowers emerge from crevices and ledges. Very similar to *T. saxatilis* is *T. bakeri* but with flowers generally of a deeper pink. The latter grows on the high, flat plains of Omalos and Lassithi, scattered across fields and meadows.

If you visit Crete in early to mid-April, you can find these tulips if you hire a car and explore the gorges, hills, and mountains, which rise to over 2400 m (7900 ft.). The trip will be an excellent introduction to wild tulips and may inspire you to learn more about these beautiful plants. It certainly had that effect on me.

3

THE TULIP PLANT

Previously a huge family with many genera, Liliaceae has now been reduced to only sixteen genera as a result of DNA (deoxyribonucleic acid) studies. These studies indicate major evolutionary groups and help in the analysis of relationships between families and genera. Genera formerly in the Liliaceae have now been placed in separate families, such as Alliaceae, Hyacinthaceae, and Colchicaceae. *Tulipa* is one of the genera that has remained in Liliaceae and is closest to *Erythronium*, the dog's tooth violets, and *Amana* (discussed in chapter 7).

Characteristics shared by the sixteen genera in Liliaceae include the formation of a bulb, corm, or rhizome; the usually leafy stems; and either a solitary flower, or a simple or branched inflorescence. The flowers are composed of six perianth segments (tepals), six stamens, and a superior ovary. A superior ovary is one that is held above the point where the tepals join the stem, so it is found within the flower. An inferior ovary is held behind this point, appearing behind the flower, as in snowdrops (*Galanthus*) and *Narcissus*, both in the Amaryllidaceae.

Tulips grow from a bulb that has a distinct outer layer called a tunic. The leaves are often few, two to four being typical, and they are quite fleshy. They are held alternately on the stem, often crowded towards the base but sometimes more spaced apart. They decrease in size up the stem and clasp it rather than having a distinct petiole. The flower is held erect and is composed of six free tepals, meaning they are not joined to each other at any point. There are no nectaries. The stamens and ovary are shorter than the tepals and held within the flower, the ovary developing into a globular or ellipsoid capsule with three compartments, each one filled with several flat seeds.

To the casual observer, the most obvious differences between tulips are size and flower colour. Plant breeders have worked on these characteristics to produce the multitude of different varieties of garden tulip that you see in bulb catalogues and planted in colourful spring bedding schemes. Dwarf and sturdy or tall and bold, these hybrid tulips have flowers in every colour except blue and true black. The tepals may be delicately fringed or deeply cut, rounded or pointed, sometimes forming elegant, waisted blooms with petals drawn out into long, fine points, as in the lily-flowered hybrids. However, tulips differ in many other respects and, to see the complete range of variation, you need to study the species; after all, it is from these that the garden hybrids have arisen.

Some tulips may have more than one flower to each stem, and in the smallest species these flowers may barely reach 1 cm (0.4 in.) from top to bottom. The leaves can be broad and rounded or narrow and linear, matt or shiny, pale green, deep green, grey, blue-grey, or grey-green, and they may have undulate margins. Sometimes the leaves are marked with brownish streaks and blotches.

Tulipa montana (left) with a solitary, bowl-shaped flower and several linear-lanceolate leaves. *Tulipa turkestanica* (top right) branching flower stem. *Tulipa sprengeri* (bottom right) flower, showing the elliptic outer tepals, the wider inner tepals, and the six stamens surrounding the single ovary.

Look even closer and you can detect less obvious differences, such as the colour of the pollen, the hairiness of the filaments that hold the pollen-producing anthers, the shape of the bulb, and the presence or absence of hairs on the leaves, stem, and bulb tunic. These minute but significant characters may not concern most gardeners, but to those with a keen interest in tulips they are what makes this group of plants so fascinating. These characters also make tulips infuriating because the various classifications of the genus are based on them, yet in many cases they are not constant. This situation can make it very difficult to decide where a species belongs within a classification and even what is a species and what is merely a variety or subspecies. The classification of tulips is dealt with in chapter 5, while this chapter looks at the parts of the tulip plant to highlight the terms used and the characters to watch out for.

The Bulb

A tulip plant replaces its bulb every year. All the food stored in the bulb is used to produce the leaves, stem, and flower. Before the plant dies down for the summer, it has to grow a new bulb, to allow it to survive without water until the following winter.

The bulb is made up of a few thick, creamy white, fleshy scales. At the centre of the bulb are the buds that will develop into the new leaves and flower. The largest bulbs can be 5 cm (2 in.) across, while the smallest may be less than 1 cm (0.4 in.) across. The size of the bulb also depends on the age and health of the plant, reflected in its capacity to produce stored food in the new bulb during the growing season.

On the underside of the bulb is the basal plate, with a semi-circular or arc-shaped zone from which the roots emerge. The bottom of the bulb is rounded but narrows towards the top, ending in a point. The outer layer of the bulb (the bulb tunic) can sometimes extend quite a distance beyond the bulb itself, forming a long, sharp point.

The features of the bulb tunic are important for distinguishing tulip species. This outer layer can be thick, tough, and leathery or thin, brittle, and papery. The colour is usually a shade of brown, sometimes almost black, and in some species it has a strong reddish tint. Carefully peel away the tunic and on its inner surface, in almost all the species, you will see some hairs. The function of these hairs is uncertain, but they could provide added protection from the heat of summer or the cold in winter.

It is common for hairs to be present at the top of the tunic and in a ring around the basal plate. *Tulipa montana*, *T. clusiana*, and *T. linifolia* have such a thick layer of hairs at the top of the bulb that they protrude in a prominent tuft beyond the tunic.

In several species, including *Tulipa fosteriana* and *T. eichleri*, the hairs are straight and form an even layer over the inside surface of the tunic. Some species, such as *T. subpraestans*, have a hairless tunic but in others the hairs can be surprisingly dense and interwoven, forming a thick felt between the tunic and the bulb scales. This latter characteristic is a feature of the species classified in section *Tulipanum*, including *T. julia* and *T. agenensis*.

In the wild it can sometimes be impossible to distinguish between two species without looking at the hairiness of the bulb tunics. Of course, to see this feature requires digging up the bulb, something you really should not

Tulip bulbs: (top row) *Tulipa sylvestris*, *T. hageri*, *T. humilis*; (second row) *T. clusiana*, *T. montana*, *T. kolpakowskiana*, *T. turkestanica*; (third row) *T. greigii*, *T. vvedenskyi* 'Tangerine Beauty', *T. fosteriana*; (bottom row) *T. kaufmanniana* 'Ancilla', *T. grengiolensis*

do. With cultivated plants you can wait until they are dormant and if you grow them in pots you can look at them when repotting.

As well as producing a new bulb every year, tulips often produce additional bulbs (offsets) of varying size. It is not unusual to find three or four bulbs in the place where last year there was one. A few of the offsets may be flowering size, the others can be grown on separately. In this way the tulip increases itself vegetatively and all the offsets will produce new plants identical to the original plant. Many species are stoloniferous, and the buds on the basal plate that form the offsets grow outwards, forming a hollow tube with a new bulb at the end. Not only does the tulip increase in this way, but it spreads as well, creating an expanding colony.

A dropper is formed when a bud on the basal plate grows downwards, producing a new bulb at a much greater depth, occasionally up to 60 cm (2 ft.) below the first bulb. This new bulb can completely replace the original and in this way the tulip can delve deeper into the ground. This process is characteristic of seedlings which in the wild need to pull themselves down into the ground to protect themselves from the heat of summer. Mature tulips prefer to be planted deep, but if they are too near the surface they too can attain their desired depth by producing droppers. Some species, such as *Tulipa tarda*, are very proficient at this.

The Leaves and Stem

You do not have to study tulips for long to realize how much the leaves vary from species to species. They emerge from the ground, the lowest leaf wrapped around the second. It may be some time before the two leaves part to reveal any further leaves and the flower bud. Bulbs that are not going to flower will only produce one leaf.

The leaves are often glaucous (blue-grey to grey-green), but in *Tulipa saxatilis* and *T. bakeri*, for example, they are shiny mid-green and in *T. tarda* they are dull green. A few species have dark markings on the leaves, forming stripes or dashes. These marks are caused by the pigment anthocyanin, which also gives red-flowered tulips their colour. The most commonly grown tulip with these markings is *T. greigii*. There is sometimes a line of short hairs along the leaf margin (ciliate). In some species like *T. lanata* and *T. ingens* the whole leaf is covered in short, fine hairs (pubescent), while others have glabrous (hairless) leaves.

In the species descriptions I have given the dimensions of the lowest leaf,

Tulipa greigii 'Red Riding Hood' leaves

as this is almost invariably the largest. The remaining leaves often decrease rapidly in size up the stem, but in some tulips they are roughly the same size. The dimensions vary enormously, from less than 1 cm (0.4 in.) wide, as in some forms of *Tulipa linifolia* and *T. clusiana*, to 16 cm (7 in.) wide in *T. fosteriana*. Leaves can reach over 30 cm (1 ft.) long but in most species they are between 10 and 25 cm (4–10 in.). The lowest leaf is joined to the stem at or just below ground level. The remaining leaves may be held close to the first like a rosette, as in *T. tarda*, or they are spaced along the stem, as in *T. montana*.

Tulip leaves come in various shapes but are always longer than they are wide. The following terms are commonly used to describe their shapes:

Linear leaves are narrow with virtually parallel sides for most of their length.

Lanceolate leaves are usually wider than linear leaves and have sides gradually coming together to form a point. They are widest near the base.

Elliptic leaves narrow at both ends and are widest at the middle.

Ovate leaves are roughly egg-shaped with a pointed tip and are widest near the base.

Obovate and **oblanceolate** leaves are the reverse of ovate and lanceolate so the widest point is near the tip.

Oblong leaves are rectangular but with rounded ends.

One feature that is often lost in cultivation is the undulate (wavy) leaf margin, especially in tulips that grow in harsh environments, such as *Tulipa systola*. Once in cultivation, where the sun may be less intense and water is

Tulipa systola in cultivation, with longer stems than it normally has in the wild. The large black blotch, narrowly margined with yellow, can be clearly seen at the base of the bright red flower.

more freely given, the leaves become 'softer' and lose this character, especially as they age.

The leaves are held on the stem, which grows from the bulb and terminates in either a solitary flower or branches to hold several flowers. The flower stem begins where the upper leaf joins, which in multi-flowered plants is where the stem may branch. Alternatively the branches can arise further up, as in *Tulipa turkestanica*.

The stem is either glabrous or pubescent and may be the same colour as the leaves or stained with a darker colour such as red or purple, especially near the flower. In the wild, where bulbs are often deep down, a large portion of the stem will be underground. The stem lengths in the species descriptions refer to the aboveground portion, which is very variable and can be different in cultivated and wild plants of the same species. In cultivation, light levels are often lower during the growing season than in the wild and can cause the stems to elongate as the flowers reach for the light. The length of the stem also varies as the flower ages. By the time the seed pods have developed, the stem can be twice as long as when the flower first opened. However, the length of the stem at flowering time gives you an idea of the size of the plant.

The Flower

In common with many other bulbous plants, tulips do not have separate sepals and petals. Instead, they have six colourful, similar-looking perianth segments (tepals). The outer tepals act like sepals, surrounding the flower in bud. As the flower opens, the inner tepals are revealed, along with the six stamens and the single ovary at the centre.

The outer tepals are often narrower than the inner three and their backs are frequently stained a different colour than the rest of the flower. In the

This yellow form of the otherwise red-flowered *Tulipa armena*, from northern Turkey, has been named *T. galatica*. This example has retained its undulate leaf margins in cultivation.

white-flowered *Tulipa biflora*, for example, the backs of the outer tepals are greyish green. In some species, such as *T. clusiana* and *T. kaufmanniana*, the otherwise white or yellow outer tepals have red or purple colouring on their backs. The red-flowered tulips are usually paler on the outside or have a buff or pink blush.

Many of the terms used to describe leaf shapes are also used to describe tepals. They can be ovate, lanceolate, obovate, or elliptic, for example. They can also be rhomboidal (diamond-shaped) or spathulate (spoon-shaped), where the tip is rounded and the tepal then narrows towards the base. The whole flower can be bowl-shaped, with a rounded base, or funnel-shaped, with a narrow base and opening wide to form a star. Funnel-shaped flowers are normally constricted just above the point where they join the stem.

Flower colour in tulips is immensely variable. For example, both red and white species have yellow forms. Pink tulips can range from almost white to lilac and purple. Red tulips can be orange-red, brownish red, scarlet, dark crimson, or blood-red.

In the majority of species, the base of the flower inside is a different colour than the rest of the flower. This area is known as the basal blotch and it varies in size, shape, and colour. It is often a shade of black, blue-black, dark brown, or olive. It can be margined with white or yellow and this margin varies in width. Some species have a yellow blotch at the base of a white flower, such as *Tulipa biflora*, *T. tarda*, and *T. turkestanica*. *Tulipa vvedenskyi* is one of the red-flowered species with a yellow blotch, and *T. saxatilis* and *T. bakeri* are both pink with a yellow blotch margined with white. The diversity of flower colours and colour combinations is one of the reasons tulips are so interesting to grow, but because colour is so variable, it is not a reliable character to use when classifying the species.

One characteristic used to differentiate species is the presence or absence of hairs on the filaments of the flower. The filaments hold the pollen-producing anthers and these two structures make up the stamens, the male reproductive part of the flower. Half the species of genus *Tulipa* have glabrous filaments. The other species have hairs on the filaments. These short hairs are usually in a tuft or boss at the base but in some species, such as *T. turkestanica* and *T. bifloriformis*, there are also wispy hairs along the whole length of the filament. Hairy filaments are usually associated with fine hairs at the base of at least the inner tepals.

The stamens surround the ovary, which is usually a shade of green, yellow, or creamy white

Tulipa vvedenskyi flower

but can have darker staining towards the tip. At the top of the ovary is the stigma, which receives the pollen. The stigma is three-lobed and in most tulips is sessile, meaning it is held directly on top of the ovary. In a few species, including *Tulipa uniflora*, a style holds the stigma above the ovary and can be up to 6 mm (0.25 in.) long. Once pollination has taken place, the ovary swells up and becomes darker. It eventually turns brown and brittle, before splitting open to release the flat, brown seeds stacked in three compartments.

By studying the flower closely you can begin to identify a tulip or at least the group to which it belongs. Looking at the filaments you can immediately assign the plant to one or other side of the genus. Also, hairy filaments are usually found in funnel-shaped flowers and glabrous filaments in bowl-shaped flowers.

The flower colour, blotch size and colour, and the presence of marks or staining on the outer tepals can also be helpful in identifying species, but remember these characters can vary within a single population. The colour, shape, length, and number of leaves are also worth noting and, looking even closer, the hairiness of the leaves and stems, the colour of the anthers and filaments, and in some cases the colour of the stigma. Do not forget to look at

The flower of *Tulipa turkestanica* has wispy hairs along the length of its filaments.

the bulb if you can, especially the hairs on the tunic. Even if you are still confused, and there is no shame in admitting that you are, at least you are getting to know the plants more intimately. Only then will you really begin to understand them.

In the species descriptions, the months of the year indicating flowering times refer to plants growing in the Northern Hemisphere. The names of the seasons are, of course, interchangeable.

Genetics

To make sense of a genus in which the species are so morphologically variable, it can be useful to look beneath the surface, to study the genetic makeup of the plants. The chromosomes of tulips have been studied since the early twentieth century and more recently, since the 1980s, the study of DNA (deoxyribonucleic acid) has been used to work out relationships between genera and the place of species within those genera.

Chromosomes are found within the nucleus of a cell and carry the genetic information, mostly in the form of DNA. The DNA carries the genetic code and so determines the exact makeup of an organism. Prior to a cell dividing, the chromosomes become visible under a light microscope and can be counted, giving the chromosome number. Tulips have a chromosome number of 24 ($2n = 24$). This is the diploid number. In normal cell division (mitosis) the resulting cells will have the same number as the original, but when a cell divides to produce gametes for sexual reproduction (meiosis), each new cell has half this number (haploid) so the nuclei of tulip pollen grains will have 12 chromosomes ($n = 12$). When the nuclei of two gametes fuse (from the pollen and egg cells), the resulting cell (the proembryo) will have the normal complement for that plant.

It was soon discovered that many tulips have more than the basic number of $2n = 24$. This situation is not uncommon in plants and is called polyploidy. Tulips may be triploid ($2n = 36$), tetraploid ($2n = 48$), or pentaploid ($2n = 60$). These polyploid plants are usually larger and more vigorous, and they often have reduced fertility so do not produce much viable seed. The plants compensate by being more stoloniferous, allowing them to spread vegetatively, but all the individuals will be exactly the same genetically.

A polyploid tulip arises from a diploid tulip so you could call it a secondary stage in the evolution of a species. The reduction of fertility suggests that polyploidy is an evolutionary dead-end. It is from the fertile diploid plants that new species will eventually evolve. Sexual reproduction involves the genes of two plants coming together to create a new individual. This is where variation among plants is initiated. The significance placed on polyploidy in the naming of tulip species varies from author to author, but without doubt the study of chromosome numbers has helped in the classification of the genus and in the understanding of its natural distribution.

The study of plant DNA (known as genetic fingerprinting) is more complex, but because it deals with the actual 'building blocks', the information is more significant. Comparing the DNA of various closely related plants can indicate how they have evolved and what their common ancestors might be. It can also show that two apparently similar plants have evolved independently of each other and are not closely related. This work is ongoing, notably at the Royal Botanic Gardens, Kew, but the conclusions so far, regarding the genus *Tulipa*, have been included in the classification in chapter 5 and in the species descriptions in chapter 6.

One conclusion that can be drawn from DNA studies is that the small genus *Amana* is clearly separate from *Tulipa*. These species, which have previously been included within *Tulipa*, are discussed in chapter 7.

4
CULTIVATION

Digging a hole, planting the bulbs, and waiting for them to flower constitute a perfectly acceptable way to grow tulips if you are going to replace the bulbs every year. This is the most common method of growing hybrid tulips, which are bred for their uniform flowers and even height but tend to decline after the first year. One of the attractions of tulip species is their ability to flower every year without loss of health or vigour. To keep them alive for more than one season you need to look after them when they are in growth, to ensure they can produce enough food to store in the bulb for the next year. You also have to provide the appropriate conditions during their summer dormant period if you want them to come back the following winter. As a general rule, tulips like plenty of light and air in winter and spring, and little or no water in summer, just like most other summer dormant bulbs.

Water

Watering is the most important task a gardener undertakes because it has to be done regularly and so offers the most opportunities to make mistakes. If you water at the wrong time, or give too much or too little, the health of the plant can be affected and you may even kill it. Correct watering is especially important for bulbs, whose requirements change dramatically during the course of the year. Fortunately, some tulips are surprisingly tolerant and most will put up with a few mistakes; it is only consistently poor watering that will finish them off.

The critical time for watering tulips is at the beginning and end of the growing season, as the plants are coming into growth or dying down. When they are dormant you can leave them dry and when in growth you will have to make a conscious effort to overwater them. The majority of widely grown species are common precisely because they are easy to grow. A few need extra care, especially those from regions of central Asia that have particularly long and dry summers, such as *Tulipa regelii* and *T. korolkowii*, or species from high altitudes, where there is little available moisture in the freezing winter. These will need more careful watering, even when in full growth.

Species like *Tulipa humilis*, *T. tarda*, and *T. sylvestris* will survive even if the soil remains moist during the summer, although it is better to keep them dry if you can. The only real exception is *T. sprengeri*, which seems to prefer some moisture in the soil when it is dormant and even a little light shade. This is the one species that grows better under deciduous trees or shrubs—not exactly a woodland plant but one for a woodland edge perhaps.

Growing tulips in the garden reduces the control you have over the amount of water they receive. You can water them if they are dry, but if it rains they are going to get wet. Growing tulips in pots gives control back to you because you can keep them under cover, in a glasshouse or cold frame, and water them only when they need it.

Root growth can start in late summer so watering should commence then or just after you have potted the bulbs. Give the pots a good soak to start them off, then leave them. Only when the soil has dried out again should more water be given. Do not just scratch the surface but stick your finger down in the pot to test the soil. If there is some moisture there, leave the pot a little longer, but if the soil is dry, give it another good soak. At this time of year it is far better to water like this than to give a dribble of water every day or so. However, it is important not to let the soil dry out completely as the new roots could be damaged if starved of water.

Once growth has appeared above ground, which in some cases is as early as November in the Northern Hemisphere, watering can be increased. Use the same method of watering but

A good dark form of *Tulipa humilis* (sold as *T. pulchella violacea*) growing in the open

now only let the top couple of centimetres (about 1 in.) of the soil dry out before watering again. Avoid getting water on the leaves as it can collect at their base and may cause them to rot. As the leaves grow, the plant will naturally draw moisture out of the soil so the need for water will increase as spring approaches. The weather will also play a part. A few mild, sunny winter days can soon dry out a pot of soil so check plants regularly, especially as growth accelerates.

During the spring keep the soil moist. This will keep the tulip growing and maximize the amount of food it can produce for the new bulb. Eventually, once flowering is over, the bulb will start drawing in the nutrients from the leaves, which in turn will start to brown around the edges. At this time watering must be reduced. Let the soil dry out before watering again. When you do water, do not completely soak the soil each time. At this stage it is better to let the soil become too dry than to keep it too wet. By early summer the tulip will have retreated into its bulb and the soil can be left dry.

How much moisture is needed during the summer will depend on the species and where the pots are kept. It is unlikely that you will have to water the soil directly, but you can keep the pots cool so the soil is not baked dry. A glasshouse can become very hot on a sunny day, causing tulips like *Tulipa humilis* to suffer. Some dryland species, such as *T. kolpakowskiana*, seem unaffected by these conditions, but it is better not to overheat the pots if you can help it. Keep them under cover but out of direct sunlight. Alternatively, tip out the bulbs, clean them, and store them somewhere cool and dry, in paper bags or envelopes.

Soil and Situation

One general rule to follow is that good drainage is essential for tulips whether they are grown in pots or the open garden. Plant them in wet, heavy soil and they will rot away in the summer. I have grown two of the more tolerant species, *Tulipa humilis* and *T. turkestanica*, in heavy clay soil and they have survived, but this soil often dries out in summer; in fact it can become rock hard. Although such growing conditions are far from ideal, they do show that rules are there to be broken or are at least open to interpretation.

If you are planting tulip bulbs in the garden, the soil may need to be amended to improve drainage. Adding sand or organic matter to the soil can open up the texture, making it lighter and allowing excess water to drain away freely. What you must avoid is having dormant bulbs sitting in sticky, wet soil.

Growing tulips in pots allows you to use the soil of your choice. A loam-based soil mix rather than peat-based is best. Add a significant proportion of sharp grit to the soil, about one-third by volume. Peat-based soil mixes are notoriously difficult to wet once they have dried out, and the watering regime for tulips, especially at the beginning and end of the growing season, when you want the soil to dry out between watering, makes their use unsuitable. The addition of grit makes the soil drain more freely and, if nothing else, lets you get away with a little overwatering now and then. As a rule, tulips prefer alkaline soil so if you have some lime available, add a good pinch to the soil mix.

Where you plant the bulbs or keep the pots is as important as the soil in which they grow. Tulips like as much sunlight as possible when in growth. In poor light the stems become etiolated, drawn out as the plant reaches upwards. When the flower opens, the stems may bend over or collapse. To minimize this effect, plant the bulbs in full sun or keep the pots in a sunny cold frame or glasshouse. Bulbs grown under cover will usually emerge earlier than those grown in the garden due to the slightly higher temperature. They are more likely to become etiolated because the days are shorter and the light is poorer than it will be a month or so later. One trick that sometimes works for the early flowering species is to repot and water in the bulbs as late as you dare so growth begins late and the leaves do not emerge until the light conditions are more favourable.

Always provide as much ventilation as possible, as damp, still air can encourage fungal disease, such as botrytis. In the garden, if the bulbs are planted in an open, sunny position, there should naturally be plenty of air movement to keep the aboveground parts of the tulip dry. Under cover, in a glasshouse or frame, air movement is restricted. A glasshouse should ideally have vents in the sides as well as the roof to ensure air moves over and around the plants. You can install fans to improve ventilation even further. Alpine plants require the same conditions, and if you grow your tulips in a glasshouse, an alpine house is the type of glasshouse you need.

A cold frame is even better as the frame lights can be completely removed in dry weather and the plants are then effectively growing in the open. If it starts to rain or snow, the lights need to be replaced but blocks can raise one side of the lights to allow some ventilation.

Most tulip species are very hardy. The only exceptions are those from lower altitudes in the Mediterranean region. The Cretan *Tulipa saxatilis*, for example, can survive temperatures of −7°C (20°F) and probably lower. Across Britain and western Europe there should be few, if any, problems with hardiness. In North America, many tulip species are reliable in the open garden in areas where winter temperatures reach as low as –29°C (–20°F). *Tulipa tarda, T. sprengeri, T. praestans, T. kaufmanniana, T. linifolia, T. clusiana,* and *T. kolpakowskiana* are among the more commonly grown species that survive in areas where the temperature can fall this low. Of course, these tulips stay safely underground in the middle of winter, not emerging until temperatures begin to rise, and snow cover will protect the bulbs from extremes of temperature.

You are more likely to have problems if temperatures do not fall to near freezing point. Tulips grow in areas where winters are usually very cold and, if they do not get their winter chill, they can sulk and refuse to flower.

Tulips in Pots

If you are going to grow tulips in pots, the first thing you need to do is find some suitable pots in which to plant them. Tulips look fantastic grown in this way, so it is worth searching out some attractive containers to show the plants off to their best. These should be large enough to accommodate the bulbs and able to support the plants when in flower. A small pot can easily become unstable with a large tulip flowering in it. Long pots are best so the bulbs can be planted deep and still have plenty of soil for the roots to grow down into. Select pots at least 15 cm (6 in.) deep for smaller bulbs and at least twice that depth for the largest.

Considering the necessity for good drainage, it should go without saying that the pot should have drainage holes. At the bottom of the pot, place some drainage material, such as sharp grit or broken pieces of

Tulipa subpraestans

clay pot, so water can drain freely through the holes. Then partly fill the pot with the soil mix; the bulbs should be planted at least halfway down. To help prevent rotting at the base of the bulb, place the bulbs on a layer of sand. This may not be necessary and I have grown tulips successfully with and without this sand layer, but it cannot do any harm and may be of some benefit, especially if the plants are overwatered at some point.

Place the bulbs in the pot, making sure they are not touching each other. It is best to leave at least 2 cm (0.8 in.) between each bulb. Then cover the bulbs with soil mix to within 2 cm of the top of the pot. The last layer is the grit mulch. This layer has several benefits. It protects the soil surface during watering, preventing wet soil from splashing out of the pot; it helps keep down weed seedlings; and, most importantly, it keeps moisture away from the base of the plant, where rot can easily set in under damp conditions.

During the growing season, the bulbs will benefit from feeding. In the wild the roots can delve deep down to obtain the nutrients the plant needs, but this is not possible in a pot. The restricted root run limits the amount of nourishment the plant can extract from the soil. Slow-release fertilizer can be added to the soil mix when potting the bulbs or a liquid feed can be applied when watering. Use a low-nitrogen, high-potash feed to promote the formation of flower buds for the next season and to help with root growth. Too high a concentration of nitrogen in the feed can encourage leafy growth at the expense of flowers. When your tulips are in full growth, feed them every couple of weeks.

When the bulbs are dormant, they can be repotted. This is the time to replace the exhausted soil and inspect the bulbs to see how healthy they are and if they have increased in size, produced offsets, or are dwindling away. It is preferable to do this every year. Tip out the pots and search for the bulbs. They may have moved so look where the original bulbs were and also at the bottom of the pot. Clean away the old bulb tunics before replanting the bulbs in fresh soil, in a clean

Tulip bulbs planted in a pot. The bulbs are placed on a layer of sand and the soil is covered with a mulch of grit.

pot. Repot your bulbs in late summer so when you water them in, root growth will begin.

Where you keep the pots will depend on the resources and space available to you, and the climate where you live. Bulbs planted in the garden will be protected from extremes of temperature by the soil above and around them. Freestanding pots in the open are likely to freeze solid, thaw out, then freeze solid again during the course of the winter. They will also get very wet when it rains and take a long time to dry out. Neither situation is good for the bulbs and will usually kill them before winter is over. Potted bulbs should have some protection from the rain and from very low temperatures.

Plunging the pots in sand can prevent them from freezing solid in winter and overheating in summer. It can also help with watering. If you use clay pots, the moisture in the plunge sand can pass through the side of the pot and reach the soil. In this way, a small amount of moisture can be given

The collection of tulip species at the Royal Botanic Gardens, Kew, showing the clay pots plunged in sand

to the plants without having to water the soil directly—a technique that is especially useful at the beginning and end of the growing season, when you may only need to provide a little water. Even in summer the plunge sand can be kept just moist for those tulips that do not need to be kept completely dry. Pots plunged in moist sand also dry out much more slowly, so you do not have to water so often.

If you do not do it already, then I would say that plunging your pots is the greatest improvement you can make to the way you grow tulips. You do not have to use sand, but it makes an excellent plunge medium because it maintains a good contact with the pot and is easy to wet. Your bulbs will be protected from extremes of temperature and they will be a lot easier to water.

The best place for your pots is in a cold frame, plunged in sand up to their rim. Cold frame designs vary, but they all protect the plants from the weather. The frame lights can be left open in wet weather to water the pots, but since winter rain can be cold and hard and thus easily damage leaves and flowers, it is far better to protect the plants and maintain control by closing down the frame lights and watering artificially.

A bulb frame is simply a term for a cold frame that is used for growing bulbs. A frame can be raised so you do not have to bend down to plunge the pots, water them, or to admire the plants. The bulb frame's base can be filled with sand to plunge the pots in or filled with soil to plant the bulbs directly into the frame.

When bulbs are planted directly into soil in a frame, they can be grown in lattice pots, the type used for growing marginal aquatics; this type of pot allows the bulbs to be lifted easily when dormant, to inspect them and refresh the soil. The great advantage of growing bulbs in lattice pots is that they allow the roots a free run, as they can grow through the sides. By the summer, the roots have shrivelled and the bulbs can be lifted out with the pot. Unfortunately, many tulips are not ideal for this method of cultivation because the formation of stolons and droppers means that they can escape the confines of the pot. The result is tulips popping up all through your frame and mingling with each other. This may look pretty for a while but the more vigorous species will drive out the others and your collection will soon be in disarray.

Pots can also be kept in a well-ventilated glasshouse. The advantage of a glasshouse is that it can be heated, but it can also get very hot when the sun shines. The protected environment is also a haven for pests, in particular aphids. If you do keep pots of tulips in a glasshouse, it is advantageous to move them out in spring, once the weather has begun to warm up. A late

Planted in the garden, *Tulipa sylvestris* can spread to form a sizeable population.

frost should not harm them, and at least it will give the aphids a shock. The pots will need to be brought back under cover once the tulips have died down, to keep the soil dry.

Growing tulips in pots allows you to specify the soil they are planted in. It means you can move them around, placing the pots in your garden when in flower and hiding them when the flowers are over. If the pots are under glass, the water they receive is controlled and they can be protected from extremes of temperature. Above all, it increases the range of species you can grow, as it gives you control over cultural conditions. However, tulips planted in a garden look far more natural, and nothing can beat an established colony scattered through a border or over a rock garden.

Tulips in the Open Garden

The range of tulip species you can grow in the open is more limited than the range you can grow under cover. How limited depends on the climate where you garden and the situation in which you plant them. If you garden in a Mediterranean or extreme continental climate, with hot, dry summers, then most commonly available species should do well planted outside. If your summers are wet, as in the maritime climate of Britain or the north-western

United States, you will be more restricted, but there is still a good variety to try, especially if you can improve drainage.

The general rule for planting bulbs is to put them at a depth equal to three times the height of the bulb itself. With tulips, I would put them deeper if possible. Even the smaller species can be planted 10 cm (4 in.) deep. Add a small handful of sharp sand at the bottom of the hole and sit the bulb on this to help prevent the bulb from rotting at the base, especially in heavier soils.

Raising a flower border above ground level will immediately improve soil drainage. Such a border can be in the form of a rock garden or raised bed, although some tulips will succeed outside as long as they are in a sunny spot and the soil is not too wet in summer. Digging in some sand or gravel will usually improve soil drainage sufficiently. The following are some of the more commonly available tulip species that can be grown in an open garden.

T. clusiana	*T. sprengeri*
T. fosteriana	*T. sylvestris*
T. humilis	*T. tarda*
T. linifolia	*T. turkestanica*
T. orphanidea	*T. urumiensis*
T. praestans	

The more you improve drainage, the more species you can grow successfully in the open. Alternatively, you can lift the bulbs in early summer and store them somewhere cool and dry. This is a dull task but it ensures the bulbs receive the dry rest they require. Tulips may do well planted permanently in your garden, but one wet summer may weaken them and you may even lose a few. If you do leave them out all year, then it is worth having a backup of your most treasured plants, kept in pots under cover for the summer.

A rock garden by its very nature creates a more natural-looking place to grow tulips, providing well-drained soil as well. In such a setting you can attempt to mimic the wild habitat of tulips. Rocky slopes, screes, ledges, and crevices can all be among a rock garden's features. Here you can experiment with planting the bulbs in different situations, tucking them between rocks or filling a planting bay to give a vibrant block of colour in spring.

A rock garden also provides the conditions needed by a range of plants that might grow naturally with tulips in the wild. Low shrubs, such as helianthemums, lavenders, and thymes, and bulbous plants like *Muscari*, *Allium*, and *Crocus* all look good alongside tulips. Some of the bulbous irises require the same conditions as tulips. You could try some of the more amenable

A yellow form of *Tulipa clusiana* growing on a narrow rock garden ledge

Juno irises, such as *Iris buchar-ica* or *I. magnifica*. The foliage of low-growing hardy geraniums or *Alchemilla*, for example, provides an attractive backdrop to tulips. Some of the smaller tulip species associate well with cushion plants, such as *Acantho-limon*, *Dianthus*, or *Draba*. The long narrow leaves of *Asphode-line lutea* contrast with the foliage of tulips, while the red goblets of *Anemone coronaria* echo the tulip's blooms.

You do not have to choose geographically correct plants to grow alongside your tulips. Why not try eriogonums and low-growing species of *Phlox* or *Aquilegia*? The list is almost endless, and nothing gives more

Tulipa saxatilis in the rock garden at the Royal Botanic Gardens, Kew

pleasure than successfully creating a natural-looking plant community in your own garden. Visit any rock garden in spring and you should come back with a host of ideas to try yourself.

A raised bed performs the same function as a rock garden in that it improves soil drainage. It is just a more formal feature. The degree of formality depends on the building material used for the walls, from rigid brick at one end of the scale to the more 'earthy' dry stone wall at the other. Both rock gardens and raised beds should be filled with gritty soil to maximize drainage. You can then grow a wider range of tulip species than you would in a normal border. The dazzling red blooms of *Tulipa ingens* or *T. eichleri*, the bright yellows of *T. ferganica* and *T. kolpakowskiana*, or the sugary pinks of *T. cretica* and *T. saxatilis* can fill the bed.

Propagation

The easiest way to increase your stock of tulips is to grow on the offsets that the bulbs naturally produce. Some species will form expanding colonies without any help from you, by producing stolons, although there is a danger that a tulip will put so much effort into spreading that it will have no energy for flowering. This danger is more likely if the climate is a little too cool or damp for the bulb's liking, or the soil too rich. For example, *Tulipa sylvestris* has become naturalized in Britain but flowering is rare unless the preceding summer has been hot and dry.

If grown in the garden, bulbs can be left to increase naturally, but if they are grown in pots you can separate the offsets at repotting time, in summer. The sizes of the new bulbs produced by a tulip will vary. Sometimes there is no increase, especially if the tulip is young, and only one new bulb is grown, but usually there are at least two where the previous year there was one. If the plant is healthy, at least one of the bulbs will be flowering size and can be replanted for the next spring. The remaining offsets can be potted up separately and grown on for a year or two, depending on how big they are, until they too have reached flowering size.

The tiniest offsets, which may be only 2 to 3 mm across (0.1 in.), need a little extra care, and the soil they are in should not be allowed to dry out completely at any time, even when the offsets are dormant. In this respect offsets are treated more like seedlings. They may take three or four years to flower.

Tulip bulb offsets will grow into plants that look exactly like the original. They are the result of vegetative reproduction so are genetically identical. Tulips grown from seed take longer to reach flowering size, and if you grow more than one species in your garden, cold frame, or glasshouse, the probability is very high that they have hybridized. The advantage of raising tulips from seed is that you end up with far more new plants from a single tulip than you do from bulb offsets.

Most tulip species readily produce seed. Polyploid tulips may be less forthcoming but even they can produce a few. The seed pods are held at the end of the stem and are usually still ripening after the leaves and roots have died back. It may be several weeks before the pods eventually dry and split to release their seeds. Tulips may be long forgotten and your garden full of summer flowers, but remember to check those pods if you want to capture the seeds before they are scattered over the ground.

Some tulips will self-sow their seeds; *Tulipa sprengeri* is particularly good at this. The following spring you will see a number of very thin, green leaves sprouting from the soil around the parent plants. Sprinkling a handful of seeds over a border is the best way of introducing a large number of *T. sprengeri* to your garden, and once established they will keep on spreading. *Tulipa tarda* also seeds itself well.

For most tulip species it is better to collect the seeds and sow them yourself. Germination normally occurs in the winter or early spring, so sow the seeds from late summer onwards. Do not prick out the new seedlings as soon as they come up, as you would with most other plants. Many bulbous plants, including tulips, are best left in their pots after germination for at least one growing season, as this gives them time to form a bulb before they are disturbed. For this reason, sow the seeds in a deep pot, to provide enough soil to keep the seedling going and to allow it to pull itself down into the soil and find its desired depth. When you do

Tulipa turkestanica seed pods

come to pot on your seedlings, do not be surprised to find the bulbs have gathered at the bottom of the pot.

Fill the seed pot with a soil mix similar to that used for the parent plant, to within 1.5 cm (0.6 in.) of the top, and firm it down with the base of another pot. Tulip seeds tend to be quite large and flat, so unless you have a huge number to sow, place seeds individually on the sand rather than sprinkling them out of your hand. This method prevents the seeds from lying on top of each other and gives each seedling the best chance of survival. Cover the seed with about 5 mm (0.2 in.) of soil, sieved to remove large lumps. Protect the soil surface with a thin layer of small grit.

After sowing, place the seed pot in a tray of water and allow the soil to soak up the water by capillary action, until you can see moisture at the surface. This ensures all the soil is thoroughly moistened. The pot can then be placed outside or in a cold frame, where it will be exposed to the cold in winter. This chilling tells the seed that winter has arrived, and when it begins to warm up the seed will germinate. If no seedlings appear, do not give up and throw out the pot. Keep it lightly watered throughout the summer and allow it another chill the following winter; the seeds may take more than a year to germinate.

The seed pot must never be allowed to dry out. The new roots and shoots are very delicate and easily killed through lack of water. The pots can be left open to the elements until the seedlings appear above ground but in dry spells some watering will be necessary. The seeds are near the surface and it does not take long for the top 2 cm (0.8 in.) of the soil to dry out on a sunny day.

When the seed germinates, the first thing you will notice is a very thin, almost hair-like leaf emerging from the soil. If the pot is in the open, bring it into a cold frame or cool glasshouse to give the young leaf some protection. Plants do not get this kind of care in the wild, but they also suffer heavy losses; you want as many of your seedlings as possible to survive.

Plunge the seed pot in sand and do not let the soil dry out. Even when the seedling bulbs are dormant, the soil should retain some moisture. In the summer a small seed pot can dry out very quickly and become overheated. Plunging helps prevent this from happening.

The following spring new leaves will appear. They may look large enough at this point to handle safely, but wait until they are dormant before disturbing the bulbs. If the leaves still look small, do not disturb them for another year. Feed the seedlings with a dilute solution of liquid feed while they remain in the same pot. This will encourage larger bulbs to form.

Once the seedling bulbs are large enough, tip them out in the summer and pot them up. Whether you put them all in a larger pot or split them into more than one pot is up to you and will also depend on how many seedlings you have. Repot them every year, giving them fresh soil. Most species should flower in another two or three years and this is when you will discover if you have raised any hybrids. In most cases it is best to remove any doubtful plants—they are normally inferior to the parents—and only keep those that are true to the original, but occasionally you might find something special.

Growing tulips from seed, or any bulbs for that matter, is a slow process but also immensely satisfying. Buying and planting bulbs are exciting, but the pleasure gained from nurturing a plant from seed to flower is far greater. There are as many ways to sow seeds and grow plants as there are gardeners. Each will have their own routine or idiosyncrasies. The above method has worked for me.

Two-year-old seedlings of *Tulipa iliensis*, ready for potting on

Pests and Diseases

I am not intolerant of pests and diseases so much as intolerant of plants that always succumb to them. I do not like to spray if I can help it, so if a plant is guaranteed to suffer from some sort of malady I would rather not grow it in my garden. Luckily, tulip species are not particularly sickly plants, but there are three major problems to look out for. Aphids attack tulips as much as any other plant and they spread virus, something anyone who has a collection of bulbs knows about. Fungal diseases can also be a problem, especially the dreaded tulip fire.

Tulip fire (*Botrytis tulipae*) distorts and stunts growth. The leaves and flowers are marked with spots and the leaf tips emerge brown and scorched. The shoot usually collapses and dies, becoming covered in mould. Nearby tulips will be infected, initially showing small brown marks on the leaves, especially in damp weather, which is perfect for the spread of spores. The disease travels down to the bulb, which also becomes marked, and new bulbs should be inspected under their tunic for black, scab-like spots.

Tulip fire can annihilate a collection of tulips. Any infected plants must be destroyed and tulips should not be replanted in a border where infected plants have been grown for at least two years. All tulips are susceptible to tulip fire, but more often the hybrids are affected. This is because the hybrids are grown in unsuitable conditions. Plant a tulip bulb almost anywhere and it will flower once. New bulbs can then be bought for the following year's display. Damp soil or poor air circulation is not a problem if the bulbs are dug up after they have flowered, but both create the conditions in which tulip fire can take hold. Tulip species are grown to flower year after year so more attention is paid to providing good drainage and an airy situation, which also happens to be the best way of avoiding tulip fire. You can also spray the leaves or dust the bulbs with fungicide if you think tulip fire might be a problem.

Other fungal diseases affect tulips and other bulbs, such as bulb rot and root rot. Again, good soil drainage and ample ventilation help to keep them under control, but it is important to check your plants for signs of rotting or for marks on the bulbs, leaves, and buds. In some cases, the buds may abort or the growth is distorted. Many of these diseases survive in the soil, so if plants are affected do not replant tulips in the same soil. Growing bulbs in pots and repotting them every year allows you to inspect the bulbs regularly and also to refresh the soil in which they are grown. Thoroughly clean the pots before replanting the bulbs to remove any soil-borne diseases.

Aphids are a common problem for tulip species. These sap-sucking insects home in on young growth. They multiply at an incredible rate and will soon cover a plant if left unchecked. They cause distortion of growth and can completely destroy a flower bud. The adults fly and move from one plant to another. If a plant has a virus, an aphid will carry that virus to a new plant. Once a virus is present, you cannot get rid of it without destroying the plant.

Tulips with virus have distorted growth and the leaves are streaked with lighter green but the most dramatic effect is seen in the flower. Here the streaks can create startling patterns of light and dark over the basic flower colour. Virus ruins a plant, weakening it and making it look ugly. The patterns caused by some viruses in cultivated tulips can look attractive, but in tulip species it just looks wrong.

A tulip with virus must be destroyed before the disease is spread to other plants. The seed of a plant with virus will be clean, so you can raise new, healthy stock, but it is worth isolating the parent from the rest of your collection until the seed has set. Controlling aphids will also prevent the spread of this disease.

A range of chemicals is available to the amateur for controlling aphids, from aerosols and liquid sprays that kill aphids on contact, to systemic soil

Tulipa vvedenskyi flower showing the effect of virus

drenches, containing the active ingredient imidacloprid, that enter the plant and kill the aphids via the sap. Professional, suitably qualified horticulturists have a more potent arsenal at their disposal and if they look after a large collection of bulbs they will need to use it, and probably have to as part of their job. In your own garden you can make your own decisions.

The simplest way to kill aphids is to squash them between your thumb and forefinger. You have to be vigilant and start squashing as soon as you spot the first one but even so, you will never kill them all. There are horticultural soap solutions for spraying on aphids and you can even use a very dilute solution of washing-up liquid, but do this too frequently and the leaves will be scorched. The soap breaks the surface tension of the water and the aphids, which breathe through pores along their sides, are drowned.

Biological control is becoming increasingly available and works well in the enclosed space of a glasshouse. A parasitic wasp, *Aphidius*, is surprisingly effective in controlling aphids. It lays its eggs in the aphids and the larvae feed on the aphid from the inside, only killing when it pupates. The aphid is mummified and the mature wasp will then cut itself out of this golden brown cocoon. This process takes from ten days to two weeks, but an adult wasp will lay a single egg in each aphid so it is not long before the colony is all but destroyed. *Aphidius* needs temperatures of 10°C (50°F) to perform, but this is quite easily attained in a glasshouse on a sunny day. Once established, this parasite will come back year after year and attack the aphids. For biological control to work, a few pests must necessarily be around for the parasites to feed on, so this approach to pest control is not favoured by growers with zero tolerance.

Cold weather is a good aphid control. One of the reasons tulips in the garden are not too susceptible is because they emerge early in the year, before aphids have built up their numbers. Tulips grown in the protected environment of a glasshouse are most at risk, so it is best to move them out as soon as the weather is mild enough. Prevention is always better than cure.

5
HISTORY & CLASSIFICATION

Study of the genus Tulipa *is beset with*
exceptionally great obstacles.
A. I. Vvedensky (1935) in *Flora of the USSR*

In *The Tulip*, Anna Pavord (1999) put it another way: 'Tulips laugh at tax-onomy'. So why is the classification of tulips so difficult? For one thing, many of them grow in inhospitable places, in remote hills and valleys, where winters are harsh and summers long and dry. There they may only flower for a short period before retreating underground. If you visit at the wrong time you will miss them. Local botanists will have a thorough knowledge of their own country's flora, but to get an overall impression of a species or group of closely related species, you need a broad view, not easy when one species may be found over a wide area, covering several countries.

When a new species of any plant is discovered and named, it has to be described in a recognized publication, such as a scientific journal or book. In other words, the name must be published along with a Latin description, and a pressed specimen must be taken and lodged in an herbarium so future botanists can refer to it. This herbarium specimen is called the type speci-men and the plant is the type of that species. To put it very simply, if a new tulip is discovered that is similar to but not exactly the same as an already described species, it should only be named as a new species if it is sufficiently different from the type of the first. Because of the complexity of the genus *Tulipa*, where plants are so variable and differ in many minor characters, it becomes extremely important to refer to type specimens when studying the species. Deciding whether one tulip is sufficiently different from another is not easy. One authority may recognize a range of species, while another may regard them as variations of one species.

Take *Tulipa biflora* as an example. This species has an immense range, extending from western China, through central Asia, to the Caucasus Mountains, eastern Turkey, and south-eastern Europe. Some plants from the Caucasus may look different from those found in the Tien Shan, but in between is a whole range of intermediate forms showing minor variations. The two extremes may have been described as separate species, as well as some of the intermediate forms, but taking a broad view may lead you to conclude that this is just one species that changes gradually across its range. Pity the poor taxonomist who has to decide whether a particular form is stable enough in its characteristics, and distinct enough from the type specimen, to warrant a species name of its own.

Of course, other large genera distributed across wide areas of the world pose the same problem, but tulips seem to be more complicated than most. It all comes down to the fact that tulips are incredibly variable and changeable, and so many different names have been published, sometimes more than one name for the same plant. Well over three hundred names of tulip species have been published, but the number of species that actually exists is probably less than one hundred. Tulips are still evolving, so the genus has not settled down into convenient, well-defined units that can easily be identified as distinct species.

Tulips are masters of naturalization, given a suitable climate. They were unknown in many parts of Europe until introduced from Asia in the sixteenth century. Today there are areas, such as Savoy in France, where they

A large-flowered form of *Tulipa biflora*, collected in Iran

appear to grow wild. These tulips have escaped from cultivation and settled down in their new home, often in fields or orchards, and have subsequently been described as new species. When traders brought tulips from central Asia to Turkey and Europe, some bulbs were inevitably cast off or lost en route. These plants were able to take advantage of the reduced competition and improved soils of cultivated areas to become established in their new home.

Fourteen tulip species are listed in *Flora of Turkey* but possibly only four are truly indigenous to that country, the others having found their way from further east. Where they came from and the wild species from which they are derived are unknown.

To make matters even more complicated, tulips readily hybridize, whether they are naturalized plants or truly wild species. In the Tien Shan, *Tulipa kaufmanniana* hybridizes with *T. greigii*, *T. tschimganica*, and *T. dubia*, resulting in a range of intermediate forms. Some tulips, described as distinct species, may only be hybrids. The 'species' described from central Europe are the result of hybridization between garden escapes that have become naturalized. All this serves to blur the boundaries between the species, often leading to a proliferation of names being published to cover all the variations.

Polyploidy, where an individual possesses one or more sets of chromosomes in addition to the normal two sets (diploid), is also prevalent in tulips. The resulting plants are often larger and more vigorous. They may not be able to reproduce sexually, but they increase vegetatively by stolons, thus increasing their ability to become naturalized in an area and to do so relatively quickly. Although they may not look exactly like the diploid plants, they are essentially the same species but with more chromosomes. Again, more names are published and more confusion is caused.

Reading this you are probably thinking the situation is hopeless, but over the last two hundred and fifty years attempts have been made to classify tulip species and divide the genus into manageable groups. Work on classification is ongoing but, dare I say, there seems to be a general consensus concerning at least the primary divisions of the genus.

Certain characteristics have proven to be fairly constant and these can be used to group species together. Unfortunately for gardeners, the most obvious features, namely, plant size, flower size, and flower colour, are the most unreliable. What appear to be minor characters, such as hairiness of the bulb tunic and presence of hairs on the filaments, are more constant and reliable. General flower shape is also significant and, in such a complex genus, geography also provides important clues.

Tulips were well known long before the Swedish naturalist Carl Linnaeus

began his studies, but he is the starting point in their classification, as he
adopted the binomial system of naming (genus and species) and used it consistently to classify all the plants and animals known to him. His survey of
plants, called *Species Plantarum*, was published in 1753. Prior to this, plants
often had long and complicated Latin names, frequently comprising several
words. Linnaeus brought similar plants together under one genus and gave
the individual forms species names. Thus he laid the foundations for taxonomy as we know it today.

The History of Tulip Classification

Linnaeus (1707–1778) included three tulip species in *Species Plantarum*:
Tulipa gesneriana, T. sylvestris, and *T. breyniana.* The last of these was soon removed from the genus and is now placed in *Baeometra*, in the Colchicaceae,
but another tulip did appear in *Species Plantarum* under the name *Ornithogalum uniflorum*, now known as *Tulipa uniflora*. *Tulipa gesneriana* has been
designated the type of the genus *Tulipa*, as it is thought to best represent Linnaeus's concept of the genus.

Other tulips described in the eighteenth century include *Tulipa biflora* in 1779; *T. suaveo-
lens,* from a cultivated plant, in 1794; and *T. australis* in 1799. The Swiss botanist, naturalist, and medical doctor Augustin Pyramus de Candolle (1778–1841) wrote the text for the first four volumes of Pierre-Joseph Redouté's *Liliacées* and among his descriptions of new species were *T. clusiana* in 1802, *T. celsiana* in 1803, and *T. agenensis* in 1804. De Candolle also wrote the third edition of *Flore Fran-
çais*, published in 1805. In this he included four tulips: *T. sylves-*

Tulipa celsiana

tris, *T. suaveolens*, *T. gesneriana*, and *T. oculus-solis* (syn. *T. agenensis*). However, the genus was not subdivided until 1847.

In the second volume of *Giornale Botanico Italiano*, published in 1847, the French aristocrat Eugenio de Reboul (1781–1851) split thirteen tulip species known from southern Europe into two groups. The first section he called *Tulipanum*; it comprised species with a woolly layer of hairs on the inside of the bulb tunic, including *Tulipa praecox* and *T. oculus-solis*. Reboul's second section, *Dulipanum*, included species such as *T. gesneriana* and *T. sylvestris* that do not have a woolly layer inside the tunic. Reboul's classification is notable because the hairiness of the bulb tunic is a characteristic still used today when subdividing the genus. The name of section *Tulipanum* appears to have been disregarded for many years until it was used by Aleksei Vvedensky in *Flora of the USSR*, in 1935.

In 1849 the German naturalist, botanist, and traveller Karl (or Carolus) Koch (1809–1879) also used the hairiness of the bulb tunic to divide the genus. His two groups were *Lanigera*, with hairy tunics, and *Leiobulbos*, with glabrous tunics.

Eduard Regel (1815–1892), one of the greatest names in the history of the genus *Tulipa*, first divided the genus into two groups based on the presence or absence of hairs on the filaments of the flower. This character is still used in modern classifications to split the genus in two, and recent studies of tulip DNA and pollen have supported this view. Regel was director of the St. Petersburg Botanic Garden from 1855. There he was in the fortunate position to receive many tulip specimens and bulbs, collected by Russian military expeditions to western and central Asia. His son Albert Regel (1845–1908) was a physician based in Kuldja, now called Yining, north of the eastern Tien Shan in western China, then part of eastern Turkestan. He also sent many tulip bulbs to his father. Among his discoveries are *T. kaufmanniana* and *T. praestans*, two of the most popular species in cultivation today. His father named the Tien Shan species *T. albertii* after him.

Eduard Regel described more tulip species than any other botanist. The names were published in the Russian journal *Acta Horti Petropolitani* and in the German magazine *Gartenflora*, where the plants were often illustrated with botanical paintings. In 1873, in the second volume of *Acta Horti Petropolitani*, Regel published a classification of tulip species. He divided the twenty-six species into two primary sections, which he did not name. In the first section are four species with hairs on the inside of the tepals and at the base of the filaments, including Linnaeus's *Tulipa sylvestris*. The remaining species have glabrous filaments, and tepals with no hairs on the inner surface. Regel used various characteristics to key out the individual species, such as hairiness of the flower stem, shape of the tepals and leaves, and hairiness of the bulb tunic, but it is the division into two main groups that is most significant. In 1882 the sections were given names by the Swiss botanist Edmund Boissier.

In the meantime, Regel was very generous with his new tulips and regularly sent bulbs to European growers and botanists, such as the naturalist, traveller, and bulb enthusiast Henry Elwes, who gardened at Colesbourne Park in Gloucestershire, England. In this way many of the new tulips entered cultivation in Europe. The Royal Botanic Gardens, Kew, were another recipient.

J. Gilbert Baker (1834–1920), botanist and keeper of the herbarium at Kew, had a particular interest in tulips and published a review of the species in the *Journal of the Linnean Society* in 1874. He included the genus *Orithyia*, established by David Don in 1836, within *Tulipa*, treating it as a subgenus. All the other species Baker placed in subgenus *Eutulipa* and divided them into five sections: *Eriobulbi, Gesnerianae, Scabriscapae, Saxatiles,* and *Silvestres*. A few years later, in 1883, Baker revised this classification in the *Gardeners' Chronicle*. Again he divided subgenus *Eutulipa* into five sections but changed the arrangement of species. His sections were now *Eriobulbae, Clusianae, Gesnerianae, Saxatiles,* and *Sylvestres*.

The details of Baker's classification are best not dealt with here, as they will only add further confusion. There is no doubt that Baker did some valuable work on the genus, describing several new species, such as *Tulipa aucheriana* and *T. sprengeri*, and writing about new introductions in *Curtis's Botanical Magazine*. A couple of his sectional names, *Clusianae* and *Saxatiles*, are still in use, but his

Tulipa aucheriana

classification has been largely discredited, as it places too much emphasis on unreliable characteristics, such as flower colour.

The work of Edmund Boissier (1810–1885), published around the same time as Baker's review of tulips, is more significant. Boissier had a particular interest in alpine plants and made many trips to the Alps, as well as Spain, the eastern Mediterranean, and the Near East. Between 1842 and 1859 he published *Diagnoses Plantarum Orientalium Novarum*, followed by the monumental *Flora Orientalis* between 1867 and 1884. For these works Boissier studied plants collected by a number of botanists including Friedrich Alexander Buhse, Georges-François Reuter, Theodoros Orphanides, Theodor von Heldreich, and Theodor Kotschy. *Flora Orientalis* covers a region that extends from the eastern Mediterranean to Afghanistan and Turkestan.

In *Flora Orientalis* Boissier named Regel's two sections of the genus *Tulipa*. The section containing species with glabrous filaments he named *Leiostemones* and the section containing those with hairy filaments he named *Eriostemones*. The name of the second section is still in use. The first has been renamed *Tulipa*, in accordance with the international rules of botanical nomenclature, which state that the initial section or subgenus containing the type of the genus must take the name of the genus. The character Boissier, and Regel before him, used to define this section is still relevant. Twenty-five species of tulip appear in *Flora Orientalis*, several of them first described by Boissier in other publications, including *T. undulatifolia*, *T. orphanidea*, and *T. cretica*.

In the late nineteenth and early twentieth centuries, the popularity of tulip species increased rapidly as new discoveries were made and introduced to cultivation. Bulb firms sold these

Tulipa orphanidea

tulips, often selecting good forms and giving them cultivar names. Foremost among these bulb traders was the Dutch firm of C. G. van Tubergen, established in 1869. Inspired by the new species discovered by collectors such as Albert Regel in Russian Central Asia, van Tubergen employed collectors to bring back bulbs, which were grown on in Holland and sold across Europe.

Some of these collectors were based in Europe but travelled to Asia to collect plants. German Paul Sintenis is one example. The Turkish *Tulipa sintenisii* is named after him and was sent by him to the German gardener and nurseryman Max Leichtlin of Baden-Baden. Van Tubergen contacted Sintenis when he heard that Sintenis was intending to travel to Transcaspia in 1905. From his base in Ashkhabad, southern Turkmenistan, Sintenis sent van Tubergen many bulbs, including *T. wilsoniana* (syn. *T. montana*).

Other collectors, like Joseph Haberhauer, were already based in the tulip heartland. Haberhauer ran a hotel in Samarkand, Uzbekistan, and in 1904 van Tubergen commissioned him to collect a large and brightly coloured tulip that he had reported seeing for sale in the markets, gathered from the surrounding mountains. This turned out to be a new species, the wonderful, red-flowered *Tulipa fosteriana*. Van Tubergen singled out a robust and especially large-flowered form of this species and named it 'Red Emperor' (syn. 'Madame Lefeber'). It is still available today.

Paul Graeber was based in Tashkent and collected for van Tubergen from 1897 to 1914. Among his collections were *Tulipa greigii*, *T. kaufmanniana*, *T. kolpakowskiana*, and *T. ostrowskiana*.

Austrian botanist and collector A. Kronenburg travelled in north-western Iran, the Caucasus Mountains, and Russian Central Asia for van Tubergen. He sent back bulbs of *T. eichleri*, *T. linifolia* in red and yellow, *T. polychroma* (a synonym of *T. biflora*), and a new species, *T. urumiensis*.

Tulipa fosteriana 'Red Emperor'

John Hoog (1865–1950) of van Tubergen described some of the new species arriving from western and central Asia, including *Tulipa ingens, T. micheliana*, and *T. tubergeniana*. Hoog is commemorated in *T. hoogiana*, sent to van Tubergen by Graeber.

This influx of bulbs from remote corners of Asia provided plenty of material for European botanists to study. Although many new species were described during this period, there was no attempt to classify these new introductions until Sir Daniel Hall produced one of the most important works ever written on tulip species, *The Genus* Tulipa, published by the Royal Horticultural Society (RHS) in 1940. Unfortunately, most of the new tulips that survived in cultivation only represented a fraction of the variation found in wild plants. To gain an understanding of these tulip species in the wild, we have to go back to the publication of volume four of *Flora of the USSR* in 1935, thankfully translated into English in 1968.

The account of *Tulipa* in *Flora of the USSR* was written by the tulip expert Aleksei Ivanovich Vvedensky (1898–1972). Although restricted to tulips from the former Soviet Union, this account includes species from the most important centres of diversity, the mountains of the Caucasus as well as the Tien Shan and Pamir Alai.

Vvedensky followed Boissier in naming his two main sections *Leiostemones* and *Eriostemones*, but he also added four smaller sections. Section *Tulipanum* included four species with bulb tunics 'profusely arachnoid-shaggy' on the inner surface, glabrous filaments, and large, brightly coloured flowers: *T. tubergeniana, T. kuschkensis, T. hoogiana*, and *T. julia*. Section *Spiranthera* contained one species, *T. kaufmanniana*, on the basis that the anthers open (dehisce) gradually and slowly from tip to base, coiling as they do so. Vvedensky created another monotypic section, *Lophophyllon*, for *T. regelii*, which has several raised, undulating ridges along the length of its one or sometimes

Tulipa hoogiana

two leaves. The last section is *Orithyia*, based on Baker's subgenus, containing *T. heteropetala*, *T. uniflora*, and *T. heterophylla*.

Vvedensky described many new species, including *Tulipa bifloriformis*, *T. dubia*, *T. ferganica*, and *T. subpraestans* and continued to study tulips until his death in 1972. He had a great understanding of the genus and his conclusions should not be dismissed lightly. Although he did not subdivide the sections, he did group the species according to their relationship to each other.

Sir Daniel Hall (1864–1942) took tulip classification a step further by introducing named sections or subsections within the *Eriostemones* and *Leiostemones*. He wrote *The Book of the Tulip* in 1929, but his masterpiece was *The Genus Tulipa*, published in 1940, in which he revised the genus but followed Boissier by placing most of the species in either *Eriostemones* or *Leiostemones*. The *Eriostemones* he divided into three sections: *Australes*, *Saxatiles*, and *Biflores*. The *Leiostemones* was divided into five: *Clusianae*, *Gesnerianae*, the *Oculus-solis* Group (equivalent to Vvedensky's section *Tulipanum*), *Eichleres*, and *Kolpakowskianae*. A third section, *Orithyia*, comprised two species now removed to the genus *Amana*. Hall had not studied the species placed in section *Orithyia* by Vvedensky so he included them in Addendum 1: Species not seen in a living state.

Hall placed a great deal of emphasis on the need to study living tulips rather than herbarium specimens, where essential characteristics can be hidden or lost. He also split species according to their chromosome number. For example, he separated the diploid *Tulipa aitchisonii* from the pentaploid *T. clusiana*, although in other respects they are similar. Hall discussed seventy-two species in detail and included a further eighty-three species in the Addendum.

There are two sides to Hall's treatment. On the one hand, he was undoubtedly thorough and went to great lengths to understand the genus. His division of the *Eriostemones* into three sections is still accepted today and he cleared up many taxonomic problems, such as the status of the 'species' in the *Tulipa humilis* group. On the other hand, his work was largely based on cultivated material, often of unknown origin and from commercial sources. As I have already mentioned, commercial stocks did not show the full range of variation of many species and often only one clone was, and still is, in cultivation. Furthermore, tulips can change in cultivation, producing larger flowers or sometimes more leaves than would normally be found in the wild. Nevertheless, Hall did a great deal to improve our understanding of the genus and no monograph on the whole of the genus *Tulipa* has been published since.

The next major work on tulips came in 1962, with the publication of *Tyul'pany* (*Tulips*) by the Russian botanist Zinaida Botschantzeva (1907–1973), translated into English by H. Q. Varekamp in 1982. This book covers the central Asian tulips in great detail but follows the classification used by Vvedensky (1935) in *Flora of the USSR*. Several new species are included and among those described by Botschantzeva herself are *Tulipa tschimganica*, *T. butkovii*, and *T. vvedenskyi*. She clearly had an intimate knowledge of these plants, studying them at the Central Asian State University, Tashkent, and undertaking several expeditions to collect plants in the mountains of the region. Vvedensky named *T. zenaidae* after her.

Late in the twentieth century, the most significant publications on tulips were floras that covered areas within the range of the genus: *Flora Europaea*, *Flora of Turkey*, *Flora of Iraq*, *Flora Palaestina*, and *Flora Iranica*. Although cataloguing the tulips from each region, these floras do not divide the genus beyond the two sections proposed by Boissier over one hundred years earlier. The only difference is that in *Flora Europaea*, *Flora Palaestina*, and *Flora of Turkey*, section *Leiostemones* is renamed section *Tulipa*. When it comes to tulips, these floras are mainly concerned with determining what is a species and which names should be treated as synonyms.

The floras do not always agree. The accounts in *Flora Europaea* and *Flora of Turkey* take a broad view of the species. For example, they treat *Tulipa orphanidea* as a variable tulip covering a range of forms previously described as individual species, such as *T. hageri*, *T. bithynica*, and *T. whittallii*. *Flora Iranica* takes a different view, often recognizing a range of similar species, varying only slightly from each other. For example, it recognizes *T. aitchisonii*, *T. oreophila*, *T. stellata*, *T grey-wilsonii*, and *T. clusiana*, which could all be regarded as variants of one species, *T. clusiana*.

Tulipa tschimganica

No major advances were made in the overall classification of the genus until the publication of two papers by L. W. D. van Raamsdonk and T. de Vries in the journal *Plant Systematics and Evolution*. The first, 'Biosystematic Studies in *Tulipa* sect. *Eriostemones*', was published in 1992 and the second, 'Species Relationships and Taxonomy in *Tulipa* subg. *Tulipa*', in 1995. Van Raamsdonk and de Vries measured thirty-five morphological characters in section *Eriostemones* and thirty-four in section *Tulipa*. They included date of flowering; height of plant; hairiness of stem, leaves, tepals, and bulb tunic; number of flowers; dimensions of the stem, tepals, and stamens; colour of anthers; and the occurrence of a blotch in the flower. They also considered geography and polyploidy when devising their classification. Not every known species was studied but most of those in general cultivation were included.

Van Raamsdonk and de Vries raised the two sections of *Tulipa* to the level of subgenus and divided each subgenus into sections. Subgenus *Eriostemones* was divided into three sections—*Australes*, *Saxatiles*, and *Biflores*—following Sir Daniel Hall's treatment. Subgenus *Tulipa* was divided into five sections: *Clusianae*, *Kolpakowskianae*, *Tulipanum*, *Eichleres*, and *Tulipa*. Section *Tulipanum* was further divided into two series, and section *Eichleres* into eight series.

Much work remains to be done on *Tulipa*, but to fully understand the genus the wild plants must be studied in detail. The vast area occupied by tulips and the variation found among them means that a thorough study is likely to be a long way off. The amount of work needed to fully understand this group of plants is phenomenal. I can only salute those who have tackled the subject and present a summary of their findings.

A Classification of *Tulipa*

Following is a classification of seventy-nine tulip species, concentrating on those available in the trade and those you are most likely to read about in popular literature, see in botanic gardens, or find offered on specialist society seed lists. This classification is based mainly on the work of Vvedensky, Hall, and van Raamsdonk and de Vries, as well as recent DNA studies carried out at the Royal Botanic Gardens, Kew. All the species listed in chapter 6 are included, but this is not a comprehensive list of all known tulips.

Tulipa subgenus *Tulipa*

The species in subgenus *Tulipa* are characterized by their glabrous filaments, which are all about the same length. The flowers are generally bowl shaped, with a rounded base, and the colour is predominantly red or yellow. Yellow forms of normally red species lack the red pigment and are equivalent to albinos.

Section *Tulipa*

T. gesneriana

T. armena (including *T. galatica*)

T. schrenkii

T. sintenisii

T. hungarica (including

    T. rhodopea, T. urumoffii)

The bulbs of species in section *Tulipa* have papery tunics, usually lined with only a few straight hairs. The flowers are generally red with a black basal blotch margined with yellow. These tulips are found growing wild mainly in Europe and Turkey, but also the Caucasus Mountains and parts of central Asia.

Tulipa schrenkii of section *Tulipa*

Section *Tulipanum* De Reboul

T. agenensis	T. kuschkensis
T. aleppensis	T. systola (including T. stapfii)
T. cypria	T. borszczowii
T. praecox	T. ulophylla (including
T. julia	T. wendelboi)

Section *Tulipanum* comprises the species with a dense layer of woolly, often rippled hairs lining the bulb tunics. Apart from this characteristic the species are very similar to those in section *Tulipa* and some of those in section *Eichleres*. Their distribution extends from Europe, through Turkey, the Caucasus Mountains, and the Middle East, into Iran and west-central Asia.

Section *Eichleres* (Hall) van Raamsdonk

T. eichleri	T. albertii
T. undulatifolia (including T. boeotica)	T. butkovii
T. micheliana	T. vvedenskyi
T. lanata	T. sosnovskyi
T. ingens	T. praestans
T. tubergeniana	T. heweri
T. hoogiana (including T. amabilis)	T. subpraestans
T. fosteriana	T. kaufmanniana
T. carinata	T. dubia
T. greigii	T. tschimganica

Section *Eichleres* is the largest in subgenus *Tulipa*. The species are similar to those in section *Tulipa* in that the bulb tunics are usually lined with a few straight hairs, but in some, such as *T. lanata*, they can form a thick layer, and in others, such as *T. subpraestans*, the tunics are glabrous. The leaves are often broad, especially in species like *T. fosteriana* and *T. greigii*, and the tepals are bright and glossy on their inner surface.

This section also has a more easterly distribution than does section *Tulipa*, with most of the species found growing wild in central Asia, particularly the mountains of the Pamir Alai and Tien Shan. Some species are found in Iran, Turkey, and the Caucasus Mountains, and one, *T. undulatifolia*, has extended its range through naturalization, into south-eastern Europe.

Aleksei Vvedensky placed *Tulipa kaufmanniana* in section *Spiranthera* on the basis that its anthers open gradually and slowly from the tip to the base.

Tulipa systola bulb tunic, showing the dense layer of woolly hairs characteristic of species in section *Tulipanum*

A beautiful red form of *Tulipa greigii* in section *Eichleres*

Zinaida Botschantzeva later added four more species to this section, including *T. dubia* and *T. tschimganica*.

Section *Kolpakowskianae* (Hall) van Raamsdonk

T. altaica	*T. tetraphylla* (including *T. kesselringii*)
T. kolpakowskiana	*T. ostrowskiana*
T. iliensis	*T. lehmanniana*
T. anisophylla	*T. zenaidae*
T. ferganica	*T. korolkowii*

The species in section *Kolpakowskianae* have narrow, glaucous leaves, often with undulate margins, and yellow, orange, or red flowers. In yellow-flowered forms the backs of the outer tepals are usually stained with red or reddish purple. The bulb tunics are lined with hairs at the tip and often at the base, although the tunic of *Tulipa altaica* is hairy all over the inner surface. These species grow mainly in the Tien Shan and Pamir Alai, but the range of the section extends northwards to the Altai Mountains of Kazakhstan and north-western China.

Tulipa kolpakowskiana, the type of section *Kolpakowskianae*

Two approaches have been taken to classify the tulips in this section. *Flora of the USSR* recognized a number of species, including *Tulipa altaica, T. kolpakowskiana, T. ostrowskiana, T. iliensis, T. anisophylla, T. ferganica, T. zenaidae, T. tetraphylla,* and *T. lehmanniana*. In contrast, van Raamsdonk and de Vries only recognized three species—*T. altaica, T. lehmanniana,* and *T. tetraphylla*—relegating the rest to subspecies, varieties, or synonyms, except *T. korolkowii*, which they do not discuss.

This group is a difficult and confusing one, with individual species showing a great deal of variation, especially in flower colour. The species also hybridize in the wild, creating even more diversity. Only a few of them are widely cultivated.

Section *Orithyia* (D. Don) Vvedensky

T. uniflora
T. heteropetala
T. heterophylla

Section *Orithyia* was originally a genus separated from *Tulipa* by the presence of an elongated style. It was reduced to a subgenus of *Tulipa* by J. Gilbert Baker and then to a section by Aleksei Vvedensky. It is named after the wife of Boreas, the Greek god of the north wind and the cold of winter, an appropriate name considering the original species, *Orithyia uniflora*, comes from the cold mountains of the Altai. With the genus *Tulipa* divided into subgenera, *Orithyia* could be treated as a subgenus, or as a section within subgenus *Tulipa*. Molecular studies at the Royal Botanic Gardens, Kew, suggest the former approach may be the most suitable.

All three species in this section are small plants, reaching 5 to 20 cm (2–8 in.) tall, with two leaves and with yellow flowers stained dingy violet or green on the outside. The species occur from the Altai Mountains to the Tien Shan and north-western China. The bulb tunics are hairy at the tip or glabrous in *Tulipa heterophylla*. All three species have glabrous filaments and a distinctive elongated style.

A fourth species, *Tulipa sinkiangensis*, may belong here. It was described in 1980 and grows in north-western China and the Tien Shan. It has three leaves and a yellow to reddish yellow or dark red flower with a slightly elongated style, up to 2 mm (0.08 in.) long. Species like *T. dasystemon* and *T. orithyioides*

Tulipa uniflora of section *Orithyia*

also have an elongated style, but because their filaments are hairy at the base, they are placed in section *Biflores* of subgenus *Eriostemones*.

Section *Clusianae* Baker

T. clusiana (including *T. aitchisonii, T. cashmeriana, T. stellata*)
T. montana (including *T. wilsoniana, T. chrysantha*)
T. linifolia (including *T. maximowiczii, T. batalinii*)

The species of section *Clusianae* have glabrous filaments. Study of their DNA at the Royal Botanic Gardens, Kew, has found that the three species represent a group clearly separated from the rest of subgenus *Tulipa*. They could be placed in their own subgenus to mark this distinction, but this is not a decision for me to make so I will leave them in a section. Suffice to say, these species, like those in section *Orithyia*, are clearly different from other tulip species and should be grouped together to indicate this.

The bulbs are distinctive, being fairly small and having a prominent tuft of hairs protruding from the top. The leaves are long and narrow and are usually spaced apart on the stem, the upper ones often attached to the stem well above ground level. The flowers may be red, yellow, or, as in *Tulipa clusiana*, white with red backs to the outer tepals.

Tulipa montana of section *Clusianae*

All three species are found in a band stretching from northern Iran to the Pamir Alai, Kashmir, and north-western India. *Tulipa clusiana* has also become naturalized in Turkey and southern Europe.

Tulipa subgenus *Eriostemones* (Boissier) van Raamsdonk

The species in subgenus *Eriostemones* have tapering filaments with a boss of hairs at the base and they may also have wispy hairs along their length. Exceptions to this include *Tulipa sprengeri* and *T. sogdiana*, which have glabrous filaments, but in all other respects they belong to this subgenus and in some cases may only be abnormal forms of species with otherwise hairy filaments.

Multi-flowered plants are common in this subgenus and all the species have funnel-shaped flowers, with a slight constriction just above the base. In the sun the flowers open wide to form a star. The inner three filaments are shorter than the outer three. The inner tepals frequently have short hairs at their base, and the outer tepals often have a dull staining on the back, usually a shade of grey-green or violet. The leaves are mostly lanceolate to linear.

Section *Australes* sensu Hall

T. sylvestris (including *T. australis*, *T. celsiana*)	*T. goulimyi*
T. primulina	*T. doerfleri*
T. biebersteiniana	*T. theophrasti*
T. patens	*T. cinnabarina*
T. urumiensis	*T. sprengeri*
T. orphanidea (including *T. hageri*, *T. whittallii*)	

The flowers of section *Australes* range from creamy white and pale yellow to bright, golden yellow and brownish red. Some bright red forms occur, such as *Tulipa goulimyi*, but they never match the rich reds and scarlets found in subgenus *Tulipa*. This section is distributed across southern Europe and North Africa, to Turkey, the Caucasus Mountains, north-western Iran, and into central Asia.

Section *Australes* can be split into two groups, one centred around *Tulipa sylvestris* and the other around *T. orphanidea*. In the first group the flowers are a shade of yellow, or creamy white in *T. patens*. The tetraploid *T. sylvestris* has become naturalized in northern Europe, reaching as far as Britain and Scandinavia, but the other forms can be separated geographically. *Tulipa patens* and *T. biebersteiniana* occur in the Caucasus, Iran, central Asia, and

Tulipa sylvestris subsp. *australis* of section
Australes

southern Siberia. *Tulipa primulina* grows in North Africa along with *T. australis*, which is also found in southern Europe. The section takes its name from *T. australis*, but this species is now included within *T. sylvestris*, usually as subsp. *australis*.

The group centred around *Tulipa orphanidea* has flowers in shades of red, brownish red, and orange, often with a dark blotch, and outer tepals greenish or buff-coloured on their back. These species are found wild in south-eastern Europe and Turkey. The recently described *T. cinnabarina* seems close to this group, although it does share some characteristics with *T. humilis* in section *Saxatiles*. *Tulipa sprengeri*, with glabrous filaments and red flowers that do not have a basal blotch, is also close in general appearance to the *T. orphanidea* group.

Section *Saxatiles* Baker

T. saxatilis	*T. humilis* (including *T. pulchella*, *T. violacea*)
T. bakeri	*T. aucheriana*
T. cretica	*T. kurdica*

The species of section *Saxatiles* have flowers in shades of violet, pink, pinkish red, or brick-red, with a yellow or blue-black blotch. As in section *Australes*, the species of this section can be split into two groups. The first three species all grow on the island of Crete, with *Tulipa saxatilis* also found on Rhodes and in south-western Turkey. *Tulipa cretica* is more like members of the second group, which are low-growing plants with narrow leaves, but it is separated geographically; the last three species are found in Turkey, the Middle East, and Iran.

The flowers of *Tulipa humilis* are constricted just above the base. This feature is typical of many species in subgenus *Eriostemones*.

Section *Biflores* sensu Hall

- *T. biflora* (including
    T. polychroma)
- *T. sogdiana*
- *T. bifloriformis*
- *T. binutans*
- *T. orthopoda*
- *T. turkestanica*
- *T. tarda*
- *T. neustruevae*
- *T. dasystemon*
- *T. dasystemonoides*
- *T. orithyioides*

Section *Biflores* comprises several species that produce many flowers from one bulb, up to twelve in some forms of *Tulipa turkestanica*. The flowers are small and yellow, or white with

Tulipa biflora, the type of section *Biflores*

a yellow blotch of varying size. This distinctive section is centred in the mountains of central Asia but has spread westwards, with *T. biflora* reaching south-eastern Europe. This complex group includes more names than those listed here, having been described to cover the myriad variations found in the wild.

Section *Lophophyllon* Vvedensky

T. regelii

This lone species, with its small, white, funnel-shaped flowers and yellow blotch, could belong to section *Biflores*, but Aleksei Vvedensky placed it in its own section because of its unusual leaves. These have raised, undulating ridges along their length, a feature not found in any other species of tulip.

The *Neo-tulipae*

The term *neo-tulipae* (new tulips) has been used to identify the naturalized tulips of Europe that have been described as species but are derived from escapes from cultivation. Strictly speaking, they should be omitted from an account of wild tulips, but because they are sometimes offered for sale and have species names I have included some of the common ones in this book.

The *Neo-tulipae* began to be recognized and named early in the nineteenth century. In 1884 Emile Levier wrote *Tulipes de L'Europe*, where he divided the genus into Edmund Boissier's two sections, *Leiostemones* and *Eriostemones*. In the first section he included seventeen species from northern Italy, mostly around Florence, and south-eastern France, in the Savoy and Hautes-Alpes regions, particularly around the market town of St. Jean-de-Maurienne. Naturalized tulips have also been recorded from Switzerland.

In the Savoy region of France and the Valais of Switzerland, these *Neo-tulipae* grow in areas also known for their cultivation of saffron (*Crocus sativus*), another plant of unknown wild origin. Saffron has been grown in this part of the world since the eighth century. It is possible that the ancestors of these tulips could have been introduced at the same time, along with the corms of *C. sativus*, but exactly where they came from is a mystery.

In 1996 Jean Prudhomme wrote a survey of French and Swiss species of tulip in the *Bulletin Mensuel de la Société Linnéenne de Lyon*. This study, illustrated with numerous photographs, gave an updated account of the tulips from the western Alps. Prudhomme considered nine of these species, plus five more from Italy, to be *Neo-tulipae*.

Flora Europaea treated all of the variants from southern France, Switzerland, and northern Italy as clones of *Tulipa gesneriana*. However, some, such as the Italian *T. maleolens*, have bulb tunics lined with a dense layer of hairs and are probably derived from species in section *Tulipanum*.

Tulipa aximensis, one of the *Neo-tulipae*

Most of these tulips only occur in very small areas and are under threat from building developments. Some have been lost in the wild forever but, fortunately, have survived in cultivation. They generally grow around 30 cm (1 ft.) tall and have a single bowl- or upturned bell-shaped flower, with glabrous filaments. The three to five leaves are glaucous and reach up to 20 to 25 cm (8–10 in.) long and 5 to 6 cm (2–2.4 in.) wide.

The Romanian and Bulgarian species, *Tulipa hungarica*, *T. urumoffii*, and *T. rhodopea*, could also be treated as *Neo-tulipae*, and *T. suaveolens*, of unknown wild origin, may belong here. The following species of *Neo-tulipae* are those most frequently offered for sale and are included in chapter 6.

T. aximensis	*T. passeriniana*
T. didieri	*T. planifolia*
T. grengiolensis	*T. platystigma*
T. marjolletii	*T. sarracenica*
T. mauritiana	

6
SPECIES DESCRIPTIONS

Tulipa acuminata Vahl ex Hornemann
HORNED TULIP

The alphabet dictates that this list of tulips begins not with a species but with a hybrid. It is included here because it carries a species name and in recent years has become a popular and well-known plant due to its unusual flower shape. The name dates from 1813, when Martin Vahl, a professor of botany, included it in a listing of plants grown at Copenhagen Botanic Garden.

Tulipa acuminata

Known as the horned tulip, *Tulipa acuminata* has exceptionally narrow, pointed tepals that are yellow, streaked to a greater or lesser extent with bright red. It is reminiscent of the slender-flowered 'needle tulips' depicted in Turkish art from the eighteenth century and bred by florists in Istanbul. *Tulipa acuminata* does not correspond to any known wild species, and its origin almost undoubtedly lies in Istanbul, from where it was exported to Europe.

In the eighth volume of Redouté's *Liliacées*, published in 1815, this tulip appears as *Tulipa cornuta*, a name that stuck with it for many years. It was also illustrated, as *T. cornuta*, in the *Botanical Register* (t. 127), in

1816, where it is written that it was introduced into Parisian gardens from Iran in 1811.

Tulipa acuminata can grow 40 to 50 cm tall and usually has three glaucous, lanceolate leaves. The solitary flower is composed of linear-lanceolate tepals that taper into a long, narrow point (acuminate), forming an elegant, dagger-like bloom. Each tepal is up to 13 cm long and the tip becomes twisted, flaring open in the sun.

This tulip is easily grown in a sunny position and free-draining soil in the garden. It is a curious rather than attractive plant, but its intriguing flower shape, unlike any other tulip, lends it a certain charm.

Tulipa agenensis de Candolle

This red-flowered tulip was known for a long time as *Tulipa oculus-solis*, but the name *T. agenensis* was published earlier and is now recognized as correct for this species. Plants found growing near the town of Agen in south-western France were described by Augustin Pyramus de Candolle in 1804 and named *T. agenensis*, the tulip of Agen, in the first volume of Redouté's *Liliacées*. Although naturalized in this area of southern France and elsewhere, this species is probably native to the eastern Mediterranean.

In France, Italy, and parts of Turkey and Iran, *Tulipa agenensis* is a plant of cultivated ground—of fields, orchards, and vineyards—but according to *Flora Palaestina*, it is also found in forests and scrub along the coastal plain from Syria to Israel and in Cyprus, indicating that it may be indigenous to this region. It was most likely introduced to mainland Europe in the sixteenth century.

A notable characteristic of this species is the outer tepals of the flower that are significantly longer and more pointed than the inner tepals. The ovate to elliptic outer tepals can be from 4 to 9 cm long and 2 to 3 cm wide, but the obovate to oblong inner tepals only reach 3 to 7 cm long and 1 to 2 cm wide. All are scarlet with a pointed, yellow-margined, black basal blotch that covers one-third to one-half of each tepal. The outside of the flower is a lighter red or yellowish, particularly at the base. The ovary is narrowed below the stigma. The three to five more or less erect leaves are glaucous-green and have flat or undulate margins. The leaves are lanceolate and up to 25 cm long and 2.5 to 4 cm wide. The whole plant grows up to 40 cm tall.

Tulipa agenensis subsp. *sharonensis* is described in *Flora Palaestina* as a smaller version of this species, usually growing 20 to 25 cm tall and with the lower leaf only 1 to 2 cm wide. The flower is also slightly smaller than that of subsp. *agenensis*. Subsp. *sharonensis* was originally described as a distinct species, *T. sharonensis*, by John Dinsmore in 1934. It is restricted to sandy soils and hills along the coastal plain of the eastern Mediterranean.

The glabrous filaments and bowl-shaped flowers of *Tulipa agenensis* are typical of subgenus *Tulipa*. The bulb tunic is densely lined with interwoven, woolly hairs, a characteristic shared by several other species, including the central Asian *T. systola* and the western Asian *T. julia*. Another close species is *T. cypria*, which is endemic to Cyprus and may well be a local variant of *T. agenensis*. All these species are placed in section *Tulipanum*.

Soon after de Candolle named this tulip, and still in 1804, Jean Saint-Amans named the same plant *Tulipa oculus-solis*. When writing volume three of the third edition of *Flora Français*, which was published in 1805, de Candolle chose to use Saint-Amans's name for this tulip rather than *T. agenensis*. Also, a painting of this tulip was later published in volume four of *Liliacées*, in 1808, under the name *T. oculus-solis*. The name *T. oculus-solis* remained in use for many years and Sir Daniel Hall even named his subsection *Oculus-solis* after this species. However, de Candolle's name was published first and takes priority.

If you can provide well-drained soil and a sunny position, then *Tulipa agenensis* should survive in the open garden. After all, this species has become naturalized in southern Europe so it doesn't need the extreme conditions experienced by many tulips from central Asia. However, it is often slow to increase, despite being stoloniferous, and will gradually dwindle away if the conditions are not to its liking. If summer rainfall is high, it is better to give the dormant bulbs some cover to keep them dry.

Tulipa aitchisonii Hall

Sir Daniel Hall treated the diploid form of *Tulipa clusiana* as a separate species and named it *T. aitchisonii* in 1938. Today it is generally included in the broad concept of *T. clusiana* but is recognized as distinct in *Flora Iranica* where it is divided into var. *aitchisonii* and var. *clusianoides*. The former has yellow flowers and the latter has white flowers, both with the outer tepals backed with a broad red band.

Tulipa albertii Regel

One of the many red-flowered species in section *Eichleres*, *Tulipa albertii* is notable for its intensely glaucous leaves, usually with undulate margins. It flowers in April on gravelly slopes and in crevices in the Tien Shan. The species was named after Albert Regel, who discovered it in the mountains near Tashkent.

The bulb of *Tulipa albertii* has a leathery tunic, lined with short, coarse hairs inside, which become more dense towards the tip. The stem is fairly short, reaching between 12 and 20 cm long, and the upper part is pubescent and stained purple. The three or sometimes four blue-grey leaves are broadly oblong to oblong-lanceolate, and their undulate margins are ciliate. The lowest leaf reaches 15 cm long and up to 7 cm wide, but the other leaves, which are held close to the lower leaf, rapidly decrease in size.

The solitary flower is variable in colour but usually a shade of orange-red with a yellow base and a muddy-brown blotch that often becomes paler towards the base of the tepals. Orange, orange-pink, yellow, and wine-red forms also occur. The rhomboidal, pointed, outer tepals are up to 8 cm long and 6 cm wide, reflexed, and pubescent on the back. The obovate inner tepals are a little shorter and concave, curving inwards. The filaments are yellow, and the anthers are usually dark purple, but in pale-flowered forms they may be yellow.

Tulipa albertii was described by Eduard Regel in 1877. Zinaida Botschantzeva described two similar species, *T. vvedenskyi* and *T. butkovii*, in 1954 and 1961 respectively. Both are from the western Tien Shan. In their 1995 paper, van Raamsdonk and de Vries treated them as synonyms of *T. albertii*. Both *T. albertii* and *T. vvedenskyi* are commercially available, and I have treated all three species separately.

Tulipa aleppensis Boissier ex Regel

This red-flowered tulip takes its name from the city of Aleppo in northern Syria, where it was discovered growing in fields by German botanist Heinrich Carl Haussknecht. It was described by Edmund Boissier in 1873.

The three or four leaves of *Tulipa aleppensis* are glaucous and erect, usually with undulate margins. The lowest can reach 30 cm long and 3 to 5 cm wide. The flowers are red with a small, rounded black blotch inside, and paler on the outside. The pointed tepals are narrowly ovate to obovate, and the outer are longer than the inner. The outer tepals reach 5 to 9 cm long and 2 to 3 cm wide, while the inner tepals are only 4 to 6.5 cm long and around 2 cm wide. The filaments are black and the pollen yellow. The whole plant grows around 20 to 30 cm tall.

Tulipa aleppensis is found in the Syrian Desert and south-eastern Turkey. Whether this region is its natural home is debatable because the species only appears as a weed of cultivated areas. It is a triploid and may be derived from, or be a variant of, a similar local species, such as *T. agenensis* or *T. julia*, or it may have come from further east, being cast off by traders travelling to Turkey and Europe.

Tulipa aleppensis is closely related to *T. agenensis*. For a long time the latter was known as *T. oculus-solis*, and in 1874 J. Gilbert Baker treated *T. aleppensis* as a variety of it (*T. oculus-solis* var. *aleppica*). It is a shorter, more compact plant than *T. agenensis* and the flowers have narrower tepals. It is also said to differ in the hairs on the inside of the bulb tunic (long and straight rather than interwoven) and in the size of the black basal blotch on the tepals, which is much smaller than in *T. agenensis* and often not surrounded by a yellow margin.

Tulipa aleppensis can be grown in a similar way to *T. agenensis*, by providing adequate drainage in the open garden or some protection from excess summer rainfall.

Tulipa altaica Pallas ex Sprengel

Tulipa altaica takes its name from the Altai Mountains, which stretch from eastern Kazakhstan, through southern Siberia and north-western China, to Mongolia. This region is at the northern limit of the range of the genus *Tulipa*, and those species that grow here experience long and bitterly cold winters. *Tulipa altaica* is extremely hardy and can be grown in the open, given excellent drainage and a sunny position. It also does well in pots kept in a bulb frame or alpine house, where it will flower in late March or early April. It received the RHS Award of Garden Merit in 1997.

This tulip usually reaches 15 to 20 cm tall. The inside of the bulb tunic is lined with short, coarse hairs, although it may be glabrous around the middle. There are three or sometimes four lanceolate to oblong, glaucous leaves, the lowest up to 4 cm wide, the others becoming progressively shorter and narrower up the stem. The flower stem is pubescent and holds a solitary flower that is primrose-yellow to orange, with the back of the outer tepals stained with

Tulipa altaica

greenish purple or pinkish red. The anthers, pollen, and filaments are yellow, and the base of the tepals may be a paler yellow. The oblong to rhomboidal tepals are 4 to 5 cm long and up to 3 cm wide, though they are often smaller. The outer three are more pointed and slightly longer than the inner three.

Tulipa altaica is found in the Altai and the mountains and steppes further south in Kazakhstan and particularly in Dzungaria, a region of Xinjiang, China. It grows in scrub and on stony slopes, at elevations up to 2600 m (8530 ft.). It was described in 1825 by German naturalist and explorer Peter Simon von Pallas in volume two of Sprengel's *Systema Vegetabilium*. In 1878 an illustration of this species was published in volume 27 of Regel's *Gartenflora* (t. 942), showing orange-red flowers with a yellow base to the tepals. Tulips sold as *T. altaica* usually have pale yellow flowers with the outer tepals backed with purplish green.

This is one of several species from the eastern part of central Asia that make up section *Kolpakowskianae*. *Tulipa kolpakowskiana*, *T. iliensis*, and *T. anisophylla* are included under *T. altaica* var. *altaica* by van Raamsdonk and de Vries, who also reduced *T. ferganica* to *T. altaica* var. *ferganica*. In *Flora of the USSR* all these species were treated as distinct. Here I have adopted the latter approach because these species names are used in the trade, although only a few nurseries offer the plants. If the names only represent different forms of one variable species, then *T. altaica*, being the oldest, is the name to use.

Tulipa amabilis B. Fedtschenko

Boris Fedtschenko, principal botanist of the St. Petersburg Botanic Garden, named this species in 1914. Plants were found on the northern slopes of the Kopet–Dag, near Ashkhabad in southern Turkmenistan. However, Aleksei Vvedensky later concluded that this species was the same as *T. hoogiana*, described in 1910, and *T. amabilis* was reduced to a synonym of that species in *Flora of the USSR*. Bulbs are occasionally still offered for sale under the name *T. amabilis*, which means 'lovely'.

Tulipa anisophylla Vvedensky

This small yellow-flowered tulip is closely related to *Tulipa altaica* and *T. kolpakowskiana* in section *Kolpakowskianae*. It is known only from the Pamir Alai, where it flowers in March.

This species is rarely offered for sale and it is a plant I have never seen. According to *Flora of the USSR*, the stem is 8 to 20 cm tall and the peduncle is glabrous or slightly pubescent. There are usually three leaves, the lowest being oblong-ovate and up to 3 cm wide. The upper leaves are much shorter, even bract-like (*anisophylla* means 'with unequal leaves'). The one or occasionally two flowers are yellow and the outer tepals are tinged with violet on the back. Each tepal is from 1.5 to 3.5 cm long and roughly elliptic, although the inner ones have a more rounded apex.

Eduard Regel named this tulip *Tulipa kolpakowskiana* var. *humilis* in 1884. It had been found in the Darwas Range, Tajikistan, at altitudes between 1200 and 1800 m (3900–5900 ft.), and the outer tepals were stained greenish to dark red. Then, in 1935, Aleksei Vvedensky raised it to species level and named it *T. anisophylla*. He could not use Regel's name and call it *T. humilis* (meaning 'low-growing' or 'dwarfish') because that name had already been used for another tulip in 1844. However, *T. anisophylla*, like *T. kolpakowskiana*, may well be just a form of *T. altaica*.

Tulipa armena Boissier

A variable, fairly low growing species, *Tulipa armena* is found on rocky slopes and screes, up to 2750 m (9050 ft.) elevation, in Turkey, the Caucasus Mountains, and north-western Iran. The stem is from 8 to 25 cm tall and holds a relatively large flower with tepals nearly 6 cm long, above glaucous, wavy-edged leaves.

The flower of *Tulipa armena* is usually red with a dark basal blotch, but yellow forms with no blotch occur and these have been described as separate species, such as *T. galatica*. In 1995 van Raamsdonk and de Vries classified the latter yellow form as *T. armena* f. *galatica*. Other tulips that have been described as distinct species but represent variations of *T. armena* include *T. confusa*, *T. karabachensis*, and *T. mucronata*. Edmund Boissier described *T. armena* in 1859 from specimens collected in

Tulipa armena

north-eastern Turkey, where they were flowering in June. It is placed in section *Tulipa*.

The papery bulb tunic of this species is thinly to densely lined with hairs. The three to six leaves are glabrous or have hairs on the upper surface. The lowest leaf reaches 20 cm long and 3.5 cm wide. The solitary flower is scarlet and inside is a small black blotch often with a narrow yellow margin. In addition to the yellow forms, there are forms with partly red and partly yellow flowers. The obovate to ovate-elliptic outer tepals are a paler red on the back and reach 5.8 cm long and 2.7 cm wide. The obovate to obovate-spathulate inner tepals are a similar width but slightly shorter, reaching 4.5 cm long. The filaments are black and the anthers are yellow or blackish.

Two varieties of *Tulipa armena* are recognized in *Flora of Turkey*: var. *lycica* and var. *armena*. They differ in the hairiness of the bulb tunic: that of var. *lycica* is densely lined with long, soft hairs, while that of var. *armena* has shorter, more bristly hairs that may be sparse around the middle of the bulb. The former is endemic to southern and central Turkey and the latter has a more easterly distribution, from north-eastern Turkey, to the Caucasus and north-western Iran.

Tulipa armena needs a hot, dry summer rest. It can be grown in the open garden if planted in sharply draining soil and a sunny position. In areas where summers are frequently wet, it will be safer to grow this species in a bulb frame or alpine house. It flowers in April.

Tulipa aucheriana Baker

This charming little tulip produces small, pink, starry flowers in April. It comes from Iran, near Tehran, and was introduced to cultivation by Henry Elwes in 1880. J. Gilbert Baker described it in the *Gardeners' Chronicle* of 1883 and named it after the French naturalist and collector Pierre Aucher-Eloy, who, Baker discovered, had collected specimens many years before, in 1838.

In *Flora Orientalis*, Edmund Boissier assigned the specimens collected by Aucher-Eloy to *Tulipa humilis*, and more recently *Flora Iranica* stated that *T. aucheriana* is probably a geographical race of *T. humilis*, essentially differing only by flower colour. However, the name *T. aucheriana* is used for commercial stocks of this plant, which can be distinguished by the generally smaller flowers than *T. humilis* and the less well defined blotch.

The two to five slightly glaucous leaves of *Tulipa aucheriana* are clustered close to the ground, almost in a rosette, but extend beyond the flower, reaching around 10 to 12 cm. The flower is held on a short stem, often only 5 to

6 cm long, and opens to a flat star, with the pointed, elliptic to ovate tepals reaching 3 cm long. The inner tepals are wider than the outer. The colour of the flower is mauve-pink or brownish pink, and the back of the outer tepals is greenish yellow. The blotch at the centre of the flower is yellow but stained with brown, which in some forms can almost completely obscure the yellow of the blotch. The filaments, anthers, and pollen are also yellow.

One of the smallest tulips available, this species makes an attractive pot-grown plant for an alpine house or bulb frame. Its flowers, like those of *Tulipa humilis*, can abort if the soil dries out when the buds are forming. Otherwise, *T. aucheriana* is a free-flowering species that is easy to grow, given some protection. It received an Award of Merit from the RHS in 1970, the Award of Garden Merit in 1993, and a First Class Certificate in 2005.

Tulipa australis Link

This diploid, upland form of the well-known European *Tulipa sylvestris* differs from *T. sylvestris* in its smaller dimensions and the violet-red staining on the back of the outer tepals. A variable tulip found in southern Europe and North Africa, it is now usually classified as *T. sylvestris* subsp. *australis*, a combination first published by Renato Pampanini in 1914.

Tulipa aximensis Perrier & Songeon

One of the European *Neo-tulipae*, *Tulipa aximensis* used to grow in a small area around the market town of Aime, in the French region of Savoy. Although its habitat has now been destroyed by a housing estate, the species survives in cultivation. It was described in 1894. The flower, which reaches 12 to 14 cm across when fully open, is dark red. Inside, the base of the flower is yellow with a dark greyish green blotch at the centre. The filaments are black, and the anthers and pollen are yellow.

Tulipa bakeri Hall

Tulipa bakeri is endemic to the Mediterranean island of Crete, where it is commonly found on the high, flat plains of Omalos and Lassithi, on cultivated land and field margins and on rocky slopes and screes. It grows at altitudes of 650 to 2200 m (2130–7200 ft.) and in April produces large deep pink to lilac-purple flowers that have a rich yellow blotch at their centre and are held above broad, glossy green leaves. It is classified in section *Saxatiles* and is very similar to *T. saxatilis*, which also grows on Crete.

Sir Daniel Hall described this tulip in 1938, naming it after G. P. Baker, of Sevenoaks in Kent, who had collected the bulbs in Crete in 1926. They had been imported as *Tulipa saxatilis*, but Baker considered them to be sufficiently different to present a bulb to the John Innes Horticultural Institution, where Hall ascertained that this tulip was diploid and *T. saxatilis* was triploid. Hall concluded that the long-known *T. saxatilis* was derived from *T. bakeri*. It is now known that both triploid and diploid forms of *T. saxatilis* occur in the wild, the form in general cultivation being triploid. Despite the tendency to treat both tulips as the same species using the older name of *T. saxatilis,* other features can be used to distinguish them apart from the chromosome number.

Tulipa bakeri has flowers that are a deeper pink than those of *T. saxatilis*, with orange-yellow rather than brownish anthers, and the blotch is less well defined, merging into a pale ring rather than being sharply delimited. Cultivated plants of *T. saxatilis* tend to be taller and have larger flowers and

Tulipa bakeri 'Lilac Wonder'

leaves, although in the wild this is not always the case. Also, *T. saxatilis* is more vigorously stoloniferous and in the wild occupies cliffs and rocky ground, often growing on the sides of gorges, at altitudes below 900 m (2950 ft.). Nevertheless, there is some variation in these plants and it is not always clear, when you see them in cultivation, which of the two species you are looking at.

The leathery bulb tunic of *Tulipa bakeri* is yellowish brown and has a few short hairs inside at the base and tip. The two to four bright green leaves are up to 15 cm long and 2.5 cm wide. The glabrous stem is from 7.5 to 20 cm tall and holds a solitary flower, composed of spoon-shaped tepals that are 4 to 5 cm long and form a shallow bowl. The yellow blotch covers up to one-third of the tepals. The outer tepals are stained green on the back and the inner tepals have a green midrib. The filaments and anthers are orange-yellow.

Tulipa bakeri 'Lilac Wonder', the form most common in cultivation, makes an excellent garden plant for a sunny position with well-drained soil. This cultivar is easily grown and freely produces its pinkish lilac flowers in April. In 1995 it received the Award of Garden Merit from the RHS. As *T. bakeri* is now more frequently treated as a synonym of *T. saxatilis*, this cultivar is often listed as *T. saxatilis* 'Lilac Wonder' or *T. saxatilis* Bakeri Group 'Lilac Wonder', but these names all represent the same plant.

Tulipa batalinii Regel

The yellow forms of the otherwise red-flowered *Tulipa linifolia* have long been known as *T. batalinii*, a name first used by Eduard Regel in 1889 and still frequently seen today. This species is now included under *T. linifolia*, but the colour of the flowers warrants some sort of recognition, so in gardens these plants are identified as *T. linifolia* Batalinii Group. There are several widely grown and attractive cultivars of this tulip, which are listed here under *T. linifolia*.

Tulipa biebersteiniana Schultes f.

This variant of *Tulipa sylvestris* grows in an area that stretches from eastern Europe, through the Caucasus Mountains and Iran, to central Asia and southern Siberia. It is similar to the Mediterranean *T. sylvestris* subsp. *australis*, having yellow flowers with the back of the outer tepals tinged with violet, but the lowest of the two or three narrow linear-lanceolate leaves is broader, reaching 2 cm wide. Up to five flowers are produced on a glabrous stem that is 15 to 30 cm long. The tepals are generally between 2 and 3 cm long, occasionally up to 4 cm.

Described in 1829, this species was reduced to *Tulipa sylvestris* var. *bieber-steiniana* by Eduard Regel in 1873. More recently it was recognized as a distinct species in *Flora Iranica* but included within the broad concept of *T. sylvestris* in *Flora of Turkey*. Like the other variants of *T. sylvestris*, the status of *T. biebersteiniana* is not fully understood and the plants in cultivation represent only a sample of the forms found in the wild.

Tulipa biflora Pallas

Tulipa biflora is an early flowering species that does well in the open garden. Grown under glass, the starry, white flowers can open in February, but planted in the garden they will be a month later. In the wild the species generally flowers in April or May and grows on grassy or rocky slopes and screes.

This species is found in a broad sweep that stretches from Macedonia in south-eastern Europe, to north of the Black Sea, into south-western Russia, down through the Caucasus Mountains into eastern Turkey, Iran, Turkmenistan, Afghanistan, Pakistan, and far western China. It is even found in the mountains of the Arabian Peninsula. It is hardly surprising that a plant with such a wide natural distribution shows some variation throughout its range.

Tulipa biflora was described by Peter Simon von Pallas in 1776 from a specimen collected in southern Russia. The name *biflora* means 'twin-flowered', although this species often has three flowers and can have up to five or six per bulb. The flowers are held on glabrous, reddish purple, branching stems and open wide in the sun, displaying glistening white tepals with a golden yellow basal blotch.

The two linear-lanceolate leaves are glaucous on the upper surface, but on the underside they are shiny grey-green and have some purple staining near the base. The leaves of cultivated plants are widely spaced, with the lower leaf at ground level and the upper leaf held someway up the stem. The lowest leaf reaches 14 to 17 cm long and can vary in width from 0.9 to 2.5 cm. The upper leaf is a little shorter and narrower, from around 12 to 15 cm long and 0.5 to 1.7 cm wide.

The buds are usually erect as they emerge from between the leaves, but in some cases they are nodding, facing the ground until they are ready to open. The backs of the tepals are bluish green when the buds first emerge, fading to a pale greyish purple as the flowers open. The outer three tepals have much more staining on their backs than do the inner three, which often have just a thin purple-grey or greenish line running up the centre. The yellow anthers are up to 5 mm long and are held on filaments that have a boss of hairs at the base.

The greatest variation in *Tulipa biflora* is in the dimensions of individual forms. The tepals vary from quite narrowly lanceolate to elliptic or broadly ovate and tend to form a funnel-shaped flower. The tepals are generally between 3 and 4.5 cm long but can be smaller, with the outer tepals between 0.3 and 1.5 cm wide and the inner tepals up to 2.5 cm wide. The flower stem may be only a few centimetres long when the flowers first open but can extend to nearly 20 cm.

In 1885 Otto Stapf described *Tulipa polychroma*, a solitary-flowered tulip from the Caucasus, Iran, and northern Afghanistan, with broad inner tepals but otherwise very similar to *T. biflora*. Both *T. biflora* and *T. polychroma* have woolly hairs on the inside of the bulb tunic, but in the latter the tunic is said to be more leathery. The distinction between these two species is unclear in the wild, with smaller-flowered forms occurring within the range of *T. polychroma*. Most botanists now treat them both as *T. biflora*.

The small-flowered forms of *Tulipa biflora* can be disappointing, their tiny blooms looking a little insipid alongside more colourful spring bulbs. The best large-flowered forms make fine plants and are usually sold as *T. polychroma*. They flower early in the year, which can cause the stems to become etiolated and prone to collapse, so it is important to grow them where they can make the most of any winter sun. Growing them under glass will protect them from wind and rain, but in the garden they will flower later, when the days are longer, and the stems are less likely to become etiolated and ungainly.

Tulipa bifloriformis Vvedensky

Belonging to section *Biflores*, this small tulip grows wild on stony slopes in the foothills of the Tien Shan, where it can flower from March to July. It is very similar to *Tulipa biflora* and *T. turkestanica*, having two glaucous-green leaves and several creamy white flowers that have a yellow basal blotch.

Tulipa bifloriformis grows from a bulb with a leathery brown tunic lined with woolly hairs on the inside. The usually pubescent stem reaches 10 to 25 cm long and the lowest of the two linear to linear-lanceolate leaves reaches 20 cm long and 1.5 cm wide. Up to eleven flowers can be produced on a branching stem but two to eight are more common. The oblong to lanceolate, pointed tepals are between 1.5 and 3 cm long, the inner between 6 and 10 mm wide and the outer between 3 and 6 mm wide. The filaments are yellow and, as in *T. turkestanica*, they have wispy hairs along their length. The anthers are usually violet, sometimes yellow.

Aleksei Vvedensky described this species in 1935 and in *Flora of the*

USSR he mentioned two other similar forms that he later described as distinct species. *Tulipa orthopoda* is a dwarf form, with a very hairy bulb tunic, erect buds, and flowers held on a short stem between the two leaves. *Tulipa binutans* has a less hairy tunic, and the buds and fading flowers are nodding.

Tulipa bifloriformis is a variable species whose identity can be difficult to confirm in cultivation, where it flowers in late February and March. It is one of the confusing *T. biflora–T. turkestanica* aggregate and may be better looked upon as a form of the latter. Although occasionally offered for sale, it is not commonly grown and not a very

Tulipa bifloriformis

showy species. A cultivar called 'Starlight' became available recently and has flowers of a clearer, brighter colour held on shorter stems than the forms generally offered for sale.

Tulipa binutans Vvedensky

As referred to previously, this species was first mentioned by Aleksei Vvedensky in *Flora of the USSR*, under the entry for *Tulipa bifloriformis*. Vvedensky eventually described it in 1952 from plants growing in the Alexandrov Range of the Tien Shan. The buds and fading flowers are nodding, a feature also found in some forms of *T. biflora*.

Tulipa borszczowii Regel

This central Asian species grows in the sandy soils of the Karakum and Kyzylkum Deserts, to the south of the Aral Sea, in western Uzbekistan, northern Turkmenistan, and south-western Kazakhstan. It is not a common plant in the wild and is rare in cultivation. In its native home it flowers in May, but grown in a bulb frame or alpine house, where winters are not so cold, it can flower before the end of February.

Along with the other species in section *Tulipanum*, this one has a bulb tunic lined with a thick mat of woolly hairs. However, in *Tulipa borszczowii* the leathery tunic is elongated at the tip to form a papery sheath around the underground part of the stem, often extending almost to ground level.

The green bud emerges on a short, glabrous stem from between the two broad, upright lower leaves. These oblong-lanceolate leaves are hairless, glaucous, and roughly 10 to 11 cm long at flowering time and 1.5 to 4.5 cm wide. The two upper leaves are much smaller, being half the length and less than 1 cm wide. When the flower first opens, the stem may be only 5 to 6 cm tall, though it can reach over 20 cm. The overlapping tepals form an elegant cup-shaped bloom.

The flower is a rich orange-yellow, and inside the basal blotch is deep reddish purple. The outer surface of the tepals is deeper orange and has a maroon-purple mark at the base that corresponds to the inner blotch. In the wild, flower colour can vary from yellow to orange-red but always with a deep purple blotch. The anthers and filaments are dark purple. Each tepal is about 5 to 6 cm long and 2 to 2.5 cm wide, the outer being ovate to rhomboidal and the inner more obovate. There is a short point, or cusp, at the tip of each tepal. The inner tepals are slightly longer than the outer, and the general flower shape is similar to that of the closely related *Tulipa systola*. In fact, in many ways *T. borszczowii* is like a yellow form of *T. systola*, but it is a wonderful rich yellow, and the flower colour, as well as the elongated bulb tunic, serve to distinguish it from the latter.

Tulipa borszczowii was described by Eduard Regel in 1868 and is named after its discoverer, the Russian explorer Borszczow, who found it flowering in May 1857, in the Karakum steppe, Turkmenistan. A few years later Regel had this species figured for the first volume of *Flora Turkestanica*, published in 1876.

Tulipa borszczowii

This detailed drawing clearly shows the elongated bulb tunic and the abruptly pointed tepal tip.

Tulipa butkovii Z. Botschantzeva

An obscure species, rarely offered for sale, *Tulipa butkovii* is similar in many ways to *T. vvedenskyi*, but the anthers gradually open (dehisce) from the tip down, as in *T. kaufmanniana*, although they do not coil as they do so. In their 1995 paper, van Raamsdonk and de Vries treated this species and *T. vvedenskyi* as synonyms of *T. albertii*.

Described by Zinaida Botschantzeva in 1961, *Tulipa butkovii* has a pubescent, glaucous stem reaching 10 to 15 cm tall and three or four glaucous, lanceolate leaves sometimes with thin, pale reddish margins. The lower leaf reaches 18 cm long and 5 cm wide. The bulb has a papery tunic lined with short hairs, especially at the base and tip. The flower is glossy red and has narrowly oblong or ovate tepals. The outer tepals reach 5.5 cm long and 2.2 cm wide, and are pinkish red on the back, especially along the midrib. The inner tepals are slightly shorter. At the base of the flower is a brownish or greenish yellow blotch that can be quite small. The filaments are a shade of red or greenish yellow, and the anthers are yellow or reddish purple.

Tulipa butkovii grows on sandy or stony slopes, at elevations up to 2000 m (6560 ft.) in the western Tien Shan. It is named after A. Y. Butkov, who

Tulipa butkovii

collected bulbs in a sandy pass in Chimgan, north-east of Tashkent, in 1954. Botschantzeva stated that this species flowers later than its close relatives, in late April, but in cultivation it can be in flower by late March.

Tulipa carinata Vvedensky

This rarely grown tulip of section *Eichleres* is found in the south-western Pamir Alai, in western Tajikistan, southeast Uzbekistan, and northern Afghanistan. It grows on rocky slopes at high altitudes, from 1500 to 2500 m (4900–8200 ft.) or more, where it flowers in May and June. Aleksei Vvedensky described it in 1935.

Tulipa carinata is related to *T. fosteriana*, which grows slightly further north, but the hairs inside the bulb tunic are more woolly. It can grow to 50 cm tall and the flower stem is covered in fine woolly hairs. The three or four glaucescent to green leaves are pubescent and have ciliate margins. These leaves have a prominent keel underneath (the botanical term for this feature is *carinate*), from which this tulip gets its name. The lowest leaf is lanceolate and 1.5 to 3 cm wide.

The solitary red flower has a yellow blotch inside or a small black blotch with a yellow margin. The tepals are 4 to 8 cm long and taper gradually to a pubescent point. The outer tepals arch out and their backs are flushed with pink. The filaments are black and the anthers yellow or violet.

Tulipa celsiana Henning

This small, yellow-flowered tulip was described in Redouté's *Liliacées* in 1803 but has been in cultivation for well over four hundred years, often under the name *Tulipa persica*. It is a form of *T. sylvestris* subsp. *australis*, but the clone in cultivation is distinct, growing around 10 to 15 cm tall and flowering in May, later than most other forms of *T. sylvestris*. The leaves curl round and lie close to the ground, and the backs of the outer tepals are tinged with red. This species was originally described from plants growing in southern France but similar forms also occur in North Africa. It can be grown in the open garden, in a warm, sunny position.

Tulipa chrysantha Boissier

Tulipa chrysantha is the name Edmund Boissier gave to the yellow form of *T. montana*. It was subsequently, and incorrectly, applied to yellow forms of *T. clusiana*, which mainly differ in their narrower tepals. The yellow forms of *T. clusiana* passed into gardens as *T. chrysantha* and are still sometimes sold under that name today.

Tulipa cinnabarina K. Persson

This newly discovered Turkish tulip was described in *The New Plantsman* by Karin Persson of Gothenburg University as recently as 2000. It grows in limestone fields and alpine steppe and on rocky slopes, at altitudes of 1700 to 1800 m (5580–5900 ft.) in the Isaurian Taurus Mountains of southern Turkey. It flowers in late April and May.

Tulipa cinnabarina appears to fall somewhere between *T. humilis* and *T. orphanidea*, in sections *Saxatiles* and *Australes* respectively. It differs from both in having two or rarely three leaves, rather than three to five. It also differs from *T. orphanidea* in having a more easterly distribution and more elliptic tepals that are brilliant orange-red with a yellow blotch. *Tulipa humilis* is more dwarf in habit, the flowers are more distinctly constricted at the base, the glaucous leaves are wider relative to their length, and forms from the Taurus Mountains have a dark centre to their flowers, often on a white background.

The leathery bulb tunic of *Tulipa cinnabarina* is dark reddish brown and lined with long, straight hairs towards the tip. The two or three linear, pale green leaves reach 18 cm long and 1.5 cm wide and are dull above but glossy beneath. In height they exceed the solitary flower, which is held only 5 to 9 cm above ground and is initially nodding in bud. The orange-red flower is slightly constricted at its base and inside it has a yellow blotch. In the sun it opens up to form a wide cup. The outer tepals are elliptic-oblong to oblanceolate-oblong and 3 to 4.3 cm long and 6 to 8 mm wide. The inner tepals are oblong-elliptic to elliptic and up to 4.7 cm long and 1.2 cm wide. The filaments are golden yellow with white hairs just above the base, the anthers bluish black, and the pollen dark yellow to black.

This same tulip was also described by two Turkish botanists, Neriman Özhatay and B. Koçak, who named it *Tulipa karamanica*, after the place where it was found. This latter name is dated 2000, but the supplement to *Flora of Turkey* (Güner et al. 2001) that the description appeared in (volume 11) was not actually published until 2001 so the name *T. cinnabarina* takes priority. In fact, the type specimen of *T. cinnabarina* was collected in 1990, with a further collection made in April 1999, but the type specimen cited for *T. karamanica* was collected in May 1999. Although it seems a shame that a Turkish name given by Turkish botanists for a Turkish plant is not valid but the name given to it by a Swedish botanist is, those are the rules.

Tulipa cinnabarina is grown at Gothenburg Botanic Garden, where it produces plenty of seed. In general appearance it seems closest to *T. orphan-*

idea but with a yellow blotch. It is said to have more brilliantly red flowers than that species, but I have seen some very bright red forms of *T. orphanidea*. Nevertheless, this is an attractive species that will no doubt become more widely grown.

Tulipa clusiana de Candolle
LADY TULIP

This charming and popular species brightens up a sheltered sunny border or rock garden and has been known in cultivation for hundreds of years. It is named after the renowned sixteenth-century botanist Carolus Clusius, who knew this plant as *Tulipa persica praecox*. In gardens it flowers in late March and April and is commonly known as the lady tulip.

The basic flower colour of *Tulipa clusiana* is white, but the three outer tepals are backed with a reddish pink band. Even when closed the flowers are attractive, with the erect, pointed, bi-coloured buds held on slender stems. This tulip reaches from 13 to 30 cm tall, and when the sun shines, the flowers open wide, with the tepals bending back as if sunbathing in the warmth. The elliptic outer tepals are 3 to 6.5 cm long (usually around 4 to 5 cm) and between 1 and 2 cm wide. The more rounded, oblong to obovate inner tepals are shorter, slightly narrower, and white on their backs. Inside the flower is a small purple blotch at the base of the tepals, and the stamens are the same colour.

The three to five leaves are glaucous, erect, linear-lanceolate, and deeply channelled. The lower two are longer than those higher up the stem. They can reach 28 cm long but are less than 2 cm and often under 1 cm wide. The bulb has a fairly tough tunic, with a few hairs around the base and longer hairs at the neck, forming a thick felt that protrudes from the top of the bulb, a characteristic shared by the related species, *Tulipa montana* and *T. linifolia*, in section *Clusianae*.

The white form of *Tulipa clusiana* is less commonly offered for sale than the yellow form. These yellow flowers still have outer tepals with a reddish pink back but lack the small purple blotch inside. White-flowered forms in which the blotch and stamens are yellow, not purple, have been described as a separate species, *T. stellata*, but are now usually included under *T. clusiana*, as are *T. aitchisonii* and *T. chitralensis*.

In keeping with its long history in cultivation, this tulip has many names associated with it. To make sense of these it seems best to start at the beginning. In 1802 the already well-known *Tulipa clusiana* was described by Augustin P. de Candolle in volume one of Redouté's *Liliacées*. This is the white-flowered plant with a purple blotch and the outer tepals backed with reddish pink. In 1827 William Hooker described *T. stellata* from the mountains of north-western India, in *Curtis's Botanical Magazine* (t. 2762), but in 1873 Regel treated it as a variety of *T. clusiana*.

Sir Daniel Hall described *Tulipa aitchisonii* in 1938. He concluded that this diploid species from Chitral in northern Pakistan, and Kashmir, had given rise to the pentaploid *T. clusiana* and the tetraploids *T. stellata* and *T. chitralensis*. *Tulipa aitchisonii* is shorter and more delicate-looking than *T. clusiana* but is otherwise indistinguishable without studying the chromosomes. Hall treated the tetraploid form with yellow flowers backed with red as a colour variant of *T. stellata*. He also described *T. aitchisonii* subsp. *cashmeriana*, from Kashmir, in which the flowers are completely yellow, without any red markings on the outer tepals.

It wasn't long before doubts were cast over Hall's treatment of this group. In 1948 J. Robert Sealy named the yellow-and-red form of this tulip *Tulipa clusiana* var. *chrysantha*, in *Curtis's Botanical Magazine* (t. NS13). He stated that intermediates between *T. clusiana* and *T. stellata* had been found in the wild and that the variation in flower colour was not reason enough to maintain them as separate species. Sealy agreed with Hall that the diploid plants (*T. aitchisonii*) were the source of the other forms in this group, but decided that taxonomically it is better to treat them as forms of *T. clusiana*.

A similar conclusion was arrived at more recently by van Raamsdonk and de Vries, who divided *Tulipa clusiana* into four formas: f. *clusiana*, f. *stellata*, the all yellow f. *cashmeriana*, and f. *dinae*. The last of these is their new name for Sealy's yellow-and-red var. *chrysantha*. *Tulipa chrysantha* was originally described as the yellow form of *T. montana*. It was also incorrectly

A diploid form of *Tulipa clusiana*, collected in Afghanistan, near Kabul

applied to yellow forms of *T. clusiana*, so a change of name for this colour form avoids any confusion with *T. montana*. However, this new name is rarely used at present, and *T. clusiana* var. *chrysantha* is still preferred in the trade. It received the RHS Award of Garden Merit in 1993 under this name.

Forma *clusiana* includes *Tulipa chitralensis* and the white-flowered forms of Hall's *T. aitchisonii*. Its range in the wild extends from Kashmir, through northern Pakistan, to Afghanistan and Iran, and it is found at altitudes of up to 3350 m (11,000 ft.). It is also naturalized in southern Europe, from Spain to western Turkey, where it usually grows in fields.

Forma *stellata*, with the yellow blotch inside the flower, is found in Afghanistan, northern Pakistan, and in the Himalaya as far east as Kumaon in northern India. The yellow f. *dinae* has a similar range, and f. *cashmeriana* is from Kashmir.

So what does all this mean for the gardener? Well, the white-flowered *Tulipa clusiana* f. *clusiana* is occasionally offered but often sells out quickly. The forms most commonly available have yellow flowers and are usually sold as *T. clusiana* var. *chrysantha* or just *T. chrysantha*. Various cultivars also have yellow flowers. 'Tubergen's Gem' is a tall form that has large yellow flowers with a bold red band on the back of the outer tepals. 'Cynthia' (RHS Award

Tulipa clusiana 'Lady Jane'

of Garden Merit, 1999) has flowers of a paler yellow, a result of crossing the white and yellow forms of *Tulipa clusiana*. 'Tinka' is primrose-yellow with a cardinal-red back to the outer tepals and dark purple pollen, and 'Sheila' is similar but with a darker yellow base to the tepals and yellow pollen.

The cultivar with flowers closest in colour to *Tulipa clusiana* f. *stellata* is the beautiful 'Lady Jane'. 'Honky Tonk' has soft, pale yellow flowers with a slight pinkish staining towards the tip of the outer tepals; it is the closest cultivar to f. *cashmeriana*.

Tulipa clusiana 'Honky Tonk'

Tulipa cretica Boissier & Heldreich

This small tulip in section *Saxatiles* only grows on Crete. Each plant produces up to three pale rose-pink flowers that peer between rocks and stones, on open slopes, cliffs, and screes, at altitudes of 500 to 2200 m (1640 to 7200 ft.), in mountains and gorges across the island. In the wild it flowers in April or early May and the stem can be less than 5 cm long, but in cultivation the flowers can appear earlier, in March, and the plants may reach over 10 cm tall at flowering time.

Tulipa cretica was described in 1854 by Edmund Boissier and Theodor von Heldreich in Boissier's *Diagnoses Plantarum Orientalium Novarum* (1842–1859). It is superficially similar to another dwarf, pink-flowered species in section *Saxatiles*, the Iranian *T. aucheriana*, but the leaves are broader, more glossy, and upright, and the flowers are a clearer, more pure pink. Also, *T. cretica* is geographically isolated from the *T. humilis* group (to which *T. aucheriana* belongs) and has more in common with the Cretan *T. saxatilis* and *T. bakeri*.

The thick, leathery bulb tunic of *Tulipa cretica* has a few straight hairs at the tip and base. The two or three glabrous, narrowly lanceolate leaves are deep green, and shiny on the upper surface. They are nearly flat, not chan-

Tulipa cretica

nelled as in the*T. humilis* group. The lowest reaches 1.7 cm wide and can be 19 cm long but is more often around 10 cm. Up to three erect buds are produced from each bulb, and the starry flowers are very pale pink, almost white inside, with a dull yellow blotch at the centre. The backs of the outer tepals are marked with green and darker reddish pink, especially towards the tip. The elliptic outer tepals are 1.5 to 3 cm long and 0.4 to 1 cm wide. The elliptic-oblong inner tepals may be 1 to 2 mm longer and wider. The filaments and anthers are yellow.

Although hardy, this pretty tulip is best grown in an alpine house or bulb frame, where the leaves and early flowers will be protected from the weather. It can be grown in a sheltered spot in the well-drained soil of a rock garden, but the small, pale flowers are likely to be lost among other plants.

Tulipa cypria Stapf

Tulipa cypria is essentially a purplish crimson or blood-red version of *T. agenensis*. It is only found in northern Cyprus, where it grows in fields and pastures and on rocky limestone slopes, among juniper and *Cistus*, and flowers in March or April. This rare, protected species is mainly confined to cultivated areas and may be a mutation of *T. agenensis*, the only other tulip found on Cyprus, but its distinctive colouring helps to differentiate it.

The whole plant grows from 20 to 35 cm tall, with usually four glaucescent leaves, the lowest reaching 30 cm long and 2 to 4 cm wide. The glabrous stem holds a solitary flower consisting of oblong-ovate tepals that are from 3 to 7 cm long and 1.5 to 3.5 cm wide. The tip of the outer tepals is more pointed than that of the inner tepals. The basal blotch inside the flower is edged with a narrow yellow margin. This purplish black blotch is smaller and more rounded in shape than in *Tulipa agenensis*, being only around 2 cm in diameter. The outside of the flower is greenish near the base. The filaments are dark purple and the pollen is yellowish.

Tulipa cypria was named by Otto Stapf, whose description was published in *Curtis's Botanical Magazine* (t. 9363) in 1934, a year after his death. It had been collected several times before, first by the Austrian botanist Theodor Kotschy in 1862, but earlier authors usually assigned it to *T. montana*. The plant painted for *Curtis's Botanical Magazine* was grown by Sir Daniel Hall at the John Innes Horticultural Institute.

Like *Tulipa agenensis*, *T. cypria* often does not do well in the open garden, unless it is grown in a climate with long, dry summers. It may survive if planted in well-drained soil, but it is better to grow this species in a frame, to keep off summer rain. On Cyprus it grows at altitudes below 300 m (980 ft.), so in cooler climates any early growth, which can appear above ground in December, can be damaged by hard frosts.

Tulipa dasystemon (Regel) Regel

This small, yellow-flowered species is close to *Tulipa tarda*. It differs from that species mainly in its fewer leaves, solitary flower, and the lack of any white on the tepals. Although available from some nurseries, *T. dasystemon* is not widely grown. It is well suited to growing in an alpine house or bulb frame, but the similar and more vigorous *T. tarda* is better for the open garden.

Growing from a bulb with few or no hairs on the inner surface of the dark papery tunic, the glabrous stem can reach 10 to 20 cm tall, although the flowers often open when held only a few centimetres above ground. The lowest of the two linear leaves reaches 10 to 15 cm long and up to 1.5 cm wide. The tepals reach 3 cm long and 1 cm wide, but the lanceolate outer three are around half the width of the oblong-ovate inner three. The tepals are yellow, sometimes quite pale, and the outer three are stained with greenish purple or dingy violet on the back. The anthers and hairy filaments are yellow.

This tulip grows in the mountains of the Tien Shan and Pamir Alai and further east in north-western China. It is found at high altitudes, growing

Tulipa dasystemon

on sunny slopes at 1800 to 3200 m (5900–10,500 ft.), where it flowers in May and June. In cultivation the flowers open in late April or early May.

The ovary of *Tulipa dasystemon* has an elongated style, and for this reason Eduard Regel initially placed this plant in the genus *Orithyia*, in 1877, naming it *O. dasystemon*. It had been collected by his son Albert, near Almaty in Kazakhstan. Three years later Eduard renamed it *Tulipa dasystemon*, following J. Gilbert Baker's decision to include *Orithyia* within the genus *Tulipa*. It is now placed in section *Biflores* because the filaments are hairy at their base.

Early in the twentieth century, bulbs sold as *Tulipa dasystemon* were actually a different, undescribed species. Otto Stapf recognized that this was a new plant and in 1933 he named it *T. tarda*. Confusion over the name of this tulip persisted in the trade for a long time. In recent years it seems to have been resolved, and when you buy bulbs labelled as *T. dasystemon* that is usually what you get.

Tulipa dasystemonoides Vvedensky

Tulipa dasystemonoides has a leathery bulb tunic that is densely woolly at the tip, and the plant can occasionally produce two flowers. Otherwise it is virtually the same as *T. dasystemon*, with two leaves and yellow flowers held on a short stem. It grows at high altitudes in the Tien Shan and was described by Aleksei Vvedensky in 1935 from material collected in the Talas Ala Tau of north-western Kyrgyzstan.

Tulipa didieri Jordan

Described in 1846 by Alexis Jordan, this was one of the first of the *Neo-tulipae* to be named as a species. It once grew 'wild' near St. Jean-de-Maurienne, in Savoy, France, but the last known locality has now been destroyed by building developments. This tulip survives in gardens. The three or four leaves are very glaucous and have undulate margins. The flower is red and the tips of the tepals are slightly reflexed. The outer tepals are tinged with crimson on the back. Inside the flower is a large dark purple blotch, narrowly margined with yellow or creamy white. The filaments and anthers are dark violet.

Tulipa doerfleri Gandoger

Only found wild on the island of Crete, *Tulipa doerfleri* is closely related to *T. orphanidea* in section *Australes*. Among the forms of *T. orphanidea*, it most closely resembles those from the Greek mainland described as *T. hageri* but differs in its wider, more ovate, less pointed tepals. Also, the backs of the outer tepals are not heavily stained with green but are greenish white towards their tips and at their bases.

The red goblet-shaped blooms of this tulip appear in grassy meadows in the Kedros Mountains of west-central Crete, where it grows in large numbers and flowers in mid-April. It was described by French botanist Michel Gandoger in 1916 and named after Ignaz Doerfler, who collected the type specimen. In 1932 August Hayek reduced it to a variety of *Tulipa hageri*, but this classification has not found favour and *T. doerfleri* is usually accepted as a distinct species. Although a beautiful sight when large groups are seen growing wild, this species is not the most attractive of the *T. orphanidea* group and is rare in cultivation.

Tulipa doerfleri

Tulipa dubia Vvedensky

This tulip is similar in appearance to the much better known and more widely grown *Tulipa kaufmanniana* and is found naturally in the same part of the world, the mountains of western Tien Shan. It is a shorter plant at flowering time than *T. kaufmanniana* and the leaf margins are strongly undulate and lie close to the ground. It also has smaller flowers that open later, in April. Zinaida Botschantzeva moved *T. dubia* into Aleksei Vvedensky's section *Spiranthera*, along with *T. kaufmanniana* and *T. tschimganica*, because, like those species, it has anthers that dehisce gradually and slowly from the tip, although they split into longitudinal strands rather than coiling or twisting.

Tulipa dubia has a dark brown, papery bulb tunic lined with hairs. The pubescent stem reaches 10 to 25 cm tall and produces two to four very glaucous, almost blue leaves. The lowest leaf is ovate to broadly lanceolate and up to 6 cm wide and 14 cm long. The solitary flower is yellow with a deeper yellow centre, and the back of the outer tepals is tinged with violet-red. Sometimes the flower can open before it has completely emerged from between the rosette of closely spaced leaves. The oblong to rhomboidal tepals are 2 to 4 cm long and 1 to 1.5 cm wide. They open wide to form a star-shaped bloom. The yellow anthers are held on orange-yellow filaments that taper to a pointed tip.

This species was described by Vvedensky in 1935. It grows in the upper mountain zone, above 1800 m (5900 ft.), in the western Tien Shan and is said to hybridize in the wild with *Tulipa kaufmanniana*. Although it is in cultivation, *T. dubia* is rarely offered for sale.

Tulipa eichleri Regel

With its large, bright red flowers and wide, glaucous leaves, *Tulipa eichleri* has become a popular species for the garden. It was described by Eduard Regel in 1874, from plants found by the traveller Eichler, in the Baku region of eastern Transcaucasia. The description and an illustration appeared in volume 23 of *Gartenflora* (t. 799). However, in *Flora of Turkey*, Wessel Marais (1984) stated that this illustration represents *T. undulatifolia*, which was described by Edmund Boissier from Turkish plants in 1844. So is *T. eichleri* a distinct species, or should it be included under the earlier name of *T. undulatifolia*?

Even though bulbs are sold under the name *Tulipa eichleri*, the prevailing view is that *T. undulatifolia* is the correct name, although there are exceptions. *Flora Iranica* (which does not cover Turkey) recognized *T. eichleri*, as did van Raamsdonk and de Vries in their 1995 paper. Furthermore, this species has given its name to section *Eichleres*.

Regel's plant, *Tulipa eichleri*, is found in eastern Transcaucasia and possibly northern Iran. The bulb tunic is lined with hairs especially at the tip and the base. The pubescent stem reaches 20 to 40 cm tall and carries three or four glaucous leaves with undulate margins. The upper one or two leaves are slightly pubescent, the lower leaf is linear-lanceolate to oblong, up to 6.5 cm wide, and can reach over 30 cm long but is typically around 15 to 20 cm.

The solitary flower is glossy scarlet with a broad, black basal blotch margined with yellow. The oblong to oblong-lanceolate tepals are around 7 cm long and 4 cm wide in cultivated plants, but they can be as short as 2.5 cm. The tips of all the tepals end in short pubescent points, but the points are more pronounced on the outer three and more rounded on the inner

Tulipa eichleri

three. Inside the flower, the black filaments hold yellow to violet anthers. The pale yellow stigmas are thick and undulate and have been described as 'ear-shaped'.

Both *Tulipa eichleri* and *T. undulatifolia* are commonly found in cultivated areas, growing among field crops, the latter species in the southern Balkans and western and central Turkey. *Flora of the USSR* also stated that *T. eichleri* is found on dry slopes. Maybe this tulip spread from central Asia, becoming naturalized further west. Plants in Turkey and south-eastern Europe were named *T. undulatifolia* and those from the Caucasus Mountains named *T. eichleri*. Whatever the correct name, forms in general cultivation are stunning tulips, tough and easy to grow, with brilliant scarlet flowers that open in mid to late April. This species does well on a rock garden or in a sunny, well-drained border and can even be used as part of a spring bedding scheme.

Tulipa ferganica Vvedensky

In far eastern Uzbekistan and over the border into south-western Kyrgyzstan and northern Tajikistan lies the Fergana Basin. Drained by the Syr Dar'ya River and surrounded by mountains, this wide, flat, fertile valley is densely populated and rich in agriculture. To the northeast is the Fergana

Range, part of the Tien Shan, and to the south the Pamir Alai. In these hills and mountains, growing on stony slopes, is the bright yellow tulip that takes its name from this region.

Tulipa ferganica generally grows 15 to 25 cm tall, with three glaucous, wavy-edged leaves and a pubescent flower stem. The dark brown bulb tunic is leathery and hairy at the tip and base. The lower leaf is lanceolate to oblong and up to 30 to 40 cm long and 6.5 cm wide. The remaining leaves are shorter and do not surpass the flower. All the leaves are covered in a fine pubescence.

The flower is golden yellow, but the outer tepals are tinged with a blush of violet, reddish purple, or orange-red. This staining becomes stronger as the flower ages. Sometimes a second flower is produced. Each oblong to rhomboidal tepal is up to 7.5 cm long and 2.5 cm wide, narrowing to a pointed tip. There is no blotch. The yellow filaments hold yellow anthers.

Aleksei Vvedensky described this tulip in 1935. It is one of the species of section *Kolpakowskianae* and is similar to *Tulipa altaica*—so similar in fact that van Raamsdonk and de Vries (1995) treated it as a variety of that species (*T. altaica* var. *ferganica*). They stated that the main differences between it and var. *altaica* are the wider stems and leaves and the larger flower parts. Also, var. *altaica* grows in the Tien Shan and northwards to the Altai Mountains, whereas var. *ferganica* is found in the southern ranges of the Tien Shan (the Fergana and Chatkal Ranges), the Fergana Basin, and the Pamir Alai.

In the wild *Tulipa ferganica* flowers in May or June, but in cultivation, especially if grown in a frame or glasshouse, it blooms in April. Like *T. altaica* and *T. kolpakowskiana*, this species can be grown outside in free-draining soil and a warm, sunny position but will do well in pots, which can be kept under cover during the summer to thoroughly dry out the soil. Comparing commercial stocks of *T. ferganica* and *T. kolpakowskiana*, the former is like a larger, more impressive version of the latter. Although *T. ferganica* is one of the pricier tulip species, I have found it increases well. When forming a large group it can make quite an impact, the golden yellow blooms opening wide in the sun.

Tulipa fosteriana Hoog ex W. Irving

This magnificent tulip has quite rightly become one of the most popular and widely grown tulip species, even though it was only described in 1906. In its larger forms, the tall, sturdy stems, huge bright red flowers, and broad leaves, up to 16 cm across, help to distinguish it from other red-flowered species. The glossy flowers can be 15 cm or more across when fully open.

It is safe to say that *Tulipa fosteriana* has embraced cultivation, adapting to a variety of soils and situations, seemingly relishing neglect and still reappearing year after year. Its tough constitution and flamboyant appearance have ensured its use in the breeding of many garden cultivars, including the Darwinhybrids. In fact, many of the taller hybrid tulips that persist in the open garden and flower regularly have *T. fosteriana* somewhere in their ancestry. Cultivars that closely resemble the species or are selected forms of it, such as the impressive 'Red Emperor', are classified in the Fosteriana Group.

Tulipa fosteriana grows wild in the western Pamir Alai, in the mountains around Samarkand, Uzbekistan, where it flowers in April or May. It can be found in deep, humus-filled pockets among rocks, at altitudes of around 1700 m (5580 ft.). This was one of the species sent to C. G. van Tubergen by Joseph Haberhauer from the Bukhara region of Uzbekistan, at the beginning of the twentieth century. It was first described in the *Gardeners' Chronicle* of 26 May 1906, but the name had been used the previous year, when the plant received an Award of Merit from the RHS. The description noted the large flowers of 'rich, intense, glowing crimson' and the robust habit. The species is named after Professor Michael Foster, who gardened at Shelford, near Cambridge.

The bulb has a leathery, dark brown tunic, densely lined with straight hairs especially at the tip. The pubescent flower stem generally reaches 20 to 35 cm tall, but some forms are taller, up to 50 cm. The three or four leaves have ciliate margins and are also covered in a fine pubescence. They can be glaucous or shiny green. The leaves decrease in size up the stem, but the lowest one is elliptic to oblong and can reach over 30 cm long and up to 16 cm wide.

The solitary red flower has tepals 4.5 to 12.5 cm long, each with a short pubescent point at the otherwise rounded tip. The outer tepals are roughly oblong,

Tulipa fosteriana

the inner tepals more obovate. The blotch inside the flower, at the base of the tepals, may be black margined with yellow or yellow throughout. The filaments are the same colour as the basal blotch, either black or yellow, and the anthers are violet.

Tulipa galatica Freyn

This yellow tulip is named after the ancient region of Galatia, in northern Turkey, where it was found in 1894. It was described by Czech botanist Josef Freyn in 1896 as having a hairy but not woolly bulb tunic, a glabrous stem, linear-lanceolate leaves reaching 20 cm long and 1.3 cm wide, yellow flowers with no blotch, yellow pollen, outer tepals up to 4.7 by 2.5 cm, and inner tepals up to 3.8 by 1.7 cm.

Although occasionally offered for sale as *Tulipa galatica*, this tulip is a yellow variant of another Turkish species, *T. armena*, and was named *T. armena* f. *galatica* by L. W. D. van Raamsdonk and T. de Vries in 1995.

Tulipa gesneriana Linnaeus

Exactly what Carl Linnaeus was describing when he included *Tulipa gesneriana* in his *Species Plantarum* in 1753 is difficult to determine. It may have been an early hybrid, one of the naturalized tulips from Europe, such as *T. hungarica*, or, because he wrote that it also came from Turkey, it seems more likely that he was describing a plant like *T. sintenisii*. The origins of *T. gesneriana* are undoubtedly in western or central Asia, but from which species it is derived is uncertain. In the third edition of *Flora Français*, published in 1805, A. P. de Candolle wrote that *T. gesneriana* was cultivated in gardens because of its beauty and variety of colours, having been introduced to Europe from the East in the sixteenth century. What is certain is that *T. gesneriana* has been designated the type species of the genus *Tulipa* and, therefore, also the type of subgenus *Tulipa* and section *Tulipa*, with *T. sylvestris*, also described by Linnaeus in 1753, being the type of subgenus *Eriostemones*.

Sir Daniel Hall gave a description of *Tulipa gesneriana* in *The Genus Tulipa* (1940), but this actually represents *T. armena* according to *Flora of Turkey*, and *T. schrenkii* according to *Flora Iranica*. The description in *Flora Europaea* takes a broad view, encompassing a range of European tulips that have been described as individual species, including *T. didieri*. *Tulipa gesneriana* is treated as a complex species or group and the tulips found in southern France, Switzerland, and Italy are considered clones.

What the true *Tulipa gesneriana* is we will probably never know. Different forms of it in Europe have been named as separate species, but the treatment in *Flora Europaea* seems to be the most sensible solution. If you imagine a 'typical' garden tulip, growing maybe 30 to 50 cm tall, with a cup-shaped flower, with or without a basal blotch, and long, oblong to lanceolate leaves, then I suspect this is as close as you are going to get to what Linnaeus was meaning. He named it after the Swiss physician Conrad Gesner, the first European to describe and illustrate a tulip, around 1561.

Tulipa goulimyi Sealy & Turrill

This beautiful but rare relative of *Tulipa orphanidea* is found in Greece, on sandy fields and stony ground in the southern Peloponnese, the island of Kythira, and extreme western Crete. It differs from *T. orphanidea* in its scarlet flowers, the distinctly undulate leaf margins, and the densely hairy bulb tunic.

Tulipa goulimyi was discovered by the Greek lawyer and amateur botanist, Constantine Goulimis, in April 1954. J. Robert Sealy and William Turrill, botanists at the Royal Botanic Gardens, Kew, described it the following year, from material collected on Kythira.

The bulb of *Tulipa goulimyi* is quite large for the *T. orphanidea* group, reaching 6.5 cm long and 3 cm in diameter. The tunic is densely lined with long, wavy hairs, similar to the species of section *Tulipanum* in subgenus *Tulipa*. The five to seven leaves are linear to linear-lanceolate and glaucous, the lowest up to 20 cm long and 2 cm wide. The leaf margins, at least in wild plants, are distinctly undulate, unlike those of other species in the *T. orphanidea* group.

The flower is held 15 to 20 cm above ground and is bright orange-red to scarlet, with a small greenish black blotch surrounded by a wide yellow margin. The tepals are elliptic-oblanceolate; the outer three reach 4 to 5 cm long and 1.4 cm wide, the inner tepals are slightly larger, reaching 4.5 to 5.2 cm long and 2.2 cm wide. The blue-black filaments have a boss of whitish hairs just above the base and hold dark anthers that produce yellow pollen.

This tulip is rare in the wild and in cultivation. It was only reported from Crete in 1990, after having its identity confirmed two years previously. I have seen the Cretan plants and they cover a fairly small area near the sea, on the western coast of the island. One building site could obliterate this population.

Tulipa greigii Regel

Tulipa greigii is a bold, large-flowered, variable, and well-known species that is easily recognized by two characteristic features. It is one of the few tulip

The distinctive flower shape of *Tulipa greigii*

species to have dark markings on the leaves, and the flower forms a distinctive shape, in bud and when it opens. Many garden hybrids are associated with this species, classified in the Greigii Group. They come in a range of colours and sizes and are the result of hybridization with *T. kaufmanniana* and *T. fosteriana*. The wild forms are a little more subtle, but there is still an extraordinary variety of colour forms growing in the mountains of the Tien Shan, the valley of the Syr Dar'ya River, and the lands between the Aral and Caspian Seas.

This species grows from a large bulb with a dark brown tunic lined with some long hairs inside especially towards the tip. The pubescent stem is often short, only 10 to 15 cm tall, but it can reach over 30 cm. The four to six glaucous leaves have ciliate margins and are usually marked with brownish or deep violet dots and dashes, although some forms can have plain green leaves. The markings are more conspicuous when the leaves are young. The lowest leaf is oblong to broadly elliptic and can reach 14 cm wide but is commonly around 4 to 5 cm wide and 15 to 20 cm long. The remaining leaves are smaller and finely pubescent.

The large solitary flower is frequently scarlet to orange-red and can reach 15 cm across or more. Inside, there may be a black blotch, forming a wedge-shaped mark at the base of each tepal. This blotch is sometimes margined with yellow or the black mark may be sitting on a yellow background. The flowers can also be yellow or cream, with a red blotch or without a basal blotch but with a red mark of varying size halfway up each tepal. In yellow and cream forms the outer tepals are backed with a stripe of red. The broad tepals can reach 11 cm long and 6 cm wide, and they have a short pubescent point at the tip. The outer tepals are ovate and pubescent on the outer surface. The inner tepals are obovate and longer than the outer. The filaments are either yellow or black, and the anthers are yellow or rarely violet.

Two colour forms of *Tulipa greigii*

The erect bud of *Tulipa greigii* has a wide, flat base and tapers gently upwards to a point. When the flower opens, the outer and inner tepals form a double bowl, with the inner tepals remaining more or less upright and the shorter outer tepals arching back and rolling in at the edges. However, in warm, sunny conditions, when the flower is fully open the 'double bowl' effect is sometimes lost and the tepals form a shallow dish.

Eduard Regel described *Tulipa greigii* in 1873 from plants collected by Sewerzow and Fedtschenko in the Karatau Mountains of southern Kazakhstan. Regel named it after General Greig, president of the Imperial Russian Horticultural Union. Only two years later, this species was featured in *Curtis's Botanical Magazine*, where J. Gilbert Baker (1875) wrote that German nurseryman Max Leichtlin of Baden-Baden was growing it 'with great success'. In April 1877, *T. greigii* received a First Class Certificate from the RHS when exhibited by Henry Elwes. Paul Graeber sent many bulbs of this tulip to C. G. van Tubergen in the early twentieth century, along with *T. kaufmanniana*, which is also from the Tien Shan. From these collections the breeding of the Greigii and Kaufmanniana hybrids began.

Tulipa greigii does well when grown in a bulb frame, where the flowers, which open in late March and April, are protected from the weather and, more importantly, the bulbs can dry off in summer. In its natural home the species may have to survive five months without rain. It is also worth trying outside, in a sheltered part of a rock garden or a raised bed, where the soil is well-drained. The hybrids of the Greigii Group are more adaptable and robust, due to the influence of *T. kaufmanniana* and *T. fosteriana*, and make fine garden plants.

Another tulip with violet spots on its leaves is *Tulipa mogoltavica*, described in 1935 by Mikhail Popov and Aleksei Vvedensky. This species takes its name from the Mogol-Tau mountains in the Tien Shan, where it was discovered. It is illustrated in *Flora of the USSR*, but Sir Daniel Hall thought that this drawing and the description were indistinguishable from *T. greigii*. In his key to tulip species, Vvedensky separated these two by flower colour (red in *T. mogoltavica*, orange-red in *T. greigii*) and the blotch (black on a yellow base in *T. greigii*, black margined with yellow or with no margin in *T. mogoltavica*). Considering the variation found in *T. greigii*, it is not surprising that *T. mogoltavica* is now treated as a synonym.

Tulipa grengiolensis Thommen

This protected tulip is only known from a small area in Valais, southern Switzerland, in the upper valley of the Rhone River. It was described in 1946, when it was discovered growing in a field of rye. It is one of the more common *Neo-tulipae* in cultivation. The flower can be red or pale yellow, but the form in general cultivation has pale yellow flowers with the edges of the tepals feathered with red. Inside the flower is a small black basal blotch. The filaments and anthers are dark violet. The entirely yellow-flowered form has yellow anthers.

Tulipa hageri Heldreich

Theodor von Heldreich, a German botanist who served as director of the botanical gardens in Athens, discovered this orange-scarlet to deep crimson relative of *Tulipa orphanidea* at around 1600 m (5250 ft.) on Mount Parnes, north of Athens, in April 1862. Later, in 1874, he described it and named it after Friedrich Hager, who was with him when he found it. The flowers are heavily shaded green on the outside and inside is a large purple-black basal blotch, margined with yellow. The tepals are up to 2.5 cm wide, making a more rounded, less star-like flower than is generally found in *T. orphanidea*. This species is now usually regarded as a form of *T. orphanidea*, but commercial stocks are widely available as *T. hageri*.

One of the most common forms in cultivation is *Tulipa hageri* 'Splendens'. The flower is coppery-red inside and scarlet with little or no green outside. Up to five flowers are produced from each bulb, although this is not a reliable feature. The plant can reach 20 cm tall, but the flowers may open when only a few centimetres above ground. Like the typical form, 'Splendens' can be grown outside in a sunny position and well-drained soil, and is the ideal size for a rock garden.

Tulipa hageri 'Splendens'

Tulipa hoogiana
B. Fedtschenko

Flowering in April or May, *Tulipa hoogiana* grows in the foothills and steppe zone of the Kopet–Dag Range, which runs along the border of Iran and Turkmenistan. It is closely related to *T. lanata* and its allies, including *T. tubergeniana*, *T. ingens*, and *T. fosteriana*. Like those species, it has large, bright red flowers.

Boris Fedtschenko described *Tulipa hoogiana* in the *Gardeners' Chronicle* of 23 July 1910, after having seen it during a visit to the nursery of C. G. van Tubergen in the spring of that year. The bulbs had been sent from the Bukhara region of Uzbekistan by Paul Graeber. The species name commemorates John Hoog.

The solitary scarlet or raspberry-red flower is held on a glabrous stem that reaches from 20 to 40 cm long. The three to six spreading leaves are also glabrous but have more or less ciliate margins. The lowest leaf is lanceolate, up to 8 cm wide and 25 cm long. The other leaves gradually decrease in size up the stem, but the upper leaf can still be 14 cm long and 2.5 cm wide. The oblong-lanceolate outer tepals are slightly narrower than the obovate inner tepals. Both are typically between 2.5 and 3.5 cm wide and can reach 8 cm long, narrowing to a pubescent point. The well-defined, elliptic black blotch at the base of each tepal is margined with yellow. The filaments are blackish violet, and the anthers are a similar colour or yellow. The stigma is yellow.

The dark brown bulb tunic of *Tulipa hoogiana* is thickly lined with reddish hairs, a characteristic that persuaded Sir Daniel Hall to place it in his subsection *Oculis-solis*, and Aleksei Vvedensky and Zinaida Botschantzeva to place it in section *Tulipanum*. However, in their 1995 paper, L. W. D. van

Raamsdonk and T. de Vries treated this species as a synonym of *T. tubergeniana* and placed it in section *Eichleres*. It is certainly very similar to that species, although the two do occupy different areas of central Asia; *T. tubergeniana* is native to the south-western Pamir Alai.

Tulipa humilis Herbert

This great little tulip for the garden is low-growing and early flowering. Clones in general cultivation are able to cope with some moisture in the soil during the summer. In fact, they seem to prefer not being baked while dormant. *Tulipa humilis* can be grown on a rock garden, in a raised bed or a sunny border, as well as in pots, and it is pretty too.

Since the species was first described by British botanist William Herbert in 1844, a number of names have been published to cover the various colour forms of *Tulipa humilis* (the species name means 'low-growing' or 'dwarfish'). The typical form described by Herbert has lilac-pink or pale purplish rose flowers, sometimes very pale to almost white, but always with a yellow base to the tepals. The filaments and anthers are yellow, like the blotch, and the four erect or curved, linear leaves are green or slightly glaucous on the upper surface. Other forms have been described as individual species, such as *T. violacea* and *T. pulchella*, but in the wild a whole range of intermediate forms occurs and *T. humilis* is now regarded as one highly variable species, encompassing all the various colour combinations. It is placed in section *Saxatiles*.

This species has its centre of distribution in the mountains of north-western Iran, in the Tabriz district, and over the border into eastern Turkey, around Lake Van, but it is also found further south and east in Iran, Syria, Lebanon, and the Taurus Mountains of Turkey. It often grows on rocky slopes and screes at high altitudes, up to 3600 m (11,800 ft.), where it can flower as late as July. In cultivation it flowers in late March or April.

Herbert described *Tulipa humilis* in the *Botanical Register*, from bulbs he was growing in Spofforth, near Harrogate in Yorkshire. He had received these bulbs in 1838 from Theodor Kotschy, who collected them in the Elburz Mountains, north of Tehran. Specimens had previously been collected by the Russian explorer Szovitz near Salmas, north-western Iran, in 1828, and these were identified as *T. humilis* by Boissier (1882) in *Flora Orientalis*.

In 1860 Boissier and Friedrich Alexander Buhse described *Tulipa violacea*, from plants collected by Buhse in south-eastern Azerbaijan in 1848. This tulip has violet to deep purplish crimson flowers with a black blotch inside the flower and the filaments are purplish or black, but it is otherwise similar to Herbert's *T. humilis*. It also occurs in Iran.

A form with white flowers, flushed with purple on the outside and with a blackish blotch and filaments, was named *Tulipa violacea* var. *pallida* by Heinrich Carl Haussknecht. This form was collected in the Rasvand Mountains near Arak, western Iran, and the name was published in 1908.

A third member of this group was found by Kotschy in 1836, in the Taurus Mountains of southern Turkey. It was eventually named *Tulipa pulchella* by Eduard Fenzl in 1874. This form has falcate (scythe-shaped) leaves spreading out on the ground, and the lowest leaf is

A Turkish form of *Tulipa humilis*

usually noticeably broader than the others, up to 1.7 cm wide. The flower is purplish crimson with a blue-black blotch on a white background.

Another name to throw into the *Tulipa humilis* pot is *T. lownei*, described by J. Gilbert Baker in 1874. This plant was collected on Mount Hermon, in southern Syria, in 1863 to 1864. Like *T. pulchella*, it has broad falcate leaves spreading out on the ground, but the flower is pale rose-pink to almost white and the blotch and filaments are yellow.

All these names are now included within the broad concept of *Tulipa humilis*. A good indication of the range of variation found in the wild is given by Brian Mathew, writing about the Bowles Memorial Expedition to Turkey and Iran in 1963. He described plants of *T. humilis* found near Tabriz as 'exceedingly variable in colour' and said, 'In just a few square yards one could obtain lilac, shell pink, deep violet, and red colour forms each with a yellow eye' (Sealy 1970). Considering this variation, it makes sense, as suggested by Hall in *The Genus* Tulipa (1940), to group all these similar tulips together under the one name.

Tulipa humilis grows from a bulb with a brittle, pale to dark brown tunic, lined with straight hairs around the base and at the tip. It has two to five leaves and the lowest is up to 20 cm long and 2 cm wide, though 10 to 12 cm long and 1 cm wide is more usual. The solitary flower is goblet-shaped, flattening out in the sun, and clearly constricted at the base. It opens close to the ground on a glabrous stem that normally only reaches a few centimetres but can be nearly 20 cm long. The tepals are between 3 and 4.7 cm long and elliptic to broadly ovate. The outer tepals are 0.5 to 1.5 cm wide, but the inner tepals are notably wider, up to 2.5 cm, and they are ciliate at the base. The bases of the filaments are densely hairy.

Bulbs are often still sold as *Tulipa violacea* and *T. pulchella*, and the various colour forms that are commercially available have been given many different names. Cultivated plants that are similar to *T. violacea* are now classified as *T. humilis* Violacea Group. However, to confuse matters, plants are sold as 'Violacea Black Base' (like the original *T. violacea*) or 'Violacea Yellow Base'. In 1966 Thomas Hoog published the invalid combination *T. pulchella violacea*, when describing an Iranian form with a black blotch. Unfortunately this name is sometimes attached to commercial stock of the deep violet form with a yellow blotch.

The more commonly available cultivars include 'Eastern Star', with yellow-centred, magenta-rose flowers; 'Liliput', with pinkish red flowers; 'Odalisque' with deep beetroot-purple flowers, yellow at the centre; and 'Persian

Tulipa humilis 'Alanya', collected in southern Turkey

Pearl', with purple flowers shaded green on the outside and with a yellow blotch. One of the most sought after forms is 'Albocaerulea Oculata', originally collected in north-western Iran, which has white flowers with a steely-blue blotch (as in *Tulipa violacea* var. *pallida*). In my experience, the demand for this last form has meant that bulbs may not be flowering size when sold, which can be disappointing. Another reason for the non-flowering of any of the *T. humilis* forms is that they are allowed to dry out just as the flower buds are developing, causing them to abort. This is less likely to occur when bulbs are planted out in the garden.

Two other tulips in the *Tulipa humilis* complex are usually referred to under their species names. *Tulipa kurdica* is from Iraq and has brick-red flowers with a small black blotch. *Tulipa aucheriana* has small pink, starry flowers, with a small yellow blotch and comes from northern Iran. I have treated the two separately here, but they are very similar to *T. humilis*.

Tulipa hungarica Borbás

Naturalized in eastern Europe, *Tulipa hungarica* is a form of the complex 'species' *T. gesneriana*. It grows in the limestone gorge of the Danube River, along the border of Romania and Yugoslavia, at the south end of the Transylvanian Alps, where it flowers in April and May. This region once belonged to the Hungarian Empire, hence the name of this tulip.

The two large, flat leaves are glaucous and usually reach 30 cm long by 5.7 cm wide. A third, smaller leaf is further up the stem. The tall stem holds a solitary, wide, yellow flower. The inner tepals are rounded with a tiny red tip. The outer tepals are more pointed and become reflexed. They are around 6 cm long and 2.5 cm wide, but can be larger. The filaments are yellow and the anthers are purple with yellow or greenish pollen.

Two other eastern European tulips, *Tulipa urumoffii* and *T. rhodopea*, grow in the Rhodope Mountains of southern Bulgaria. The former has yellow flowers and the latter has brownish scarlet flowers with a dark blotch. Both species, also naturalized, are best treated as forms of *T. hungarica*, which was described by Vinczé Borbás in 1882. L. W. D. van Raamsdonk and T. de Vries (1995) classified the red-flowered form as *T. hungarica* subsp. *rhodopea*.

Tulipa iliensis Regel

This tulip is a slightly smaller version of the better-known *Tulipa kolpakowskiana*, and L. W. D. van Raamsdonk and T. de Vries (1995) regarded these two tulips as forms of *T. altaica*. Both, however, are offered in the trade

Tulipa iliensis

as distinct species. *Tulipa iliensis* was described by Eduard Regel and is native to the Tien Shan and north-western China, growing on grassy or stony slopes and in semi-desert, up to 1400 m (4590 ft.).

The original description of *Tulipa iliensis* appeared in volume 28 of Regel's *Gartenflora*, in 1879, where it was also illustrated (t. 975). The whole plant grows 10 to 20 cm tall. The three or four glaucous, deeply channelled, linear-lanceolate leaves are up to 1.5 cm wide but tend not to reach higher than the flower, as they usually do in *T. kolpakowskiana*. Another difference between these two species is the flower stem, which is pubescent in *T. iliensis*, although it can be hairless. Furthermore, some plants sold as *T. kolpakowskiana* have a slight pubescence on the stem, thus blurring the boundaries between these two species and reinforcing the view that they are variations of *T. altaica* (which also has a pubescent flower stem).

The flower of *Tulipa iliensis* is yellow, with the outer tepals tinged with red or purple on the back, with a touch of green near the base. Each tepal is 2.5 to 3.5 cm long and from 0.4 to 2 cm wide, the inner being more rounded than the outer. The filaments are slightly dilated in the middle and narrow towards each end. They are yellow and hold yellow anthers.

Though not particularly showy, this species does well in a pot kept under glass, where the bulbs can dry off completely in the summer. It can be grown in the open garden, in very free draining soil, but may be overlooked unless planted in a raised bed or on a rock garden, where the small flowers can be more closely studied. It flowers in early April.

Tulipa ingens Hoog

Paul Graeber collected this tulip in 1901, in the high mountains of the Bukhara region of Uzbekistan, where it was flowering in the first week of

Tulipa ingens

May. John Hoog described it in the *Gardeners' Chronicle* the following year and gave it the name *ingens*, which means 'enormous', 'on account of its very large flowers' (Hoog 1902a). It is similar to the closely related *Tulipa lanata*, *T. tubergeniana*, and *T. fosteriana*, which were collected for C. G. van Tubergen from Bukhara around the same time but, unlike those species, the prominent black blotch inside the flower of *T. ingens* does not have a yellow margin.

The dark brown bulb tunic is lined with long, silky hairs towards the tip and at the base. The pubescent flower stem reaches 20 to 35 cm tall and holds three to five glaucous leaves that are densely covered in tiny white hairs and have ciliate margins. The lowest leaf is lanceolate, around 15 to 25 cm long and 2 to 5 cm (occasionally up to 9 cm) wide.

The solitary flower, which forms a loose cup, was described by Hoog as 'bright scarlet-vermilion'. Each tepal is around 4 cm wide and can be up to 11 cm long. There is a pubescent point at the tip. The oblong-rhomboidal outer tepals have a soft yellowish coloured band on the back and are slightly wider than the obovate to elliptic inner tepals. The filaments are black and the anthers produce deep brown-purple pollen. The stigma has a slight yellowish tinge and is held on a pale red ovary.

Tulipa ingens is found in the Pamir Alai, in the Zeravshan Mountains and the Kashkadar'ya Basin, south of Samarkand, Uzbekistan. It grows on clayey slopes up to 2500 m (8200 ft.). Like the other species from this region, it can be grown in well-drained soil, in a sunny, sheltered part of a rock garden. It also does well in pots kept in a bulb frame, where the large flowers are protected from the weather and the bulbs are kept dry in summer. It usually flowers in mid to late April.

Tulipa julia C. Koch

This red-flowered species grows on stony and grassy slopes from north-western Iran to eastern Turkey and north into the Caucasus Mountains; it is the most widespread tulip in Armenia. It flowers from April to June in the wild and can be found at elevations up to 2500 m (8200 ft.).

The brown, papery bulb tunic is densely lined with the matted, shaggy hairs typical of the species in section *Tulipanum* in which *Tulipa julia* is placed. The glabrous stem has a pinkish purple blush. It can reach 30 cm tall but is often half this height or less, making it one of the shorter species in this section. The three to four leaves are glaucous and broadly lanceolate, the lower leaf reaching from 13 to 20 cm long and up to 4 cm wide. The margins are sometimes undulate and often ciliolate, especially towards the tip. The upper leaves are narrower and more linear, reaching less than 1 cm wide.

Tulipa julia

The solitary flower of *Tulipa julia* is orange-red to deep scarlet, with a short, rounded, brownish black basal blotch margined with yellow. The outside of the flower is paler red or pinkish and yellow at the base. There are also forms with yellow flowers and a brownish blotch. The outer tepals are ovate to rhombic-elliptic and pointed. They are typically around 4 to 5 cm long and 1.3 to 2 cm wide. The inner tepals are a few millimetres shorter, spathulate to obovate, and generally with a rounded tip. The glabrous filaments are brownish black, and the anthers are violet or yellow.

Tulipa julia was described by Karl Heinrich Emil Koch in 1849. Koch was born near Weimar in Germany and had a broad range of interests, including botany. From an early age he had a dream to see the Caucasus and went on to make two expeditions to that region, discovering many new species on the way, including this tulip.

The bulbs need to be kept dry during the summer so it is best to grow this tulip in a bulb frame or alpine house. It can be grown in free-draining soil outside, where summers are dry.

Tulipa kaufmanniana Regel
WATERLILY TULIP

Commonly known as the waterlily tulip, this is one of the best-known and most popular species in cultivation, with many cultivars available in colours ranging from white and yellow, to pink, orange, and red. Wild forms are almost as variable, and some approach or even equal the splendour of the garden forms. This is one of the easier tulips to grow in the open garden and, as long as the soil is free-draining, will gradually increase, producing large, showy flowers in March, held 15 to 25 cm above the broad leaves.

Tulipa kaufmanniana was described by Eduard Regel in 1877 from plants collected by his son Albert near the Chirchik River, east of Tashkent, in the western Tien Shan. The species name commemorates General von Kaufmann, the then governor-general of Tashkent Province, Uzbekistan. In 1883 J. Gilbert Baker wrote about this species in the *Gardeners' Chronicle* saying that this new tulip was 'as yet very little known to us in England', and 'We shall, no doubt, hear further about the plant' (Baker 1883). How right he was! It received a First Class Certificate from the RHS in 1897 and an Award of Garden Merit in 1923. Now there are so many different forms available that a separate group of cultivated tulips (the Kaufmanniana Group) has been created for its cultivars and hybrids.

The true species is restricted in the wild to the western Tien Shan, growing in the mountain shrub belt, on stony, grassy slopes and flowering in April and May. It grows from large bulbs, up to 4 cm across, that have tunics lined with hairs. The two or three broad, glaucous leaves are lanceolate, oblong, or oblong-elliptic, the lowest usually between 4 and 8 cm wide and 10 to 16 cm long. The pubescent flower stem is often tinted violet and holds a single flower composed of lanceolate to oblong tepals.

When it comes to flower size and colour, *Tulipa kaufmanniana* shows a great deal of variation. The basic flower colour can be white, cream, or yellow and the centre of the flower is deep golden yellow. Sometimes red marks in the form of a spot or V shape occur on the inside of the tepals, corresponding to the edges of the yellow blotch. The outer tepals are backed with bright carmine, crimson-red, or dingy violet, either as a wide, bold stripe or an irregular smudge along or around the midrib. Some forms have greenish staining on the backs of the outer tepals, surrounded by a red zone. Forms with orange to bright red, yellow-centred flowers have also been found in the wild.

The tepals are generally 5 to 8 cm long and 1.5 to 2.5 cm wide, but they can be larger, up to 11 cm long and 5 cm wide. When the flowers open wide in the sun, the tepals arch back, the outer tepals more so than the inner, to form a beautiful star-shaped bloom, displaying the deep yellow centre. The yellow filaments hold long, linear, yellow anthers that dehisce gradually and slowly from the tip to the base, becoming contorted or twisted as they do so. This feature led Aleksei Vvedensky to place *Tulipa kaufmanniana* in a section of its own, section *Spiranthera*, to which Zinaida Botschantzeva later added four more species, including *T. dubia* and *T. tschimganica*.

Despite the variation found in *Tulipa kaufmanniana*, it is still a distinctive species. The large colourful flowers with their characteristic shape and markings, the compact form, and broad glaucous leaves make this tulip easily recognizable. It is one of the earliest large-flowered species to bloom in

Tulipa kaufmanniana

the garden and can be grown in a sunny border among other early flowering perennials and bulbs. It also makes a fine pot plant, kept in the shelter of a frame or cold glasshouse to protect the flowers until they are ready to put out on display.

Tulipa kolpakowskiana Regel

This attractive and variable small tulip is the most widely available and best-known species in section *Kolpakowskianae*. In the wild, flower colour varies from yellow to orange and brownish red, sometimes with a small, yellow basal blotch. The form in general cultivation has bright yellow flowers, with the outer tepals stained with reddish pink on the back. The yellow-flowered forms of *Tulipa clusiana* have a similar colour scheme, but the staining on the outer tepals is stronger and more defined than in *T. kolpakowskiana*. It was treated as a synonym of *T. altaica* by L. W. D. van Raamsdonk and T. de Vries in 1995, but is usually sold as *T. kolpakowskiana*.

Like *Tulipa altaica*, this species can be grown in the open garden if the soil is very well drained, and it has also received the RHS Award of Garden Merit, in 1993. However, the bulbs seem to revel in hot, bone-dry conditions during dormancy, and the plant does well and often looks best when grown in a pot. If the pot is kept in a bulb frame or alpine house, this species will flower in early April.

Described by Eduard Regel in 1877 from plants found in the Tien Shan, *Tulipa kolpakowskiana* also occurs further north in Kazakhstan, in the Altai Mountains, and over the border into north-western China. *Flora Iranica* also reported it from north-eastern Afghanistan. It grows on sunny, stony slopes and in semi-desert, up to 2600 m (8530 ft.).

This species grows 15 to 20 cm tall, sometimes up to 35 cm, from bulbs that have a leathery tunic extending beyond the bulb to form a prominent point. Inside, the tunic is lined with straight hairs around the base and especially at the tip. There are usually three erect, linear-lanceolate, glaucous leaves, the lowest being over 20 cm long and 1 to 3 cm wide. The upper leaves are shorter but often reach higher than the flower.

The slender, glabrous stem holds a solitary flower with tepals commonly 3.5 to 4 cm long and around 1.5 cm wide, although they can reach 6 cm long. The outer tepals are oblong to oblong-rhomboidal, with a sharp point. The inner tepals are more rounded and slightly broader. The anthers are pale yellow and the filaments bright yellow to dull orange-yellow.

Although flower colour in commercially offered plants of *Tulipa kolpakowskiana* is fairly uniform, in the wild it is more variable, and the species hybridizes with *T. ostrowskiana*, producing even further combinations of flower colour and shape. In 1878 this species was illustrated in volume 27 of Regel's *Gartenflora* (t. 951). The painting showed a bunch of flowers in yellow-orange, brown-red, and yellow with pinkish red staining on the back of the outer tepals, reflecting the mixture of colours in wild populations.

Tulipa korolkowii Regel

This striking red tulip is found in the western foothills of the Tien Shan and Pamir Alai (the Zeravshan Mountains), up to 1700 m (5580 ft.), growing on sandy or gravelly slopes and flowering in March and April. In this region, where the Syr Dar'ya River begins its long journey around the eastern and northern edges of the Kyzylkum Desert before flowing into the Aral Sea, plants are adapted to survive long, hot and dry summers. These conditions have to be imitated in cultivation if *Tulipa korolkowii* is to be grown successfully.

This species is in section *Kolpakowskianae*, appearing to be closest to red-flowered forms of *Tulipa lehmanniana*. The tough, leathery, dark brown bulb tunic extends to form a point above the bulb and is lined with hairs at the tip. The three glaucous, channelled leaves are lanceolate to narrowly linear,

the lowest reaching 17 to 25 cm long but only 1.4 to 1.7 cm wide. In the wild these leaves lie close to the ground and have very undulate margins. The long, pointed flower bud emerges from between the leaves and then droops down as the red colouring strengthens through the glaucous bloom. It straightens up before opening 11 to 18 cm above ground on a glabrous stem.

The rhomboidal to obovate outer tepals are 5 to 6 cm long and 3.1 to 3.5 cm wide, sometimes with a short point at the otherwise rounded tip. The vaguely triangular inner tepals have a more prominent point at

Tulipa korolkowii

the tip and are slightly longer, up to 7 cm, and 3.4 to 3.6 cm wide, although the margins tend to roll back, making them look narrower and giving the flower an attractively tousled appearance as it ages. At the base of the tepals is a small black blotch without a yellow margin. The anthers are yellow and the filaments are black, sometimes with a red zone just below the anthers.

Eduard Regel described *Tulipa korolkowii* in 1875 from material collected by Korolkow and Krause near Farish in southern Kazakhstan. Yellow forms also occur in the wild and some with a mottled flower colour. In 1901 a form with deep yellow flowers, a scarlet blotch, and tepals shaded orange-scarlet on the exterior gained an Award of Merit from the RHS under the cultivar name 'Bicolour'.

This species is perfectly hardy, but the bulbs must be kept dry when dormant, and even during the winter and early spring, when plants are in full growth, the soil must not be too wet. Consequently, it is essential to water this tulip carefully and grow it under cover, either in an alpine house or bulb frame. Growth appears above the soil early, usually in December, and the buds are just visible between the leaves in January, although the flowers will not open until late March or early April. This bright, attractive species is suitable for an alpine house but unfortunately is not often seen in cultivation.

Tulipa kurdica Wendelbo

I have grown bulbs sold to me as *Tulipa kurdica* that have turned out to be the deep violet form of *T. humilis*. This was annoying, but it did not come as a complete surprise as, apart from flower colour, this species is practically identical to *T. humilis*. In the true *T. kurdica* the flower is brick-red to orange-red, a colour not otherwise found in *T. humilis*.

Tulipa kurdica is endemic to the mountains of northern Iraq, growing on igneous rock and limestone, often near melting snow, at altitudes of 2400 to 3000 m (7900–9840 ft.). It flowers in May and June in the wild, earlier in cultivation at low altitudes. It was first described by Per Wendelbo in 1974.

This tulip grows from a small bulb, about 1 cm in diameter, that has a brown tunic lined with straight hairs towards the tip. The glabrous stem can reach 10 to 15 cm long and is often stained brownish purple in the upper part. There are three to five glabrous, channelled, dark green leaves, the lowest reaching 6 to 15.5 cm long and 0.5 to 1.5 cm wide. The upper leaves are a similar length but much narrower.

The tepals are brick-red to orange-red and inside the flower is a blue-black blotch. The outer tepals are elliptic and up to 4.5 cm long and 1.2 cm wide. The inner tepals are slightly shorter and much broader, up to 2 cm wide. They also have a ciliate base. The pubescent filaments are blue-violet and the anthers are greenish, with yellow pollen.

Tulipa kuschkensis B. Fedtschenko

This is another red tulip in section *Tulipanum*. By all accounts it is a beautiful species, but unfortunately it doesn't appear to be in cultivation at present. Sir Daniel Hall grew it and included it in *The Genus* Tulipa (1940) but noted that it was difficult to maintain in the open. In the wild this species can reach a great age, and there are reports of it flowering for fifty to sixty years in the same spot.

Tulipa kuschkensis comes from Turkmenistan, eastern Iran, and northern Afghanistan, where it grows in clay or loamy soil or on stony slopes. The flower is a brilliant vermillion-scarlet and inside there is a large, rounded black blotch, margined with yellow. The edges of the outer tepals roll back when the flower is fully open. Each tepal is about 7 to 8 cm long and 3 to 4 cm wide, and the inner segments are only slightly smaller than the outer. Usually four narrow, glaucous leaves grow on a stem that reaches around 15 to 20 cm above ground.

This tulip takes its name from the town of Kuschka, on the border of Turkmenistan and Afghanistan. It was here that Boris Fedtschenko found the species. He named it in 1914, although the first full description didn't appear until 1932. This tulip was beautifully illustrated for *Curtis's Botanical Magazine* in 1934 (t. 9370) from plants grown by the John Innes Horticultural Institution that flowered in 1931. These bulbs originally came from the van Tubergen firm.

Tulipa lanata Regel

It can be hard to distinguish between many of the red-flowered tulips in section *Eichleres*, let alone choose a favourite, but *Tulipa lanata* must be among the best. The large, luxurious-red, slightly waisted flowers are produced above the wide glaucous leaves in late March or April. This species grows in the Pamir Alai and north-eastern Afghanistan at altitudes of up to 2000 m (6560 ft.). It was described by Eduard Regel in 1884 from plants collected by his son Albert in the Pamir Alai in the spring of 1883. Albert found it in ravines in red sandstone slopes, where it was growing with anemones, irises, fritillaries, and eremurus; it must have been a wonderful spring sight.

The leaves of *Tulipa lanata* have ciliate margins and are covered with soft, fine hairs. The flower stem is also pubescent. The species name means 'hairy', referring to the inside of the bulb tunic, which is thickly covered with long hairs, especially towards the tip. Sir Daniel Hall, in *The Genus Tulipa* (1940), placed *T. lanata* in his subsection *Oculis-solis* (syn. section *Tulipanum*), but the hairs are not always as dense and woolly as those found in the species of that section and it is better placed in section *Eichleres*, which also includes the well-known *T. fosteriana*. However, Hall did mention that the hairs inside the bulb tunic are not so woolly or felted when this tulip is grown in cultivation and C. G. van Tubergen (1947) has written that the woolly layer beneath the tunic can reach 2.5 cm thick. Hall also wrote that this triploid tulip rarely forms seed capsules but is stoloniferous and increases freely this way.

The usually four leaves decrease in size up the stem. The lowest is lanceolate and reaches around 6.5 cm wide and 13 cm long. The pubescent stem can reach over 40 cm long and holds a solitary red flower. The tepals are 7 to 8 cm long by 2.5 to 3.2 cm wide, narrowing abruptly to a sharp, pubescent point, although some cultivated forms have tepals up to 12 cm long. The rhomboidal to oblong-rhomboidal outer tepals are slightly broader than the oblong-obovate inner tepals and are flushed pale pink on the outside. Inside, at the base of the flower, is a rounded black blotch, margined with a thin yellow border. The filaments are black and the pollen is yellow.

This species was featured in *Curtis's Botanical Magazine* in 1928 (t.9151), where Otto Stapf wrote that in 1901 C. G. van Tubergen employed a collector, Paul Graeber, to bring back various bulbs and tubers from the Bukhara region of Uzbekistan. According to Stapf, from these and later collections *Tulipa lanata* came into general cultivation but under different names, including *T. tubergeniana*, *T. hoogiana*, *T. ingens*, and *T. fosteriana*, and he considered them all to be strains of the same species. However, these alternative names were included by Aleksei

Tulipa lanata

Vvedensky in *Flora of the USSR* and are still upheld today; *T. fosteriana* is now a popular and widely grown tulip. Vvedensky placed *T. tubergeniana* and *T. hoogiana* in section *Tulipanum*, but van Raamsdonk and de Vries, in their 1995 paper, treated *T. hoogiana* as a synonym of *T. tubergeniana*, placing it in section *Eichleres*. All these beautiful species are undoubtedly closely related, differing in minor characteristics, such as the shape of the blotch, the presence or absence of a yellow margin around it, and the colour of the stigma (colourless in *T. lanata*).

Stapf also recounted an interesting story regarding bulbs of *Tulipa lanata* that the Royal Botanic Gardens, Kew, received from Kashmir in 1925. These had originally been collected by Maurice McNamara, director of sericulture to the Kashmir government, from the roof of a mosque that collapsed during a flood in 1905. Apparently this species had been imported from central Asia, maybe as far back as the sixteenth century, and planted on mosques, temples, and sometimes house rooftops. It has now become naturalized in this region. Clearly, the beauty of this tulip has long been appreciated. And although only occasionally offered for sale, if it can be obtained it makes a fine plant for growing in pots in a bulb frame or in the well-drained soil of a warm, sheltered part of a rock garden.

Tulipa lehmanniana Mercklin

This rarely grown species in section *Kolpakowskianae* has a wide distribution across central Asia, where it grows in stony desert and on rocky outcrops, flowering in April. It is found from Iran and Afghanistan to the Kyzylkum region in the north, and east to the Tien Shan. It was first described in 1851 by the Russian paleobotanist Karl Eugen von Mercklin, from material collected by Alexander von Bunge near Bukhara in southern Uzbekistan.

The bulb tunic of *Tulipa lehmanniana* has a covering of woolly hairs at the tip. The top of the tunic extends beyond the bulb, sometimes reaching ground level. The four glaucous leaves are lanceolate to linear-lanceolate. The lowest leaf is around 15 to 18 cm long and up to 2.7 cm wide, but the remaining leaves rapidly decrease in size up the stem, becoming narrow and pointed. The stem is glabrous and reaches 15 to 25 cm above ground.

This species can have yellow, orange, or red flowers, and the tepals are generally 5 to 6 cm long and 4 cm wide. Inside the flower, at the base of the tepals, is a small, distinctive brown-black or blackish violet blotch, without a yellow margin. The anthers are yellow and the filaments are yellow, sometimes blackish violet towards the tip.

Sir Daniel Hall knew this plant and evidently grew a red-flowered form

('Light Nasturtium Red'). He states that this little-known tulip is closely related to *Tulipa korolkowii.*

Tulipa linifolia Regel

Tulipa linifolia, with its wide, bright red flowers, is one of the best of the smaller tulip species for growing in the open garden and received the RHS Award of Garden Merit in 1993. As long as it is planted in free-draining soil, it will survive in areas with fairly high summer rainfall. Clumps will gradually increase in size, and the bulbs will reliably flower every year in April or early May. The plant does well in a sunny position on a rock garden and, like the closely related *T. montana,* it is also a fine species for pot cultivation, growing only 10 to 20 cm tall.

Yellow forms of this species have become well known under the name *Tulipa batalinii.* Eduard Regel described *T. linifolia* in 1884 and *T. batalinii* in 1889. Also in 1889, Regel described *T. maximowiczii.* All three species are now gathered together under the name *T. linifolia.*

Tulipa linifolia was described from plants found in the Pamir Alai, in present-day Tajikistan. The bulb has a tuft of woolly hairs at the apex and produces six to eight glaucous, linear leaves, often with undulate margins. The lower leaves are up to 12 cm long but only 6 to 10 mm wide. The orange-red to scarlet tepals are all more or less the same size, up to 5 cm long and 2

Tulipa linifolia

cm wide, and rhomboidal to ovate. At the centre of the flower is a small, dark purple blotch. The anthers are yellow.

Tulipa maximowiczii was described from plants found in the same part of the world. According to Regel it differs from *T. linifolia* in its more erect leaves that are spaced apart up the stem and usually surpass the flower, rather than being held close together like a rosette near the ground. Also, the leaf margins are not undulate, the tepals have a more pointed tip, and the anthers are purple.

The flowers of *Tulipa batalinii* are pale yellow. The outer tepals may be more pointed and slightly longer than the inner. There is a darker yellow or brownish blotch at the centre of the flower and the anthers are yellow. The species is named after Professor Batalin, a former director of the St. Petersburg Botanic Garden.

As early as 1925, in an article for the *Journal of the Royal Horticultural Society*, William Dykes stated that *Tulipa linifolia* and *T. maximowiczii* were almost identical and that *T. batalinii* was merely a yellow form. Sir Daniel Hall agreed with this point of view and in *The Genus* Tulipa (1940) wrote that the characters used to distinguish *T. maximowiczii* are also shared by forms of *T. linifolia*. Furthermore, he said that *T. batalinii* 'is undoubtedly an albino form of *T. linifolia*'.

So *Tulipa linifolia* is a variable, red- or pale yellow-flowered species with narrow, glaucous leaves. It comes from northern Iran, Afghanistan, and the Pamir Alai of central Asia. In the red-flowered forms the dark blotch at the centre of the flower may have a yellow or creamy white margin. The numerous narrow leaves help to distinguish this species from *T. montana*, which has fewer, wider leaves. The more pointed, ovate tepals give the flowers of *T. linifolia* a distinctive shape, and in the sun the flower opens wide, forming a shallow, gleaming bowl, up to 8 cm across, with the outer tepals bending back. The red forms are a gorgeous colour but not the intense, rich red of *T. montana*.

Van Raamsdonk and de Vries (1995) named the yellow forms *Tulipa linifolia* var. *chrysantha*, but they are still commonly sold as *T. batalinii*. Flower colour alone, as I'm sure you have realized by now, is not reason enough to distinguish tulip species but to the gardener it is very important. To maintain the distinction between the colour forms in cultivation, the yellow-flowered plants are now classed as *T. linifolia* Batalinii Group. Under this name are various cultivars, resulting from crosses between the yellow and red forms that have produced some popular and beautiful tulips:

'Apricot Jewel' has flowers of orange-red outside and golden yellow inside.

Tulipa linifolia Batalinii Group 'Bright Gem'

'Bright Gem' is one of the most widely available and has flowers of sulphur yellow, flushed with orange. It received the RHS Award of Garden Merit in 1995.

'Bronze Charm' has yellow flowers feathered with bronze outside.

'Red Gem' has rich-red flowers with a black blotch and pale yellow veins inside. The anthers are yellow.

'Red Hunter' has bright scarlet flowers and was chosen by the Royal Horticultural Society for its bicentenary plant collection in 2004.

'Yellow Jewel' has bright yellow flowers that are greenish yellow towards the base inside and tinged with pink outside.

Tulipa marjolletii Perrier & Songeon

Along with *Tulipa grengiolensis*, this species is one of the most common of the *Neo-tulipae* in cultivation. It was described in 1894 from near the town of Aime, in the Savoy region of France. The firm of van Tubergen received bulbs of this tulip from Baron Eduard Perrier de la Bathie at the beginning of the twentieth century. Perrier had a special interest in the tulips of Savoy. *Tulipa marjolletii* is now thought to be extinct in the wild but is grown in Holland.

The buds of this late-flowering tulip do not open until May. The flower reaches 10 to 12 cm across when fully open. The primrose yellow tepals are edged with a feather of rosy red, especially towards the base. The flowers become paler as they age, but the red margins become darker and gradually spread towards the centre of each tepal. The small blue-grey blotch inside the flower is poorly defined. The filaments are blue-grey and the anthers are yellow.

Tulipa mauritiana Jordan

Another of the *Neo-tulipae*, this species was described in 1858 from near the town of St. Jean-de-Maurienne, in Savoy, France. The flower is red with a yellow base. The filaments are violet and the anthers yellow.

'Cindy' is a form raised in cultivation from seed of this species. The tepals are lemon yellow outside and primrose yellow inside. Inside the flower the base is lemon yellow with greenish yellow veins. The tepals are narrowly edged with red when they first open, but as the flower ages this colour gradually spreads, eventually staining most of the tepal. The anthers are bluish black.

Tulipa maximowiczii Regel

When Eduard Regel described *Tulipa maximowiczii* in 1889, he used several minor features to distinguish it from *T. linifolia*, including its longer, more erect leaves and the purple rather than yellow anthers. The two species are very similar and as *T. linifolia* is now known to be quite variable, *T. maximowiczii* is included within its range of variation. It is rarely recognized as a distinct species, although some suppliers still sell bulbs under this name.

Tulipa micheliana Hoog

John Hoog described this species in the *Gardeners' Chronicle* of 31 May 1902 and named it after Marc Micheli of Geneva, a 'distinguished botanist'. It was growing in the nurseries of Messrs. van Tubergen. Hoog wrote, 'There have been flowering this spring in these nurseries a great number of new and rare bulbs sent home by their collector from the steppes of Trans-Caspia and the mountain range which divides that vast country from North Persia'. *Tulipa micheliana* was originally collected by Paul Sintenis near Ashkhabad in southern Turkmenistan, but its range extends from Iran to the north-western Pamir Alai, growing at altitudes up to 1800 m (5900 ft.). It flowers in the wild in April or May.

This tulip is one of the few species to have anthocyanin markings on the foliage, the best known of which is *Tulipa greigii*. In *T. micheliana* the markings form long, unbroken, deep violet stripes on the upper surface of the three or four glaucous leaves. Occasionally plants will have plain green leaves but, in any case, the stripes fade as the leaves mature. The lowest leaf is lanceolate, around 15 cm long and 4 to 6 cm wide. The upper leaves are narrower and linear-lanceolate.

The whole plant can reach over 30 cm tall but is usually shorter, around 10 to 15 cm tall, often even less in the wild. The solitary flower is scarlet or raspberry-red and held on a pubescent stem. The tepals reach up to 10 cm long (in the flower Hoog described they were 6 to 8 cm long) and narrow abruptly to a pubescent point. The outer tepals are oblong-ovate to rhomboidal and tinged with lilac on the outside. The inner tepals are obovate to oblong-lanceolate. Inside the flower, the prominent, large black blotch can reach half way up each tepal and is lanceolate or may be three-pointed. It has either a broad yellow margin or only a faint trace of yellow around it. The filaments are black and the anthers black to violet, with yellow pollen.

Tulipa micheliana grows from a bulb that has a tunic lined with long, buff-coloured hairs, particularly at the base and tip. It is closely related to *T. eichleri*, which has a more westerly distribution, although the ranges of the two species overlap in northern Iran. L. W. D. van Raamsdonk and T. de Vries (1995) concluded that these two species are very similar and they reduced the more dwarf *T. micheliana* to a variety of *T. eichleri* (*T. eichleri* var. *micheliana*).

Tulipa montana Lindley

This is the perfect little red tulip. The flower colour has been described variously as crimson, vermilion-scarlet, and brilliant blood-red, and John Lindley, who named this species in 1827, claimed that it was more brilliant than any other flower of the season. At the centre of the flower is a small black blotch and surrounding the greenish yellow ovary is a ring of yellow anthers that produce bright yellow pollen. The whole plant grows to only 10 to 12 cm tall. It is most likely to survive in cultivation if grown in pots in a bulb frame or alpine house, where it will flower in late March and April, though in the wild it can flower as late as June.

Tulipa montana grows from a small bulb with a thick, dark brown tunic. Like *T. clusiana* and *T. linifolia* (the other species in section *Clusianae*), this species has matted hairs around the apex of the tunic that protrude like a small beard from the top of the bulb. The four, five, or occasionally six leaves are evenly spaced up the stem. They are glaucous and backed with purplish brown, particularly when they first emerge. The lower leaf reaches 20 cm or more long and is up to 2 cm wide. The remaining leaves are progressively shorter and narrower up the stem. These leaves are held erect and overtop the flower, although the longer, lower leaves will bend in the middle and flop over.

The tepals are all roughly the same size, usually 4 to 5 cm long and around 3 cm wide. They form a small, bright, cup-shaped flower that opens wide in the sun. The outer tepals are oblong to rhomboidal, with a rounded tip and a tiny point at the apex. They have a faint pinkish sheen over the red on their backs. The inner tepals are more ovate and instead of a point at the apex they often have a shallow notch. The glabrous filaments are notable, as the top half of each one is red and the lower half is black. They hold the chunky, bright yellow anthers. This really is one of the most alluring of the smaller tulip species.

Tulipa montana grows wild in the mountains to the south-east of the Caspian Sea (the Kopet–Dag Range) and in Iran, particularly the north, typically on stony mountain slopes, up to 3150 m (10,335 ft.) above sea level. Lindley called this species the crimson mountain tulip when he described it in the *Botanical Register* (Lindley 1827). He studied plants received by the Horticultural Society of London in 1826 from Sir Henry Willock, who was living in Tehran. They flowered in Chiswick in April 1827.

Yellow-flowered forms of *Tulipa montana* also exist, and in the wild both yellow and red variants can be found growing together. In *Flora Orientalis*,

Tulipa montana

Edmund Boissier (1882) called these yellow forms *T. chrysantha*. Per Wendelbo named them *T. montana* var. *chrysantha* and this combination was published in *Flora Iranica*. Unfortunately, in gardens the name *T. chrysantha* became (and still is) confused with the yellow form of *T. clusiana*.

In the *Gardeners' Chronicle* of 26 July 1902 John Hoog described a new species of tulip, collected by Paul Sintenis and imported by van Tubergen from the mountains of the Kopet–Dag. Hoog named it *T. wilsoniana*. However, a look at this description, which mentions the 'deep and full vermilion-scarlet' flowers, the small black blotch, and the red and black filaments, indicates that this plant is in fact *T. montana*. The confusion was soon realized, notably by Sir Daniel Hall, but surprisingly the name *T. wilsoniana* is still often used in the bulb trade today. Whether you buy bulbs labelled *T. montana* or *T. wilsoniana*, you will receive this beautiful red tulip. Almost as certain is that if you buy bulbs labelled *T. chrysantha* you will get the yellow form of *T. clusiana*.

Tulipa neustruevae Pobedimova

An attractive, bright yellow-flowered species, *Tulipa neustruevae* comes from the Chatkal and Fergana Ranges in the western Tien Shan and northern Pamir Alai. It is similar to *T. dasystemon*, but it grows at lower altitudes in the wild and in cultivation does well on a rock garden or raised bed, flowering in late March and April.

Like *Tulipa dasystemon*, this species has two linear leaves and a yellow flower, but the leaves are a fresh, glossy green and the flower is a brighter golden yellow. In cultivated plants the lower leaf can reach 15 to 16 cm long and 2.5 cm wide. The second leaf is narrower but can be a centimetre or two longer.

This species can produce up to three star-like flowers. They open when only 5 to 6 cm above ground, but the glabrous stem soon elongates to 15 cm or more above ground as the flower ages. The tepals are typically 3 cm long, the inner around 1.2 cm wide and the outer 9 mm wide, although some plants can have tepals half this size. The ovate outer tepals are backed with greenish brown except at the margins, and the lanceolate inner tepals have a narrow green line running up the centre. There is no basal blotch inside the flower, and the anthers and filaments are yellow. The style is elongated.

This tulip is mentioned by Aleksei Vvedensky in *Flora of the USSR* under *Tulipa dasystemon*, and although he intended to describe it, apparently as *T. paradasystemon*, he never did. It was Eugenia Pobedimova who named it *T. neustruevae* in 1949, the description based on a single cultivated plant.

Tulipa neustruevae

The only differences Vvedensky mentioned between this tulip and *T. dasystemon* are the firmer, leathery bulb tunic and bright yellow flowers of the former. It may well be only a low-altitude form of *T. dasystemon*.

Tulipa oculus-solis St. Amans

This name was used for many years for a tulip that should be called *Tulipa agenensis* (see under that species for an explanation). To make matters more complicated, the name *oculus-solis* has also been applied to several other tulips, such as *T. undulatifolia* and *T. didieri*. In the *Botanical Register* in 1817, t. 204 was labelled *T. oculus-solis* but actually depicts *T. praecox*. *Oculus-solis* means 'eye of the sun', an apt name for a tulip that has a red flower with a black basal blotch surrounded by yellow. Unfortunately, this name cannot now be used for any tulip.

Tulipa orithyioides Vvedensky

A rarely grown tulip from the Zeravshan Mountains in the western Pamir Alai, *Tulipa orithyioides* is closely related to *T. dasystemon* and *T. tarda* in section *Biflores*. Like *T. tarda*, it has white flowers with a yellow blotch, but otherwise it is more like *T. dasystemon*, having two leaves, a solitary flower, and an elongated style. It grows on stony slopes at altitudes of around 3000 m (9840 ft.).

The bulb tunic of this species is papery and finely cobweb-hairy on the inner surface. The glabrous stem reaches 10 cm long, and the lower leaf is linear-lanceolate and up to 1.5 cm wide. The single flower opens in June in the wild and is fairly small, the tepals only reaching 2.4 cm long. The outer tepals are lanceolate and dingy violet on the back. The wide inner tepals are oblanceolate. The filaments are yellow and have long hairs at the base. The anthers are violet.

Aleksei Vvedensky described *Tulipa orithyioides* in 1935. It has a very long style and the species name refers to the genus *Orithyia*, which was distinguished by this characteristic until included within *Tulipa* by J. Gilbert Baker in his revision of 1874. Vvedensky placed this species in section *Eriostemones* because, unlike those in section *Orithyia*, it has filaments that are hairy at the base.

Tulipa orphanidea Boissier ex Heldreich

Tulipa orphanidea was the first species to be named in a group of closely related tulips within section *Australes*. The predominant flower colour in this group is dull orange-red with a dark blotch inside, and the back of the outer tepals is usually greenish or buff-coloured. Like the other complex group in this section centred around the yellow-flowered *T. sylvestris*, the *T. orphanidea* group may be represented by only one species, encompassing a range of similar forms that have been individually named, including *T. hageri* and *T. whittallii*.

Some forms of *Tulipa orphanidea* may be a subdued brownish red, but others are very beautiful, with bright red flowers. These funnel-shaped flowers open wide in the sun to form attractive starry blooms. The plant does well in a sunny part of the garden if the soil is free-draining, and it is not too large for a rock garden. It is also a good plant for growing in pots in a bulb frame or alpine house. The flowers open in late March or April.

This variable tulip is named after Theodoros Orphanides, professor of botany in the University of Athens, who discovered it in 1857 on Mount

A Turkish form of *Tulipa orphanidea*

Malevo, near Agios Petros in the Greek Peloponnese. Edmund Boissier named and described it in 1862. It grows on stony ground in fields and open pine forests at elevations up to 1700 m (5580 ft.) in the south-eastern Balkans and western Turkey.

The tough bulb tunic is lined with a few straight hairs around the base and at the tip. Up to seven leaves are produced, the lowest reaching 32 cm long and 2 cm wide. The second and third leaves from the base can be almost as long, but further up the stem they become shorter. They are linear-lanceolate or linear-oblong, channelled, and glaucous. The flower is held 15 to 20 cm above ground and the bud is buff-coloured or greenish yellow. When the bud opens, the dusky-red to orange-red inner surfaces of the tepals are exposed, with a blurred, purplish black basal blotch margined with yellow. The elliptic to oblong, pointed tepals are usually between 4 and 5 cm long but can reach 6 cm. The inner tepals are slightly broader than the outer, reaching 2 cm wide. The filaments are black and the anthers violet, with violet or yellowish pollen.

The stem and ovary of this species are typically glabrous, but in some plants they are hairy. These variants have been described as separate species, *Tulipa thracica* and *T. hellespontica*, but intermediate forms also occur in the wild so these two are best considered forms of *T. orphanidea*.

Another closely related species is *Tulipa hageri*. This tulip, which is widely available commercially, was discovered by Theodor von Heldreich in 1862 on the slopes of Mount Parnes near Athens, growing with *T. orphanidea*. It was described as having deep crimson flowers tinged with green on the outside and a large, yellow-margined, purple-black blotch that reaches one-third of the way up the inside of the tepals. Most floras now treat it as a synonym of *T. orphanidea*.

Both diploid and tetraploid forms of *Tulipa orphanidea* occur, and one of the tetraploid forms from near Izmir, on the western coast of Turkey, has been described as a separate species, *T. whittallii*. Named after Edward Whittall who sent it to Henry Elwes from Turkey, this tulip is distinguished by its greater height and vigour and the orange-brown, rounded flowers. It too is widely available in the trade and makes an attractive plant for the garden. Most floras also treat it as a synonym of *T. orphanidea*.

Tulipa orphanidea 'Flava'

Tulipa orphanidea 'Flava' is a yellow form of this species in cultivation. The colour is greenish yellow on the outside, tinged with red along the edges and towards the tip of the tepals. Inside, the flower is lemon yellow with a small bronze-coloured blotch. 'Flava' often produces more than one flower per bulb and, like the typical form of the species, it is easy to grow in the open garden.

Tulipa orthopoda Vvedensky

This tulip is closely allied to *Tulipa bifloriformis* and in cultivation flowers early in the year. In the *Flora of the USSR*, under the entry for *T. bifloriformis*, Aleksei Vvedensky mentioned a tulip from the Karatau Range in Kazakhstan that is very squat, with erect buds, leaves that usually surpass the flower, and a very hairy bulb tunic. He formally described it in 1971, naming it *T. orthopoda*, meaning 'upright'.

The two leaves are bluish green and stained with purplish red on their undersides. They are held close together and reach 6 to 8 cm long at flowering time and 2 cm wide, the bud appearing between them and opening when very close to the ground. The hairy stem is only 1 to 2 cm long at this stage, so the whole plant barely reaches 4 cm tall. The one or two flowers are typical of section *Biflores*, being small and white, with a yellow centre and outer tepals backed with grey-green and a tinge of purple. The outer tepals are lanceolate, around 2 to 2.5 cm long and only 5 mm wide. The inner tepals are slightly shorter, wider, and more triangular, typically 1.8 cm long

Tulipa orthopoda

by 1 cm wide and with a green midrib. The yellow anthers are held on creamy yellow filaments that have a ring of whitish hairs.

Tulipa orthopoda is grown at the Royal Botanic Gardens, Kew, but is rare in cultivation, and its small size and unremarkable flowers will ensure that it stays this way. Appearing in February or even late January, the flowers can easily be damaged by harsh winter weather and the whole tiny plant would be lost in the smallest garden. Hence this species is best kept in a bulb frame, where it will be safely ignored by all but the most devoted tulip fans.

Tulipa ostrowskiana Regel

This species in section *Kolpakowskianae* is very similar to *Tulipa kolpakowskiana* itself. The most obvious difference is the flower colour, which in *T. ostrowskiana* is scarlet to orange-red, with a small brownish black basal blotch. However, both species are reported to hybridize in the wild, resulting in a mixture of flower colours.

Tulipa ostrowskiana occurs in the northern Tien Shan, on stony slopes, flowering in April and May. It was described by Eduard Regel in 1884, having been discovered by his son Albert in 1881, in eastern Turkestan. It is named after Ostrowski, a minister in the Russian government.

The glabrous stem can reach 30 cm long or more, but the flowers may open when held only 5 cm above ground. The bulb tunic has hairs at the apex and around the base, in common with the other species in this section. The two to four glaucous leaves are spaced apart up the stem but not surpassing the flower. They are linear-lanceolate to lanceolate, and the lowest is up to 4 cm wide and 20 to 30 cm long.

The bud is nodding at first but straightens up before opening to form a cup-shaped flower consisting of roughly equal tepals. These are 5 to 8 cm long, 2 to 3 cm wide, and pointed. The outer tepals are rhomboidal and the inner obovate. Colour is variable but generally a bright red with a small brownish black blotch at the base, margined with yellow. The filaments are yellow or blackish and the anthers are violet. When the flower opens wide the tepals become slightly reflexed. Regel illus-

Tulipa ostrowskiana

trated this species in volume 33 of his *Gartenflora* in 1884 (t. 1144), clearly depicting the scarlet blooms with a small black blotch.

Flower colour is an unreliable characteristic to use when distinguishing between tulip species, and the similarity between *Tulipa ostrowskiana* and *T. kolpakowskiana* suggests that these two may be variations of the same species. In *The Genus* Tulipa, Hall (1940) reported that *T. ostrowskiana* had been distributed under the name *T. kolpakowskiana coccinea*. However, *T. kolpakowskiana* is diploid and *T. ostrowskiana* tetraploid. More recently, van Raamsdonk and de Vries (1995) classified *T. ostrowskiana* as a subspecies of the tetraploid *T. tetraphylla* (*T. tetraphylla* subsp. *ostrowskiana*).

Tulipa passeriniana Levier

This member of the *Neo-tulipae* was described in 1884 from northern Italy by Emile Levier in his study of European tulips. The flower is red with a yellow-margined, black basal blotch. The species is named after Professor G. Passerini, who collected it and initially identified it as a form of *Tulipa didieri* in 1871. It flowers in April but is rarely offered for sale.

Tulipa patens Agardh ex Schultes f.

Growing in south-western Russia, northern Kazakhstan, and the Altai Mountains, this variant of *Tulipa sylvestris* is similar to the yellow-flowered

T. biebersteiniana. These two closely related tulips differ mainly in flower colour, which in *T. patens* is white with a yellow centre. The back of the outer tepals is stained with pale or purplish green. Also, in *T. patens* the lowest of the narrow linear-lanceolate leaves only reaches 1 cm wide. Both species are usually included within the broad concept of *T. sylvestris*.

Tulipa planifolia Jordan

This taller member of the *Neo-tulipae* sometimes reaches 60 cm. It has a dark red flower with a large black blotch, not margined with yellow. The filaments and anthers are violet. *Tulipa planifolia* was described in 1858 and was discovered near St. Jean-de-Maurienne, in Savoy, France.

Tulipa platystigma Jordan

One of the French *Neo-tulipae*, *Tulipa platystigma* was described in 1855 from plants growing near Guillestre in the Hautes-Alpes region of southeastern France. It is the only tulip endemic to this region. Like *T. planifolia*, it can reach 60 cm tall. The flowers are lilac-pink and inside at the base is a blue-black blotch on a white background. The tepals are sometimes suffused with orange at the margin. The filaments and anthers are violet. The species flowers in May.

Tulipa polychroma Stapf

Tulipa polychroma is the name Otto Stapf gave to a small white-flowered tulip from the Caucasus Mountains, Iran, and northern Afghanistan. Apart from its wider inner tepals and solitary flowers, it is very similar to *T. biflora*. It is now included within the broad concept of *T. biflora*, but the name is often seen in bulb catalogues. Bulbs sold as *T. polychroma* usually have two leaves, and the one or more flowers have wide tepals at the larger end of the range found in *T. biflora*.

Tulipa praecox Tenore

Popping up in southern Europe and western Turkey, usually on cultivated ground but sometimes on mountain slopes, this triploid, stoloniferous tulip is closely related to *Tulipa agenensis* and is probably derived from it. It differs in having relatively broader tepals and a narrow yellowish band running from the tip to the base of the inner tepals. It also has broader leaves, up to 8 cm wide.

Tulipa praecox was named by Michele Tenore, director of the University Botanic Garden in Naples, in 1811. His description appeared in the first volume of *Flora Napolitana* and was accompanied by a painting depicting a stocky plant with four wide leaves, a thick stem, and a dull red flower. Tenore's description is of a plant growing near Naples. This species is also found from southern France to Greece and Turkey.

As with *Tulipa agenensis*, the inside of the bulb tunic of *T. praecox* is densely hairy. The stem is 6 to 8 mm wide and reaches 30 to 50 cm tall, holding the solitary flower. The three to five leaves can reach over 30 cm long and are broadly lanceolate. The flowers are red or orange-red, paler or greenish outside and with a small brownish black blotch inside, edged with yellow. The outer three tepals are from 4 to 8 cm or more long and 2 to 5 cm wide. They are longer, broader, and more pointed than the inner three, which are 3.6 to 7 cm long and 1.4 to 3.4 cm wide. The filaments are brownish black, and the pollen is dull yellow.

Tulipa praecox is rarely offered commercially, despite being fairly easy to grow in the open garden. The reasons for this are probably its dull colour, not the bright, vibrant red of some species, and its stoloniferous nature, which means the plant can become a bit of a weed in some situations.

Tulipa praestans Hoog

Tulipa praestans must be one of the most widely grown tulip species. Several named forms are available and all are easily grown in the open garden, in borders, beneath shrubs, or in grass. The most notable feature of the plant is its multi-flowered habit, with up to seven flowers per bulb in the popular cultivar 'Fusilier'. Although multi-flowering is not unique in tulip species, most of those that do produce several flowers are in section *Biflores*, whereas *T. praestans* is in section *Eichleres* and the flowers are bright red or orange-red.

This species grows on rocky slopes, screes, and in light woodland, to over 3000 m (9840 ft.) above sea level, in the southern Pamir Alai. In the late nineteenth century, Albert Regel sent specimens of this tulip to his

Tulipa praestans

father Eduard, who originally considered it to be a form of *Tulipa suaveolens*. Eduard later realized that this was a new species but never described it. John Hoog named it *T. praestans* in 1903. It soon became a popular plant and the firm of van Tubergen distributed several forms that had been collected by Joseph Haberhauer in Tajikistan, including 'Fusilier' and 'Zwanenburg Variety'.

The bulb of *Tulipa praestans* has a thick, leathery tunic with few hairs on the inside at the base and tip. The stem is usually between 15 and 40 cm tall but can be much taller in some forms. The upper part of the stem is pubescent and so are the three to six broad, grey-green leaves. The lower leaf reaches 25 cm long and can be up to 10 cm wide. The other leaves gradually decrease in size and all are channelled with a prominent keel and have ciliate margins.

The orange-red or scarlet cup-shaped flowers have no basal blotch. The tepals are all a similar size and shape—oblong to obovate and up to 7 cm long and 3.5 cm wide. The filaments are red or occasionally black, and the anthers are yellow or violet.

Some forms of this variable tulip are short and many-flowered while others are taller but with fewer flowers. 'Fusilier', which received the RHS Award of Garden Merit in 1993, grows to about 25 cm tall and generally has

Tulipa praestans 'Fusilier'

the most blooms but these tend to be slightly smaller than in other forms, such as 'Van Tubergen's Variety' or the taller, vermilion-flowered 'Zwanenburg Variety'. 'Unicum' is a sport of 'Fusilier' and has variegated leaves with pale yellow margins.

Tulipa praestans, in all its forms, is tolerant of a range of soil types and situations, persisting for many years in the open ground, although the number of flowers per bulb will usually decrease over time. It flowers in early to mid-April.

Closely related to this species is the multi-flowered *Tulipa heweri*, named after Tom Hewer, who collected specimens with Chris Grey-Wilson in the Salang Pass of northern Afghanistan in 1971. It was originally assigned to *T. kolpakowskiana* but in 1998, after studying herbarium specimens, L. W. D. van Raamsdonk described it as a new species, closer to *T. praestans*. It has up to five yellow or ochre flowers, with yellow filaments and anthers. The leaves are smaller and have less densely ciliate margins than *T. praestans*.

Tulipa primulina Baker

This Algerian tulip in section *Australes* is one variant of *T. sylvestris*. Henry Elwes collected it near Batna in 1882, and J. Gilbert Baker described it the same year. It has three to six linear leaves that reach 20 cm long. The flowers are pale primrose-yellow, with red staining on the back of the outer tepals. It is an attractive plant that can be grown in the open garden, in a warm, sunny position.

Tulipa pulchella Fenzl

Described in 1874 from plants found in the Taurus Mountains of southern Turkey, this species is now regarded as a form of the variable *Tulipa humilis*. It has purplish crimson flowers with a blue-black blotch on a white background and falcate leaves spreading out on the ground.

Tulipa regelii Krassnow

This small species is rarely seen in cultivation, being found only in a few specialist collections. However, it is noteworthy because it possesses a distinctive feature not found in any other species of tulip. The white funnel-shaped flower with a yellow centre and hairy filaments indicates its close relationship with the species in section *Biflores*. The feature that distinguishes it from these species, and all other tulips, is the broad blue-grey leaf that has several undulating, raised crest-like ridges running along its length.

Tulipa regelii grows from a bulb with a leathery tunic lined with short hairs at the base and tip. The oblong-elliptic or elliptic-lanceolate leaf measures up to 11 cm long and 1.5 to 4 cm wide. It lies close to the ground and is occasionally accompanied by a second, much smaller leaf that has less well-defined ridges or none at all. The solitary white flower is also held close to the ground. The lanceolate tepals are around 3 cm long, but the inner tepals are up to 1.4 cm wide while the outer tepals reach only 8 mm wide. The back of the outer tepals is flushed with greenish purple, sometimes tinted pink at the tip. Inside the flower the yellow blotch covers the lower third of the tepals, and the filaments and anthers are also yellow.

Tulipa regelii

Botanist and plant collector Andrej Krassnow collected this tulip in 1886 and described it the following year, naming it after Eduard Regel. It grows in semi-desert and on stony mountain slopes in the Lake Balkhash area of Kazakhstan. In *Flora of the USSR*, Aleksei Vvedensky placed *Tulipa regelii* in a section of its own, section *Lophophyllon*, separated from section *Eriostemones* on the basis of its unique leaves. In classifications where *Eriostemones* is rated as a subgenus, this species could be placed in its own section within it or included in the similar section *Biflores*.

Coming from a part of the world with very cold winters and hot, dry summers, this tulip is not suitable for growing in the open garden (unless you happen to garden in Kazakhstan). Even in winter the bulbs do not want too much moisture, and in summer they must be sheltered from any rainfall. Pots can be kept in a bulb frame or alpine house in full sun so the bulbs are baked during dormancy. Growth begins early and can become etiolated in low light conditions, but leaving the repotting of this species until late autumn can delay this growth until light levels are higher. The flowers open from late February, and although not the showiest species, the unusual foliage makes this a particularly intriguing tulip.

Tulipa rhodopea Velenovsky

This red-flowered form of the *Tulipa gesneriana* complex grows in, and is named after, the Rhodope Mountains of Bulgaria. It was named by Prague botanist Joseph Velenovsky in 1922. L. W. D. van Raamsdonk and T. de Vries (1995) classified it as *T. hungarica* subsp. *rhodopea*, and in *Flora Europaea* it is treated as a synonym of another Bulgarian tulip, the yellow-flowered *T. urumoffii*.

Tulipa sarracenica Perrier

Described in 1905 by Eduard Perrier de la Bathie, this *Neo-tulipae* is similar to *Tulipa planifolia*. It too has made its home in the Savoy region of France, but the flowers are scarlet with a grey to olive basal blotch.

Tulipa saxatilis Sieber ex Sprengel

Tulipa saxatilis has long been known in cultivation and was grown as early as the beginning of the seventeenth century, when it was known as the tulip of Candie (Candie, or Candia, is the old name for the Mediterranean island of Crete). It then seems to have disappeared from cultivation until reintroduced by George Maw in the 1870s. He first flowered it in 1878. As well as Crete, this tulip has been found in south-western Turkey and on the island of Rhodes.

The leathery bulb tunic is dark brown and lined with short, straight hairs at the tip and around the base. The two to four shiny green, glabrous leaves can reach 38 cm long and 4.5 cm wide. They emerge erect, but as they grow they bend over until the tip touches the ground. The glabrous stem, which can reach over 30 cm, holds one, rarely two or three flowers.

The green buds are nodding but turn upwards as they open. The flow-

Tulipa saxatilis

ers are pink to lilac-purple and have a large, sharply delimited, egg-yolk yellow blotch. The tepals form a cup shape, but in warm sunshine they open out to almost flat. The elliptic outer tepals are up to 5 cm long and 2 cm wide. The obovate inner tepals are larger, up to 5.5 cm long and 3 cm wide, narrowing to a pubescent claw. The filaments are yellow with a hairy boss at the base and the anthers dark yellow to brown.

In the wild this tulip grows in rocky places, usually below 900 m (2950 ft.), and is often found on the sides of gorges, clinging to ledges or pushing through cracks and between rocks, the glossy green, strap-like leaves hanging down. It is very similar to the Cretan endemic *Tulipa bakeri*, which tends to grow at higher altitudes and has darker flowers. Sir Daniel Hall described the latter species in 1938, finding it to be diploid and *T. saxatilis* to be triploid. This is certainly true of most *T. saxatilis* in cultivation, and they do not set viable seed, but in the wild diploid forms of this species also occur. *Tulipa saxatilis* and *T. bakeri* are now often treated as the same species, with the former being the earlier and therefore correct name; Czech naturalist Franz Sieber named it in 1825.

Tulipa saxatilis needs a hot, sunny position and well-drained soil. It is more stoloniferous than *T. bakeri* and in cultivation can produce an abundance of leaves but few flowers. To increase flowering this tulip needs to be planted in a confined space, such as between rocks on a rock garden or surrounded by pieces of slate underground. Here the bulbs will become congested and this seems to promote greater flower production. The same effect can be produced in pots by under-potting slightly. When it comes to repotting in summer, you will find the stolons have reached down to the bottom of the container, producing a cluster of small bulbs that can be separated and potted up.

Tulipa saxatilis is usually the first tulip to emerge above ground, the distinctive leaves often appearing in early November, but the flowers will not open until April. It is surprisingly hardy considering its natural home, and the leaves are undamaged by frosts. The popular cultivar 'Lilac Wonder' was originally assigned to *T. bakeri* but is now more frequently associated with this species.

Tulipa schrenkii Regel

The clone of this species in general cultivation is a striking and distinctive tulip. The scarlet tepals are edged with orange-yellow along their margins and the flowers are large for a plant that may only be 10 cm tall. It can be grown outside on a rock garden or raised bed and flowers in early to mid-

April. However, in the wild the flower colour of this tulip is extremely varied and includes shades of red, pink, and yellow.

The natural range of *Tulipa schrenkii* extends from the European part of Russia, including the Crimea, through the Caucasus Mountains to the steppes and semi-deserts of western Siberia and central Asia. It is named after Alexander Gustav von Schrenk, who collected the plants Eduard Regel described in 1873. In 1879 this species was featured in *Curtis's Botanical Magazine* (t. 6439) where J. Gilbert Baker wrote that wild specimens at the Royal Botanic Gardens, Kew, collected by Schrenk, had flowers of a uniform pale yellow. The plant painted for the magazine, which was sent to Kew by Regel, is larger and bright crimson, with a yellow throat.

Tulipa schrenkii is in section *Tulipa*, and the dark brown bulb tunic has short, stiff hairs on the inside, especially towards the tip. The stem is glabrous or slightly pubescent and can reach 40 cm tall. There are three or four glaucous, undulate leaves and the lowest is linear-lanceolate to oblong, usually around 10 cm long and 3 cm wide, occasionally up to 20 cm long and 6 cm wide. The solitary flower has tepals up to 5.8 cm long and 2.7 cm wide that narrow abruptly to a pubescent point. The outer tepals are oblong to elliptic and the inner tepals are oblong-obovate. Inside, at the base of the flower, there is a black or yellow blotch or no blotch at all. In yellow forms the base of the flower is darker yellow than the rest of the flower. The filaments and anthers are black or yellow.

In *The Genus Tulipa*, Sir Daniel Hall (1940) treated *Tulipa schrenkii* as a synonym of *T. suaveolens*, described from a cultivated plant in 1794, and this was also the opinion of van Raamsdonk and de Vries (1995). In 1805 *T. suaveolens* was illustrated in *Curtis's Botanical Magazine* (t. 839) and this painting is remarkably similar to today's commonly grown form of *T. schrenkii*, with its red, yellow-edged tepals. However, the original *T. suaveolens* was not of wild origin and, like *T. acuminata*, may even have been an early hybrid; it was originally thought to be one of the 'Duc van Thol' race. Consequently, it is better to treat it as a cultivar, with *T. schrenkii* recognized as a wild species.

Tulipa sintenisii Baker

Belonging to section *Tulipa*, this species is found on cultivated land in central and eastern Turkey at altitudes up to 2440 m (8000 ft.). It is named after Paul Sintenis, who collected it near Erzurum, north-eastern Turkey, and sent bulbs to nurseryman Max Leichtlin of Baden-Baden, Germany. Leichtlin in turn sent bulbs to the Royal Botanic Gardens, Kew, where J. Gilbert

Tulipa sintenisii

Baker described them as a new species in the *Gardeners' Chronicle* in 1891. One of the plants grown at Kew was painted for *Curtis's Botanical Magazine* the same year (t. 7193).

Tulipa sintenisii is a stoloniferous species with a bulb tunic lined with soft hairs at the base and tip. The glabrous stem reaches 10 to 30 cm tall. The three or four glaucous, channelled leaves are lanceolate, and the lowest reaches 30 cm long and 6 cm wide. The margins are frequently undulate and the upper leaves may be ciliolate. The flower is bright scarlet or orange-red on the inside and dull red, pinkish, or creamy orange on the outside. Inside is a black basal blotch usually margined with yellow. The ovate-elliptic to ovate-rhomboid outer tepals vary from 4 to 10 cm long and 1.6 to 4.2 cm wide. The obovate to oblong inner tepals are smaller, from 3 to 8.5 cm long and 1.2 to 3 cm wide. The filaments are black, and the anthers are yellow or dark, with olive or yellow pollen.

As this species is known almost exclusively from cultivated land, it is difficult to know its true origin. *Tulipa armena* is similar and comes from more natural locations in the same area of Turkey. There is a possibility that the larger, stoloniferous *T. sintenisii* arose from *T. armena*, becoming established in fields and orchards, where it was found by Sintenis. In cultivation, both species require similar conditions. *Tulipa sintenisii* flowers in early April but is rarely offered for sale.

Tulipa sogdiana Bunge

Tulipa sogdiana is one of two species in subgenus *Eriostemones* that does not have hairs on the filaments, the other being *Tulipa sprengeri*. In all other respects it belongs to this subgenus and is placed in section *Biflores*, close to *T. biflora*.

The dark brown leathery bulb tunic is woolly hairy on the inside. The glabrous stem reaches 15 to 25 cm long, and the lowest of the two or three linear-lanceolate leaves reaches around 20 cm long and 1 cm wide. The leaves may become twisted towards their tip, and their margins are slightly undulate. The one or two flowers are white, sometimes faintly tinted rose-violet, and the blotch is yellow. The lanceolate to ovate tepals are 1.5 to 3 cm long, and the narrower outer tepals are tinged dull violet on the back. As with other species in subgenus *Eriostemones*, the inner tepals are slightly ciliate at their bases. The filaments and anthers are yellow.

This rarely grown species is found from central Iran to northern Afghanistan and north to the Karakum and Kyzylkum Deserts of central Asia, growing in sandy or gravelly soils and flowering in March or April. It was described in 1851 by Russian botanist Alexander Bunge, who distinguished it from *Tulipa biflora* by the glabrous filaments. However, forms of *T. biflora* with glabrous filaments have been found within populations of typical plants and this puts a question mark over the validity of *T. sogdiana* as a distinct species.

Tulipa sosnovskyi Akhverdov & Mirzojeva

This species grows on rocky hillsides in the Caucasus Mountains of Armenia, flowering in May. It belongs to section *Eichleres* and was only described in 1950. The flowers are deep red, and inside they have a black basal blotch with no yellow margin. Also inside the flower is an irregular brownish grey mark at the centre of each tepal.

Tulipa sosnovskyi grows to 35 to 40 cm tall, with three or four glaucous, lanceolate leaves, the lowest reaching around 30 cm long and 3 to 4 cm wide. The stem is tinged with red and bends irregularly so that often the bud is held close to the ground until it opens and becomes erect. Occasionally a second flower is produced. The pointed, broadly lanceolate tepals reach up to 9 cm long, and the outer three are a little longer and more pointed than the inner. The filaments are dark purple to black but have a distinctive yellow tip. The anthers are also dark purple to black.

This species is little known in cultivation but is offered occasionally, at a price. It can be grown in very well drained soil in a sunny position in the garden but will usually do better in a bulb frame, where it can be kept dry in summer.

Tulipa sprengeri Baker

The last of the species tulips to flower is a beautiful plant and easy to grow. It readily naturalizes in a sunny or semi-shaded border, in grass, or on a rock garden, being one of the few tulips to self-seed in significant numbers. It has become well-established in many gardens, producing its brilliant scarlet flowers in May and early June. In 1993 it gained the RHS Award of Garden Merit. It is lucky that *Tulipa sprengeri* is so easy to keep going, as for many years it was thought to be extinct in the wild, and the stocks that persist in gardens today are all derived from collections made in the late nineteenth and early twentieth centuries.

Growing from a bulb with a papery, chestnut-brown tunic that is glabrous or only slightly hairy on the inner surface, the green, glabrous stem reaches 30 to 40 cm tall. Up to six linear leaves can be produced and these are bright shiny green, the lowest up to 25 cm long and 2.5 cm wide. The funnel-shaped flower is shiny scarlet and has no contrasting basal blotch inside. The oblong-elliptic outer tepals are buff or yellowish on the back and reach 6.5 cm long by 2 cm wide. The obovate inner tepals are wider, reach-

Tulipa sprengeri

ing 7 cm long by 3 cm wide. The glabrous filaments are red like the tepals and are topped with bright yellow anthers.

Tulipa sprengeri was collected in the 1890s in the area around Amasia in northern Turkey and introduced by Damman and Company of Naples, Italy, in 1894. J. Gilbert Baker described the species that year in the *Gardeners' Chronicle*, noting the plant's close resemblance to *T. hageri*. Baker named the new species after Carl Sprenger of Damman and Company. It was soon available for sale and grown in various gardens. It is likely that more than one collection was made around this time, but since the start of the First World War no new material has been introduced and *T. sprengeri* was presumed extinct in the wild. However, there are reports that it has recently been rediscovered growing wild in Turkey.

The slender, funnel-shaped flower of *Tulipa sprengeri* is typical of those in subgenus *Eriostemones*. Although the filaments are not hairy, they are swollen at the base where the boss of hairs would be expected. Recent molecular work at the Royal Botanic Gardens, Kew, has confirmed *Eriostemones* as the correct half of the genus in which to place this tulip. Judging by the flower colour and general habit, it appears to be closest to the species centred around *T. orphanidea*, in section *Australes*.

Tulipa sprengeri can be grown in various soils and situations, from grassy banks to herbaceous borders, under deciduous trees, among shrubs, and on a rock garden. The soil should drain freely, but this tulip does not need the summer baking required by many other species and does well in soil that does not dry out completely. The fat seed capsules generate plenty of seeds that germinate freely, and you will soon see the tiny thread-like leaves of seedlings surrounding mature plants in spring. These seedlings can flower in only four years. The easiest way to introduce this species to your garden in large numbers is to sprinkle the seed around and lightly rake it in. It is certainly worth finding space for the plant, as the elegant, brightly coloured flowers provide a final boost to the tulip season.

Tulipa stapfii Turrill

This species, named by William Turrill in 1934, commemorates Austrian botanist Otto Stapf. Although available to buy as *Tulipa stapfii*, it is now usually regarded as a synonym of *T. systola*.

Tulipa stellata Hooker

Tulipa stellata is the white form of *T. clusiana* with a yellow rather than purple blotch and stamens. It was described by William Hooker in 1827. Like

T. aitchisonii, it was recognized as distinct from *T. clusiana* in *Flora Iranica* but, as intermediate forms occur in the wild, it is generally considered to be a form of that species (*T. clusiana* f. *stellata*).

Tulipa suaveolens Roth

This name was given to a cultivated tulip of unknown origin by Albrecht Roth in 1794 and considered at the time to be one of the 'Duc van Thol' race. The species name means 'sweet scented' and was subsequently used for a range of wild, dwarf, early tulips that were introduced from southern Russia.

Sir Daniel Hall considered the wild form of *Tulipa suaveolens* to be the tulip described by Eduard Regel as *T. schrenkii* in 1881, in which case the plants sold as *T. schrenkii* today should be given the older name of *T. suaveolens*. L. W. D. van Raamsdonk and T. de Vries, in 1995, also treated *T. schrenkii* as a synonym of this species and, therefore, the account I have given of *T. schrenkii* also serves to describe *T. suaveolens*. However, because the source of the original *T. suaveolens* is unknown, it makes more sense to disregard it as a wild species and maintain *T. schrenkii*.

Tulipa subpraestans Vvedensky

As you might guess from the name, this tulip is closely related to *Tulipa praestans*. It has broad, glaucous leaves and red flowers with no basal blotch. It was originally described as having only a solitary flower, but it can have two, three, or rarely more. It grows on stony ground in the southern Pamir Alai, Tajikistan, and flowers in late April.

Tulipa subpraestans grows 30 to 40 cm tall from a bulb with a dark, leathery bulb tunic that is glabrous on the inner surface. The stem is glaucous-green and pubescent in the upper part. There are three or four linear-lanceolate, deeply channelled leaves, the lowest sometimes reaching over 40 cm long and 12 cm wide, although around 30 cm long by 4.5 cm wide is typical. The point at which the leaf joins the stem is usually well above ground level. The remaining leaves, spaced widely apart up the stem, decrease in size, and the upper leaf may be very reduced, resembling a bract, less than 2 cm long and only a few millimetres wide. The leaves are glaucous and pubescent.

The flowers are deep, glossy red and open to form a star. If there is more than one, they are held on branches that arise from the axils of the upper leaves. The tepals are oblong to lanceolate and taper to a pubescent point at the tip. Where they are attached to the stem, they are yellow, but this minute mark is hidden by the stamens. The outer tepals are paler pinkish red or buff on the back, especially along the midrib, and reach 6 cm long and 2.8 cm wide. The inner tepals are slightly shorter. The filaments are red, sometimes yellow at the base, and the anthers purplish black or yellow.

Aleksei Vvedensky described *Tulipa subpraestans* in 1935 from plants collected by Victor Botschantzev in 1933. It is a very attractive, brightly coloured species that can be grown in the free-draining soil of a rock garden or raised bed and also does well in pots, kept in a bulb frame or cold glasshouse. It readily increases, forming droppers. When repotting you are likely to find a number of new bulbs around the base of the pot.

Tulipa subpraestans

Tulipa sylvestris Linnaeus

Tulipa sylvestris is the yellow-flowered 'wild tulip' of central and northern Europe, described by Carl Linnaeus in 1753. This tetraploid plant increases readily by stolons and is one of the best species for naturalizing in the garden. In a warm, sunny location it can form a sizeable population that produces a dazzling display of yellow blooms in late March and early April, especially if the previous summer was hot and dry. It does not do so well in grass or in shadier, cooler positions, where there may be plenty of leaves but few flowers.

This tulip grows up to 45 cm tall from a bulb with a tough tunic lined with a few straight hairs at the tip. The two to four linear-lanceolate, channelled leaves reach 30 cm long and 1.8 cm wide. They are dull green or slightly glaucous. The glabrous stem holds one or two green nodding buds, and this green colour remains on the back of the outer tepals when the flowers open. The flowers are otherwise entirely golden yellow. The elliptic outer tepals can reach over 6 cm long and 1.8 cm wide, and the tip often becomes reflexed, even when the flowers are not fully open. The inner tepals are elliptic to oblanceolate and reach up to 7 cm long and 2.6 cm wide. The anthers and filaments are yellow.

Tulipa sylvestris was already well-known before Linnaeus named it in his *Species Plantarum*. It was recorded as early as the mid-sixteenth century around Bologna in Italy and has, with the help of man, gradually spread and become naturalized across Europe. Historical records indicate that it reached southern Scandinavia in the mid-eighteenth century and Britain in the late eighteenth century, if not earlier. It also appears further east, in south-western Asia, and has even become naturalized in North America, in the eastern states of Maryland, Massachusetts, and Pennsylvania.

A similar form, with lemon-yellow flowers backed with green, was introduced by van Tubergen in 1933 from north-western Iran. It was found growing in large numbers in orchards and was sold in bunches in shops and on the streets of Tabriz. It is known as *Tulipa sylvestris* 'Tabriz Variety'.

The exact origin of *Tulipa sylvestris* is uncertain, as plants are usually found on cultivated or waste ground, particularly vineyards, roadsides, and meadows. If you look at *T. sylvestris* in its broader sense, you can begin to find some clues to the story of this fascinating plant. As a much more widespread species, it encompasses a range of smaller diploid forms that are found from the Iberian Peninsula, through North Africa and Europe, to western and central Asia. These variants are the true wild forms of *T. sylvestris*, but several have been described as separate species, such as *T. australis*, *T. celsiana*, and *T. primulina*. Commercial stocks of these individual forms are fairly distinct, but in the wild there is a wide range of variation, making their separation difficult.

Tulipa australis was described by German botanist Johann Link in 1799. This species occurs at higher altitudes than the typical *T. sylvestris* and differs in being smaller and in having violet to crimson, rather than green, staining on the back of the outer tepals. It grows in grassy and rocky places in southern Europe and the mountains of North Africa. The stem is not more than 2 mm wide (at least 2.5 mm in *T. sylvestris*), the lower leaf is less than 1.2 cm wide, the outer tepals reach only 3.7 cm long and 9 mm wide, and the inner tepals are up to 3.8 cm long and 1.6 cm wide. The filaments and anthers are also smaller, reaching 8 mm and 4 mm respectively (14 mm and 9 mm in *T. sylvestris*).

Tulipa australis is diploid and in *The Genus* Tulipa, Sir Daniel Hall (1940) concluded that the tetraploid *T. sylvestris* of central and northern Europe is derived from this species. Renato Pampanini reduced *T. australis* to a subspecies of *T. sylvestris* in 1914, and although Hall maintained it as a distinct species, *T. sylvestris* subsp. *australis* is the name most often used today.

It is usually easy to differentiate between plants of *Tulipa sylvestris* subsp. *sylvestris* and subsp. *australis* in cultivation, based on the above characters, but in the wild the boundaries are not so clear. A tulip I found in Tunisia in 1989 resembles subsp. *australis* in general appearance, but the tepals are backed with green. Looking more closely at this plant reveals that its dimensions are slightly larger than those described for subsp. *australis*, except for the sizes of the filaments and anthers. Although outside the range of typical *T. sylvestris*, this plant appears to be that species and was named *T. sylvestris* subsp. *sylvestris* 'Mount Zaghouan', after the mountain it was growing on.

Another species now included within the broad concept of *Tulipa sylvestris* is *T. celsiana*, named by Johann Henning in 1803. This plant, described

Tulipa sylvestris 'Mount Zaghouan'

from specimens growing in southern France, is like subsp. *australis*, but the leaves curl round and lie close to the ground. Although treated as a form of *T. sylvestris* in recent floras, it is still sold as *T. celsiana*. This cultivated form grows 10 to 15 cm tall, displaying small, deep yellow flowers in May.

Tulipa biebersteiniana and *T. patens* are among the names applied to diploid variants of *T. sylvestris* in Asia. The former was described by Julius Schultes in 1829. This tulip has up to five yellow flowers, the outer tepals backed with violet. It grows up to 30 cm tall, with two or three narrow linear-lanceolate leaves, the lowest of which reaches 2 cm wide. The tepals can reach up to 4 cm long. The species grows in a large area, stretching from eastern Europe, through the Caucasus Mountains and Iran, to central Asia and southern Siberia.

Tulipa sylvestris, collected on the Greek island of Naxos

The eastern part of this range overlaps with that of *Tulipa patens*, a similar species described by Carl Agardh, also in 1829. *Tulipa patens* differs from *T. biebersteiniana* in its white flowers that are yellow at the base and tinged or streaked with pale or purplish green on the back of the tepals. It grows to 25 cm tall. The two or three leaves are narrowly linear-lanceolate and up to 1 cm wide.

Various species have been described from the Atlas Mountains of North Africa. They include *Tulipa primulina*, described by J. Gilbert Baker in 1882. This tulip was collected by Henry Elwes in May of that year, in the mountains west of Batna, north-eastern Algeria, where it was growing on ridges and in open glades of cedar forests. The flowers are pale primrose-yellow and the outer tepals are stained with red. The filaments are yellow and the anthers are orange-yellow.

In *Flore de L'Afrique du Nord*, published in 1959, René Maire treated all the North African tulips as subspecies, varieties, and formas of *Tulipa sylvestris*. So, for example, *T. primulina* becomes *T. sylvestris* subsp. *primulina* and *T. celsiana* becomes *T. sylvestris* subsp. *australis* var. *celsiana*. This complex approach reflects a desire to recognize the various forms of *T. sylvestris*, but with the boundaries between each subspecies being blurred it becomes unsatisfactory. In its broadest sense, *T. sylvestris* has the widest natural range of any tulip, so some variation is not surprising. Although cultivated forms are fairly distinct, in the wild they are not so easy to differentiate. Cultivar names can be used to identify distinct clones in cultivation.

This account is by no means the full story of *Tulipa sylvestris*. Many other names and combinations have been published for the tulips in this group, but those included here are the ones you are most likely to encounter.

Tulipa systola Stapf

This beautiful red tulip grows wild in the steppe and forest zones of northern Iraq and western Iran, on mountain slopes, among rocks, in oak forest clearings and sometimes in fields and on waste ground, flowering in April and May. It has also been reported from other parts of western Asia, and even Egypt, but at least some of these are likely to be naturalized plants. As with many tulips, it is difficult to determine the true range of the species; *Tulipa systola* may be naturally widespread throughout much of the Middle East.

The species is placed in section *Tulipanum*. The inside of the brown bulb tunic is densely covered in woolly hairs. Usually four, but occasionally up to seven, glaucous leaves are spaced apart up the stem, and they are blue-green to markedly blue-grey in colour, especially when young. There are prominent short hairs along the margins. The lower leaf has an undulate margin and can reach 30 cm long but is more often around 15 to 20 cm long and 3 cm wide. The leaves decrease in size up the stem so the upper leaf is less than half the length of the lowest, and much narrower, typically 4 to 5 mm wide.

The solitary flower of *Tulipa systola* is held on a stem that in cultivation reaches 15 to 20 cm long at flowering time. This stem is not very sturdy, which means the plant can become a little floppy, especially where light levels are not as high as in its natural home. In the wild this can be a very compact plant, with the flowers held just a few centimetres above ground.

The bowl-shaped flowers are bright scarlet with a large, dark purple-black blotch at the base, which may or may not be edged with yellow. The ovate outer tepals are more pointed and slightly shorter than the obovate inner tepals. They can vary from 2.5 to 7 cm long but are typically around 4 cm long and 2 to 2.5 cm wide. The outside of the flower is a duller pinkish red and yellowish at the base. The filaments and anthers are dark purple, and the pollen can be yellow or purple.

This species needs a dry summer rest, so cultivation under glass is usually necessary, or the bulbs must be lifted after the leaves have died back. It is not difficult to grow in pots and makes a beautiful plant for an alpine house.

Tulipa systola was described from Iranian material by Otto Stapf in 1885. In the same year Stapf described another species from Iran, *T. cuspidata*. However, this latter name was invalid as it had already been used by Eduard Regel for a different tulip (in the *T. sylvestris* group) the previous year, so in 1934 William Turrill renamed Stapf's plant *T. stapfii*. The description and a painting of *T. stapfii* appeared in *Curtis's Botanical Magazine* (t. 9356). Stapf

Tulipa systola

used the name *cuspidata* for this tulip because the tips of the tepals narrow abruptly to a short, rigid point or cusp.

Tulipa stapfii differs from *T. systola* mainly in the wider lower leaves, which can be up to 8 cm or more across and crowded near the base of the stem, but it is otherwise very similar. It is now generally accepted that the two represent extreme forms of the same species, with intermediate forms found in the wild. The older name, *T. systola*, should be used for these plants. Bulbs labelled *T. systola* are rarely offered commercially, but as *T. stapfii* they are sometimes available.

Tulipa tarda Stapf

The star-like flowers of *Tulipa tarda* appear close to the ground in mid to late April and early May. They are surrounded by a number of linear, green leaves. This species does well in the open garden in a sunny spot, but due to its small stature it needs to be planted at the front of a border or raised bed, where it is not lost among other plants.

The finely pubescent stem can reach 20 cm tall but is commonly less than 10 cm and often only 4 to 5 cm. Up to seven leaves can be produced and these are crowded together at ground level like a rosette. The upper sur-

Tulipa tarda

face of each leaf is dull green, but the underside is a bright, glossy green. The leaves reach 21 cm long and between 0.8 and 2.1 cm wide.

Up to eight flowers may open from one bulb and these are white but with a large yellow blotch in the centre that can cover most of the tepals, leaving only white tips. The back of the outer tepals is greenish, flushed with purple, and the inner tepals are yellowish green on the back towards the base, with a narrow green line running up the centre. The lanceolate to oblong-lanceolate outer tepals reach 1.1 cm wide and 4.5 cm long and are narrower than the ovate to oblong inner tepals, which reach 1.7 cm wide. The filaments are yellow and densely hairy at their base. The anthers are also yellow.

The dark, leathery bulb tunic of *Tulipa tarda* is glabrous on the inner surface or slightly hairy at the tip. The bulb is very proficient at producing droppers to reach down to the desired depth. When repotting this species, you will find the droppers at the base of the pot and the original bulbs left as hollow shells where you planted them. Of course, bulbs in the garden will soon find their own depth, and clumps of this stoloniferous species will gradually increase to form a dense colony over the years.

Tulipa tarda grows on rocky slopes in the Tien Shan. It was known in cultivation long before it was recognized as a distinct species, masquerading under the name of another tulip, *T. dasystemon*. Otto Stapf in 1933 cleared up this mistaken identity and named this tulip in *Curtis's Botanical Magazine* (t. 9321). It is now popular and widely available, and received the RHS Award of Garden Merit in 1993. The species name refers to its late flowering. It is not the last of the tulip species to flower but is certainly later than most of those in section *Biflores*, to which it belongs.

Tulipa tetraphylla Regel

Tulipa tetraphylla is another yellow-flowered species in section *Kolpakowskianae*. It grows wild on stony slopes and gravelly areas in the Tien Shan and into western China, flowering in April and May. The species is a tetraploid but is otherwise similar to the other members of the section, in particular *T. kolpakowskiana* and *T. altaica*.

Tulipa tetraphylla was described by Eduard Regel in 1875. The species name means 'four-leaved'. In fact this tulip can have up to seven glaucous leaves, crowded together at the base of the glabrous flower stem. They grow from a bulb with a blackish tunic that has hairs at the tip. The linear to linear-oblong leaves have undulate margins and tend to surpass the flower. The lowest leaf is around 15 to 20 cm long and 1 to 1.5 cm wide.

The glabrous stem grows from 10 to 30 cm tall or more and can carry up to four flowers from one bulb, although one or two is more common. From nodding buds the flowers open to display pale yellow, oblong to oblong-rhomboidal tepals that reach up to 4 cm long but less than 1 cm wide. The back of the tepals is greenish, particularly along the midrib and at the base, and the outer tepals are also stained with violet-red. The tip of the outer tepals bends right back when the flower is fully open. Inside the flower is a small greenish basal blotch. The anthers and filaments are yellow.

In 1878 Regel described *Tulipa kesselringii*, naming it after his son-in-law, J. Kesselring, a *cultivatori eruditissimo*. The fol-

Tulipa tetraphylla

lowing year he featured a painting of this species in volume 28 of *Gartenflora* (t. 964), showing the narrow leaves with undulate margins, the dark bulb tunic, and the outer tepals stained reddish on the back and with a green median stripe. The species was collected by Albert Regel in 1878 and the same year bulbs were sent to Henry Elwes at Colesbourne and to the Royal Botanic Gardens, Kew. *Tulipa kesselringii* was featured in *Curtis's Botanical Magazine* (t. 6754) in 1884. Eduard Regal described the flowers as having oblong-lanceolate tepals, 4.5 cm long and 1.4 cm wide, but little else differentiates it from *T. tetraphylla* and the two are now regarded as the same species.

Tulipa ostrowskiana is another tetraploid species in section *Kolpakowskianae* and was classified as a subspecies of *T. tetraphylla* by L. W. D. van Raamsdonk and T. de Vries in 1995. *Tulipa tetraphylla* subsp. *ostrowskiana* is said to differ from subsp. *tetraphylla* by its more erect, less undulated leaves and its more westerly distribution in the Tien Shan. However, commercially available stocks of these plants are sold under their individual species names, with *T. ostrowskiana* having red or orange-red flowers. It is worth noting that plants sold as *T. tetraphylla* are remarkably similar to those sold as the more widely available *T. kolpakowskiana* and require the same conditions in cultivation.

Tulipa theophrasti Candargy

Tulipa theophrasti is a little-known tulip from the Aegean island of Lesbos off the western coast of Turkey. Belonging to the *T. orphanidea* group, it is characterized by its purple-red flowers with a blue-black basal blotch. It is otherwise similar to *T. orphanidea*, with four linear, channelled leaves reaching 1.5 cm wide and oblong-lanceolate tepals that are around 4 cm long.

This species was described in 1897 from specimens found on Mount Olympus, Lesbos. It is rarely seen in cultivation but is grown at the Royal Botanic Gardens, Kew, where unfortunately it does not reliably flower. A few bulbs planted on the rock garden a few years ago have gradually increased to form an extensive colony that sends up a mass of individual leaves every spring but few flower buds. This is all the more frustrating as this material came from Gothenburg Botanic Garden where it does flower well.

Tulipa tschimganica Z. Botschantzeva

Flowering in late April, *Tulipa tschimganica* grows in stony or sandy soils in the western Tien Shan, at altitudes of 1400 to over 2700 m (4590 to 8860 ft.), and takes its name from Chimgan valley, east of Tashkent. Zinaida Botschantzeva described this species in 1961 and placed it in section *Spiranthera* because, like the similar *T. kaufmanniana*, the anthers dehisce gradually and slowly from the tip down.

It is sometimes said that *Tulipa tschimganica* differs from *T. kaufmanniana* in having red, inverted V-shaped marks on the inside of the tepals. However, the latter species can have the same markings and this is often clearly evident on the hybrids in the Kaufmanniana Group. Both species are very similar but occupy different ecological niches in the wild, *T. tschimganica* generally growing at higher altitudes, flowering as the snow melts around it. It also differs from *T. kaufmanniana* in having anthers that tend not to coil or twist as they dehisce. In cultivation the flowers open towards the end of March or in early April, a little later than *T. kaufmanniana*.

The flower emerges from between the three or four glaucous leaves, the lowest leaf being broadly lanceolate, up to 7.5 cm wide, and sometimes over 20 cm long. Although the flower initially opens near ground level, the pubescent stem can eventually reach over 20 cm long, growing from a bulb with a papery, dark brown tunic that is sparsely lined with long straight hairs.

From conical buds the flowers open to form a wide star, and the basic colour can be yellow or orange-red. It is the yellow forms that have the inverted V-shaped marks inside the flower, and the back of the outer tepals is feathered with bright red, particularly along the midrib. The red forms have a yellow base to the tepals, while in the yellow forms they are darker yellow or orange at the base. The tepals are up to 8.5 cm long and between 2.8 and 4 cm wide, the inner a little wider and shorter than the outer. They are lanceolate to oblong or narrowly ovate. The yellow anthers are very long, reaching 2 cm, and are held on yellow filaments, surrounding the long, yellowish green ovary.

Tulipa tubergeniana Hoog

This tulip was one of the species sent back from Bukhara in southern Uzbekistan by Joseph Haberhauer for C. G. van Tubergen at the beginning of the twentieth century. It received an Award of Merit from the RHS on 17 May 1904, and the description appeared in the *Gardeners' Chronicle* on 4 June the same year. It seems that the plants collected in Bukhara were cultivated specimens; in *Flora of the USSR*, Aleksei Vvedensky stated that the true range of this species is the south-western Pamir Alai.

Tulipa tubergeniana, named after van Tubergen, is one of the group of showy, red-flowered species centred around *T. lanata* in section *Eichleres*, a group that also includes *T. hoogiana*, which was described in 1910. However, Vvedensky placed *T. tubergeniana* and *T. hoogiana* in section *Tulipanum*, and Sir Daniel Hall separated them by placing the former in his subsection *Eichleres* and the latter in his subsection *Oculis-solis* (syn. section *Tulipanum*). In 1995, L. W. D. van Raamsdonk and T. de Vries concluded that these were both the same species, with the earliest name of *T. tubergeniana* taking priority, and placed it in section *Eichleres*.

The papery, brown bulb tunic of *Tulipa tubergeniana* is covered with long, silky hairs inside. The stem reaches 15 to 30 cm long and the upper part is pubescent. The three or four leaves are falcate, glaucescent, and more or less pubescent, with ciliate margins. The lowest leaf is lanceolate, up to 4 cm wide and 22 cm long. The solitary flower is described by John Hoog in the *Gardeners' Chronicle* as forming 'a fine cup or dish, rich orange-crimson'. He also described the bud before opening as having the outer tepals reflexing at their tips, exposing the tips of the inner tepals. The tepals are up to 10 cm long, narrowing to a pubescent point. The rhomboidal or deltoid outer tepals are slightly wider than the obovate to oblong inner tepals. Inside the flower is a well-defined black blotch with a distinct yellow border. The filaments are black and the anthers violet. The stigma is reddish or purple.

Although very similar, *Tulipa hoogiana* does differ from *T. tubergeniana* in several subtle ways. For example, the stem and leaves are glabrous and the stigma is yellow rather than reddish or purple, but perhaps the most convincing argument to maintain these two as separate species is their natural distribution. Whereas *T. tubergeniana* grows wild in the mountains of the south-western Pamir Alai, *T. hoogiana* is found in the central and western Kopet–Dag, in north-eastern Iran, and southern Turkmenistan; their ranges are separated by the Amu Dar'ya River.

Tulipa tubergeniana is an attractive species that can be grown in a warm, sheltered part of the garden, where the soil is very well drained. In this situation it will flower in late April or early May. In a bulb frame or cold glasshouse, where the large flowers will be protected from the weather, it can flower up to a month earlier.

Tulipa turkestanica Regel

The individual flowers may not be the showiest, but they are produced in such profusion, with several flowers from each bulb, that this tulip deserves a place in the garden. It also happens to be one of the easiest species to grow in the open and received the RHS Award of Garden Merit in 1993. It belongs to section *Biflores* and is similar to *Tulipa biflora*, but the plants in general cultivation are more vigorous than that species, producing thick leaves with slightly undulate margins, and many-flowered stems.

Tulipa turkestanica, described by Eduard Regel in 1875, grows wild in the central Asian mountains of the Pamir Alai and Tien Shan, on stony and clay slopes, flowering in March and April. Its range covers southern Kazakhstan, Uzbekistan, and Kyrgystan, an area once included in the old region of Turkestan, from which this tulip takes its name. This is the heartland of the genus *Tulipa* and, although section *Biflores* takes its name from *T. biflora*, which was described almost a hundred years earlier, it is probably from *T. turkestanica* that the closely related species in this group evolved, spreading south and west.

As in *Tulipa biflora*, the bulb of this species usually produces two leaves that are glaucous on the upper surface and shiny green beneath, with maroon-purple staining towards the base. These leaves are 15 to 25 cm long at flowering time and between 1 and 3 cm wide. They are held close together when flowering begins, but as the pubescent stem lengthens they become more spread out. The flower buds emerge from between the two leaves, and although the stem lengthens as more flowers open, it tends not to exceed the leaves. The whole plant can reach 25 to 30 cm tall, but some forms are much shorter.

The flowers of *Tulipa turkestanica* do not reach the size of the largest forms of *T. biflora*, but it is not unusual for a bulb to produce five or six flowers or even up to twelve. They are creamy white with a yellow centre. The pointed tepals are lanceolate to ovate and around 2.5 cm long, and the inner three are twice the width of the outer three, from 6 to 13 mm wide. The outer tepals are backed with greyish or violet-green.

Like *Tulipa bifloriformis*, this species differs from *T. biflora* in having wispy, white hairs along the length of the filaments, and the purplish green flower stem is pubescent. The anthers are up to a centimetre long and may be yellow with a dark violet tip or occasionally completely violet, like those of *T. bifloriformis*. The tough, leathery bulb tunic is a wonderful reddish brown colour and has thick, woolly hairs inside, particularly towards the tip.

Tulipa turkestanica does well in a sunny border, even flourishing in fairly

Tulipa turkestanica

heavy clay soil, as long as it doesn't become waterlogged. This is a great tulip for planting in a winter garden as the first flowers will open in early March, before the last snowdrops (*Galanthus*) have finished. The bulbs will gradually increase to create dense patches, and the small star-like flowers make an attractive sight when they open wide on a sunny spring day.

Tulipa ulophylla Wendelbo

Tulipa ulophylla was described in 1967 by Norwegian botanist Per Wendelbo, who found it at an altitude of 600 m (1970 ft.) in the Haraz valley of Māzandarān Province in northern Iran. Here, where the Elburz Mountains fall away to the southern shores of the Caspian Sea, Wendelbo came across this species flowering on 26 April 1959 and in fruit three months later. It has also been found south of the Elburz Mountains, but this tulip is endemic to Iran and is rare in cultivation.

The inside of the leathery, dark brown bulb tunic is hairy, as in the other species in section *Tulipanum*, although these hairs are relatively sparse when compared to the dense, woolly covering found in species such as *Tulipa julia*. The stem can reach 16 to 26 cm long but is often shorter. There are usually six long, narrow leaves up to 1 to 2 cm wide with undulate margins. The solitary flower forms a shallow bowl composed of purplish red tepals. The elliptic-ovate outer tepals are 4 to 5.8 cm long and around 2.2 cm wide, with a short point at the tip. The inner tepals also have a short point at the tip but are more rounded, being a few millimetres shorter and wider.

Wendelbo's original description of *Tulipa ulophylla* stated that inside the

The form of *Tulipa ulophylla* grown at the Royal Botanic Gardens, Kew, and collected by Per Wendelbo in Iran

flower the black basal blotch (which is 1 to 2 cm long) has a yellow margin, the filaments are dark violet, and the pollen is yellow. However, a tulip grown at the Royal Botanic Gardens, Kew, that came from Gothenburg Botanic Garden as *T. ulophylla* and was collected by Wendelbo in Iran, has violet pollen and the yellow margin of the blotch is reduced to just a hint of yellow at each side of the blotch. Otherwise, this plant has the six leaves and purplish red flower typical of this species. It is not, though, dissimilar to *T. wendelboi*, described by Farideh Matin and Mousa Iranshahr in 1998, in the *Iranian Journal of Botany*.

Tulipa wendelboi, named after Per Wendelbo, is said to differ from *T. ulophylla* by having up to seven leaves, a shorter stem (7 to 13 cm), a notched basal blotch with a narrow yellow margin, and shorter filaments holding anthers that produce violet pollen. It was collected in Māzandarān in 1996, where it was growing on rocky slopes at an altitude of 800 m (2625 ft.). The differences between these two species are minor, and *T. wendelboi* may well end up being treated as a variant of *T. ulophylla*.

Of course, variation in a species is far from unusual in tulips, and *Tulipa ulophylla* is considered by L. W. D. van Raamsdonk and T. de Vries (1995) to be a form of the more widespread *T. systola*. The flower colour, the more numerous leaves, and the less densely hairy bulb tunic of the former help to distinguish the two.

Tulipa ulophylla should be grown in a bulb frame or a well-drained raised bed to ensure the bulbs are kept dry in summer. Like *T. systola*, it makes a fine alpine house plant.

Tulipa undulatifolia Boissier

This tulip is a weed of cultivated ground in western and central Turkey and has also spread westwards into the southern Balkan Peninsula. It was described by Edmund Boissier in 1844 from plants he found flowering in May 1842 near Izmir, on Turkey's western coast. Boissier described the Balkan plants as a separate species, *Tulipa boeotica*, in 1859, but these are now included under *T. undulatifolia*.

Tulipa undulatifolia is in section *Eichleres*. The bulb tunic is sparsely hairy inside except at the base where there is a ring of hairs. The stem is pubescent, especially in the upper part, and reaches around 20 to 40 cm above ground. The three or four leaves are glaucous, ovate-lanceolate, with undulate margins and are usually minutely pubescent on the upper surface. The lowest leaf reaches 20 cm long and 4.5 cm wide.

The flower is orange-red to scarlet, and the ovate to ovate-lanceolate

This form of *Tulipa undulatifolia* was collected by Wessel Marais in Turkey-in-Europe.

tepals narrow gradually to a point, reaching up to 7.5 cm long and 2.8 cm wide. The outer tepals are slightly longer than the inner. The outer surface of the tepals is a pale red or bluish red. Inside the flower is a black blotch usually surrounded by a yellow margin. The filaments are black and the anthers violet, with greenish yellow pollen.

This tulip was introduced into cultivation in England in 1875 by Henry Elwes, who found it between 1200 and 1500 m (3900–4900 ft.) above sea level on Boz Dağ, about 100 km (60 miles) east of Izmir. Like *Tulipa aleppensis* and *T. praecox*, it too has an uncertain natural habitat. It has colonized cultivated areas in Turkey and south-eastern Europe but doesn't appear to occur in more natural locations. In 1874, Eduard Regel described *T. eichleri* from eastern Transcaucasia and Iran, but according to Wessel Marais (1984) in *Flora of Turkey*, this is the same plant as Boissier's *T. undulatifolia*. If these two names represent the same species, the range of *T. undulatifolia* extends further east, towards central Asia, its probable natural home.

Tulipa uniflora (Linnaeus) Besser ex Baker

This dwarf tulip is found at the cold northern and eastern limits of the range of the genus *Tulipa*, growing in thickets and on exposed stony slopes, up to 2400 m (7900 ft.) above sea level. The small flowers and narrow leaves give this species a deceptively delicate appearance, but in the wild it braves the elements in the Altai Mountains of Kazakhstan, southern Siberia, over the border into north-western China, and in Mongolia, flowering in May or June.

Tulipa uniflora was grown as long ago as the late eighteenth century and was known to Carl Linnaeus, who named it *Ornithogalum uniflorum*. It was apparently then lost to cultivation until reintroduced to England in 1835 from bulbs sent by Carl von Ledebour, director of the Imperial Botanic Garden, Dorpat (Tartu), Estonia. It was on these bulbs, grown at the Chelsea Physic Garden in London, that David Don based his new genus *Orithyia* in 1836, naming this plant *O. uniflora*. It eventually received its current name in 1874 in J. Gilbert Baker's revision, where he included *Orithyia* within *Tulipa*.

The main characteristic Don used to distinguish the genus *Orithyia* was the elongated style, which can be a third of the overall length of the ovary. This species is otherwise similar in general appearance to some forms of *Tulipa biflora*, but the flowers are yellow and the filaments are glabrous, not hairy at the base. When Baker transferred *Orithyia uniflora* to *Tulipa*, he placed it in subgenus *Orithyia*. In *Flora of the USSR*, Aleksei Vvedensky reduced this to section *Orithyia* and included two other species with elongated styles and glabrous filaments: *Tulipa heteropetala* from the Altai, and *T. heterophylla* from the Tien Shan and north-western China.

Tulipa uniflora grows to 10 to 20 cm tall from a bulb with a blackish brown, papery tunic, hairy inside towards the tip. The glabrous flower stem is stained violet and holds the solitary flower. Two or occasionally three glabrous, glaucous-green, narrowly linear-lanceolate leaves are produced, and they are usually held close together near the base of the stem. The lowest leaf reaches 12 cm long and 1.3 cm wide. The second leaf is only a little shorter and narrower.

The flower is nodding in bud but opens to expose the yellow tepals with no basal blotch. The lanceolate to oblanceolate outer tepals are up to 3.3 cm long and 8 mm wide. They are heavily stained with dingy greenish violet on the back. The obovate inner tepals are a similar length but reach 1.3 cm wide and are feathered with greenish violet on the back. The anthers and glabrous filaments are yellow. The ovary is green, but the elongated style is pale yellow and can reach 6 mm long.

The small flowers of *Tulipa uniflora* would be lost in the garden and are best appreciated in a pot in an alpine house or bulb frame, where the bulbs can be kept dry in the summer. Like other species from high altitudes, this tulip needs to be treated more like an alpine plant, with careful watering in late autumn and winter. In cultivation it flowers in March.

Tulipa urumiensis Stapf

This small yellow tulip was found at Salmas on the northern shores of Lake Urmia in north-western Iran and collected by A. Kronenburg for the van Tubergen firm. In 1928 John Hoog sent a flowering specimen to the Royal Botanic Gardens, Kew, for identification, and later some bulbs. The species was described by Otto Stapf in 1932, in *Curtis's Botanical Magazine* (t. 9288) where its similarity to *Tulipa australis* was noted. Stapf wrote, 'If it were proposed for taxonomic reasons to treat it as a component of the latter, no serious objection could be raised'. Strangely, it has never been found in the wild again, although other forms of *T. sylvestris*, including *T. biebersteiniana*, are known from Iran.

Tulipa urumiensis has survived in cultivation and is commonly available in the trade. It is a low-growing tulip with a stem reaching 10 cm tall. The bulb tunic is lined with only a few hairs near the base. The two to four dull green, linear, channelled leaves reach 12 cm long and 1.5 cm wide. They are held close together, almost forming a rosette near ground level. Inside the flower is clear yellow, but the back of the outer tepals is stained with olive green and red. The outer tepals are lanceolate to narrowly oblong and reach 4 cm long by 1.3 cm wide. The inner tepals are lanceolate and slightly shorter, reaching 3.5 cm long but up to 1.75 cm wide. The anthers and filaments are yellow.

Although not difficult to grow, I have found this species can be shy to flower. In a pot full of bulbs only two or three flowers may appear each year. In a good year, two or more flowers may grow from each bulb, but they are held close to the ground. This species received the Award of Garden Merit from the RHS in 1993 so in the right situation it must be a garden-worthy species. The cultivar 'Tity's Star' is said to be a brighter yellow and can have up to eight flowers per bulb.

Tulipa urumoffii Hayek

This tulip is named after Professor Urumoff who collected it near Belovo in the Rhodope Mountains of Bulgaria. It was described in 1911 by the Austrian botanist August Hayek, who in 1932 reclassified it as *Tulipa hungarica* var. *urumoffii*. The red-flowered *T. rhodopea* from the same mountain range is usually treated as a synonym of *T. urumoffii*, and both species, along with the similar *T. hungarica* from the Danube Gorge, are naturalized tulips and part of the European *T. gesneriana* complex.

Tulipa urumoffii grows to 30 cm tall and has three or four glabrous, glaucous leaves, the lowest broadly lanceolate and reaching 20 cm long and 4 cm wide. The flower is yellow with no basal blotch, and the ovate-lanceolate tepals reach 6 cm long and 2.5 cm wide. *Tulipa rhodopea* differs only in flower colour, which is brownish scarlet with a black, yellow-margined basal blotch and purple, rather than yellow or greenish, pollen.

Tulipa urumoffii is occasionally offered for sale and can be grown in well-drained soil outside. It flowers in March or April.

Tulipa violacea Boissier & Buhse

Found in Iran and south-eastern Azerbaijan and described in 1860, this tulip is now treated as a form of *Tulipa humilis*. It has violet to deep purplish crimson flowers with a black blotch. Bulbs are still sold as *T. violacea*, but cultivated plants are more correctly classified as *T. humilis* Violacea Group.

Tulipa vvedenskyi Z. Botschantzeva

Three closely related species in section *Eichleres* all grow in the Tien Shan: *Tulipa albertii*, *T. butkovii*, and *T. vvedenskyi*. The last of these was described by Zinaida Botschantzeva in 1954 and named after Aleksei I. Vvedensky. The bulbs were collected at 1500 m (4900 ft.) above the village of Tyurk in the valley of the Angren River, south-east of Tashkent, Uzbekistan. They were growing on rocky slopes with a thin covering of fine soil. This species is endemic to the western Tien Shan.

The papery bulb tunic of *Tulipa vvedenskyi* is sparsely lined with hairs except at the tip where they are more dense. The glaucous, pubescent stem reaches 20 cm tall and bears four or five lanceolate leaves, held close together. These are also glaucous and often have undulate margins. The lowest leaf reaches up to 25 cm long and 6 cm wide, and the other leaves are similar in length, maybe a little longer, but much narrower; the upper leaf often less than 2 cm wide.

The solitary flower is bright orange-red with a yellow base. A dark brown blotch of variable size, shape, and intensity may be present but, certainly in cultivated plants I have seen, this dark blotch is often absent, leaving just a golden yellow base to the flower. The outer tepals are rhomboidal, tapering at the base and with a small pubescent point at the tip. They can reach up to 10 cm long and 6 cm wide, and are a paler shade of red on the back. The inner tepals are obovate and more rounded at the tip but still end in a pubescent point. These are longer than the outer tepals, reaching 11.5 cm long and 5.2 cm wide. The filaments are yellow or brown, and the anthers and pollen can be yellow, brown, or dark violet.

In the late 1970s Kew botanist and bulb expert Wessel Marais said, '*Tulipa vvedenskyi* is a "species" in which I have never believed'. He would probably agree with L. W. D. van Raamsdonk and T. de Vries, who in 1995 treated this species and *T. butkovii* as synonymous with *T. albertii*, which was described in 1877. *Tulipa albertii* is said to differ in its shorter but broader leaves and its slightly smaller flowers with a more prominent dark basal blotch.

Tulipa vvedenskyi 'Tangerine Beauty'

Tulipa vvedenskyi can be grown in well-drained soil on a rock garden or raised bed, but it is better to give it the protection of a bulb frame or alpine house, where the large flowers will be sheltered from the elements. It flowers in late March or early April.

This species is sometimes available commercially, but the cultivar 'Tangerine Beauty', which received the RHS Award of Garden Merit in 1997, is more frequently offered. It has large orange flowers, with only a tiny yellow blotch at the centre. There can be up to six glaucous leaves with undulate margins. The long pointed bud opens to reveal the rich orange tepals that are typically 9 to 10 cm long and 5 to 6 cm wide. The anthers are violet and held on yellow filaments.

Tulipa whittallii Hall

This tetraploid form of *Tulipa orphanidea* was found near Izmir, on the western coast of Turkey. It is stronger and taller than typical *T. orphanidea*, with three or four glaucous, channelled leaves, the lowest reaching 20 cm long and 2 cm wide. The bright orange-brown flower has a rounded shape, with pointed tepals, and is held up to 30 cm above ground. The back of the outer tepals is stained green or buff, and inside the flower is a dark olive basal blotch with a pale margin.

Tulipa whittallii is named after Edward Whittall, who established a nursery near Izmir in the late nineteenth century and sent bulbs of this plant from Turkey to Henry Elwes. Although the name was in use in the 1920s and Sir Daniel Hall referred to it in *The Book of the Tulip* (1929), this species was not described in any detail until Hall included it in *The Genus* Tulipa (1940). He then expanded upon this description in 1943, in *Curtis's Botanical Magazine* (t. 9649). Commercial stocks of this tulip are often sold as *T. whittallii*, but taxonomically this tulip is now accepted as a form of *T. orphanidea* and is identified as *T. orphanidea* Whittallii Group.

Tulipa whittallii

Commonly available today, *Tulipa whittallii* is a good garden plant and more attractive than its description suggests. It can look quite effective when several bulbs are planted together in a sunny border, where it will flower in April. It received the Award of Garden Merit from the RHS in 1999.

Tulipa wilsoniana Hoog

This species was described by John Hoog in 1902. It is identical to *Tulipa montana* and is included under that name.

Tulipa zenaidae Vvedensky

Belonging in section *Kolpakowskianae*, this species is close to *Tulipa lehmanniana*. Like that species, it has glaucous leaves that rapidly decrease in size up the stem and do not surpass the solitary flower. The stem is glabrous, and the flowers can be yellow, orange, or red. So similar are *T. zenaidae* and *T. lehmanniana* that L. W. D. van Raamsdonk and T. de Vries (1995) treated them as the same species, with *T. lehmanniana* being the oldest and therefore correct name. However, Botschantzeva (in *Tulips*) and Vvedensky (in *Flora of the USSR*) indicated certain characteristics that distinguish the two.

Tulipa zenaidae sometimes has a small black or yellow blotch inside the flower. The tepals can reach 6.5 cm long and are more oblong than those of *T. lehmanniana*. The outer tepals are stained reddish pink on the back, along the midrib. When the flower opens, the top third of the outer tepals bends back, while the inner tepals are only slightly reflexed. The anthers are yellow, and the filaments are yellow or black. The stem eventually reaches 15 cm above ground, often less at flowering time, and usually holds three oblong to oblong-lanceolate leaves, the lowest reaching 6 cm wide. The bulb tunic is lined with straight hairs at its tip.

Aleksei Vvedensky named this tulip after Zinaida Botschantzeva in 1935. It grows in the Tien Shan, particularly the Kirghiz Range along the border of Kyrgystan and Kazakhstan, and flowers in April and May. It is rarely seen in cultivation.

7

THE GENUS *AMANA*

The species of *Amana* have all previously been classified as tulips. The first species to be recognized was originally described as *Orithyia edulis* by the Dutch botanist Friedrich Miquel in 1867. The genus *Orithyia* was established by David Don in 1836, based on *O. uniflora* (now *Tulipa uniflora*) and was distinguished from *Tulipa* by the elongated style on the ovary. In 1874, when J. Gilbert Baker transferred *Orithyia* to *Tulipa*, *O. edulis* went with it, becoming *T. edulis*. However, *T. edulis* differed from all other tulips in that it had two or three small leaf-like bracts on the stem, just behind the flower.

The plant Baker named *Tulipa edulis* was from Japan, but in 1875 he named a Chinese form of it *T. graminifolia*. The same year Baker described another new species, which had been collected in 1873 in a snowy valley in the Zhejiang Province of China. He named it *T. erythronioides*, noting the two *Erythronium*-like leaves and a whorl of bracts behind the flower. In 1904 Tomitaro Makino described *T. edulis* var. *latifolia*, also from Japan but with shorter and broader leaves than the typical form and three or four bracts in a whorl on the stem. It also has a pale stripe along the midrib of each leaf. A few years later, in 1914, Makino raised it to a species in its own right, naming it *T. latifolia*.

All four of these species, *Tulipa edulis*, *T. erythronioides*, *T. graminifolia*, and *T. latifolia*, differ from other tulips in two major respects. They all have bracts on the stem, behind the flower, and they are found considerably further east than any other tulip. The genus *Tulipa* reaches the far west of China and the western Himalaya, whereas these four species occur in eastern China, Manchuria, Korea, and Japan. In 1935 Japanese botanist Masaji Honda moved the Japanese species *T. edulis* and *T. latifolia* into a new genus, *Amana*.

This separation from *Tulipa* was accepted by Sir Daniel Hall, who recognized *Amana edulis* and *A. graminifolia* in *The Genus* Tulipa (1940), but more recent works, such as *Flora of Japan*, have included *Amana* within

Tulipa. In 1980, in *Flora Reipublicae Popularis Sinicae* (Flora of China), Zu Mei Mao reduced *Amana* to a section of the genus *Tulipa*, containing *T. edulis* and *T. erythronioides*. It is only recently that DNA studies at the Royal Botanic Gardens, Kew, have concluded that *Amana* should be maintained as a distinct genus.

Amana graminifolia is now regarded as a Chinese form of *A. edulis* and is treated as a synonym. Likewise, the wide-leaved *A. latifolia* can be regarded as a rare Japanese form of the Chinese *A. erythronioides*, leaving only two species in *Amana*: *A. edulis* and *A. erythronioides*.

Neither species of *Amana* is widely grown, but *A. edulis* is the one you are more likely to come across. It flowers very early and is not suitable for the open garden in most climates where tulips are grown. The small pale flowers need to be studied closely to appreciate their delicate markings, so this is a plant for pot-cultivation.

Amana edulis (Miquel) Honda

Amana edulis blooms earlier than most tulips, often producing its flowers by the end of January if grown in a bulb frame or glasshouse. When the flowers first appear they are held on a short, thin stem, barely a centimetre above the ground. They need a little warmth and some sunshine to open fully, and in the short, dull days of winter the stems rapidly elongate, causing the blooms to flop over. However, on those rare winter days when the sun does shine, they can open wide, alongside snowdrops (*Galanthus*) and early spring crocus.

The one, two, or occasionally three buds emerge from between the two leaves, immediately exposing two or three leaf-like bracts on the stem. These bracts are actually wrapped around the bud at first, but as the stem lengthens the flowers leave

Amana edulis

them behind. Even if the flowers remain tightly closed, they display intricate markings on the outside of the tepals. The two grey-green leaves are only 10 to 12 cm long when the first flowers open, but they continue to lengthen, eventually reaching 25 cm and far exceeding the flower stem. The lower leaf is about 1 cm wide, and the upper leaf a little narrower. The leaves are lightly stained with dull purple on the back and along their straight margins.

The pinkish green flower stem is between 1.5 and 4 cm long at first but, like the leaves, it will continue to grow, reaching 14 to 15 cm, with the bracts up to 5 cm behind the flower. The green linear bracts are about 3 cm long and tightly curled up lengthways. They appear to be only 2 to 3 mm wide but are actually nearer 6 mm wide when opened out. They are held opposite each other on the stem or in a whorl if there are three.

The narrowly elliptic to lanceolate tepals are greyish white with a pattern of feathered, brownish purple lines on the back, particularly of the outer tepals. On the insides they are stained yellow at the base, but the staining is only apparent when the flowers are wide open. The outer tepals are around 3 cm long and 7 mm wide, with the inner tepals very slightly shorter. At the centre of the flower are the bright yellow anthers, each one 5 to 6 mm long and held on a glabrous filament that is expanded at its middle.

In the wild *Amana edulis* grows in meadows and along stream banks. It is used to conditions that are more moist than those of most tulips and should be grown in soil that is free-draining but doesn't dry out completely at any time. This is a hardy species but, because it flowers so early, it is best kept in a bulb frame or cool glasshouse, where the blooms are protected from harsh winter weather. It needs as much light as possible at this time to prevent it becoming too etiolated, but the dormant bulbs will appreciate some shading on warm sunny days in summer.

8

GARDEN HYBRID TULIPS

The most widely grown and well-known tulips in gardens today are hybrids. Selection and breeding of tulips are known to have been carried out in Persian and Turkish gardens in the fifteenth and sixteenth centuries. The preferred flower shape in this period was one with long, pointed tepals, forming dagger-like blooms, and known as 'needle tulips'. Over the last four hundred years it is in Holland that the most work has been done on the development of tulip hybrids.

For many years the most sought after tulips were those with 'broken' flowers, known as florists' tulips. In these flowers, the anthocyanin pigment, which provides the red and purple colouring, withdraws to the edges of the tepals, allowing the ground colour, a shade of yellow or white, to show through. Wonderful patterns are formed, called flames or feathers. These are the tulips portrayed in seventeenth-century Dutch flower paintings. The cause of this breaking, the tulip breaking virus (TBV), was unknown until the 1920s, and broken flowers appeared to arise by chance. This gave them an aura of mystery and led to hugely inflated prices being paid for particular treasured forms.

The plain-coloured tulips that gave rise to the broken flowers were called breeder tulips and were grown by florists in the hope that they would break. It was in the late nineteenth century that attention turned to breeders as garden plants in their own right. Today a bewildering variety of tulip hybrids is offered, differing not only in flower colour but in height, flowering time, and flower shape.

It was a Dutch grower, E. H. Krelage, who led the way in the 1880s, concentrating on breeders rather than the fancy florists' tulips. He gave his new tulips the name 'Darwin' and in 1889, at the Great Exhibition in Paris, he planted a bedding display to publicize his collection. These Darwin tulips flowered in May. Using tulips in mass bedding schemes was a new idea that soon caught on. Other breeder tulips were sought, often those discarded or forgotten by florists, and they became known as Cottage tulips, named after the cottage gardens in which they were often found. They were crossed with Darwins and eventually the boundaries between these two groups became blurred and they were merged together as the Single Late Group in 1981.

To produce earlier flowers, the Darwins were crossed with Single Early tulips. The resultant hybrids are called Triumphs, first named in 1923 and sometimes referred to as mid-season tulips. At the beginning of the twentieth century, new species from central Asia were collected and introduced, such as *Tulipa fosteriana, T. kaufmanniana*, and *T. greigii*. These were crossed with existing cultivars to breed a new race of tulips. The Darwinhybrids were the result of this influx of new genetic material, although cultivars from any group, in particular the Single Early and Triumph Groups were used, as well as Darwins. All the Darwinhybrids have a similar shape and constitution. The influence of the wild species in their makeup means they can be relatively long-lived in the garden.

The lily-flowered *Tulipa* 'Ballerina'

Raising a hybrid tulip from seed can take seven years, but new tulips are not only produced by hybridization. Many are sports, which arise spontaneously, as offsets on a tulip bulb. These will be similar to the parent in size and flowering time but often differ in flower colour. The anthocyanin pigment in sports is usually reduced, gathered along the midrib of the tepal, particularly at the base, forming a flame of deeper colour on a paler background, and can be absent altogether, leaving the ground colour only. Once noticed, these sports need to be separated and bulked up, which can take many years. Commercial production of new hybrids is a long process.

Tulip hybrids are bred to produce plants of uniform height and with regular flowers. This reflects their main use, which is in formal, orderly spring bedding that is replaced every year, but there are other ways to grow hybrid

White-flowered *Tulipa* 'Snowstar' (Triumph Group) and red-flowered *T.* 'Apeldoorn' (Darwin-hybrid Group) planted in a spring bedding scheme

tulips. For example, they look great in pots or planted more informally, among herbaceous perennials or alongside other bulbs. The classification system for hybrid tulips gives you some idea of the size, form, and flowering time of the various cultivars, but the best way to choose your plants is to look through a well-illustrated bulb catalogue or visit gardens to borrow ideas. Almost any colour is available, so the choice of combinations is only limited by your imagination and your budget.

The Classification of Hybrid Tulips

Tulips are now divided into fifteen divisions, according to when they bloom, their height, and the shape or form of the flower. Three groups are based on the species they most closely resemble, the Kaufmanniana Group, the Fosteriana Group, and the Greigii Group. The final division, called Miscellaneous, includes all the species, their cultivars, and the hybrids between them.

The flowering times referred to in this chapter are based on tulips growing in northern Europe, in particular Holland, where most of these hybrids are produced. Different climates will have an affect on the flowering time, but the order of flowering, from the Single Early Group to the Single Late and Double Late Groups, should remain the same.

Single Early Group

These tulips have single flowers and are among the first hybrids to flower, sometimes as early as late March but usually in April. The flower stems are fairly short, generally between 20 and 40 cm (8–16 in.) tall, and they hold a simple, cup-shaped flower. As in all of the following groups, these flowers come in a range of colours.

The Single Early Group does not contain a large number of tulips but, in my opinion, it includes some of the most attractive cultivars. They are neat, compact plants, with richly coloured flowers. Due to their early blooming, they are more likely to be damaged by adverse weather. The later tulips will enjoy more pleasant conditions, but strong winds or heavy rain may batter the early groups, bruising the flowers and shredding the leaves, even though the plants are quite sturdy. Find a sheltered part of the garden or raise them in pots in a cold frame or cool glasshouse, to give them some protection.

The popular cultivar 'Apricot Beauty', with salmon-pink flowers tinged with red, is typical of the tulips in this group. 'Generaal de Wet', an older

Tulipa 'Flair' (Single Early Group)

cultivar, raised in 1904, is a wonderful orange, faintly stippled with red and flushed with a pink blush on the outside of the tepals. 'Flair' is a more recent creation, raised in 1978, and has flowers of golden yellow, flamed with deep red along the midrib of each tepal, inside and out.

Single Early tulips predate Darwin tulips, and some of the oldest known cultivars, the 'Duc van Thol' race, are classified in the Single Early Group. Some of these date from the seventeenth century, and they come in a variety of colours, including orange, red, primrose, salmon pink, and rose. The Duc van Thols are very rarely offered for sale but can be seen in historical tulip collections, such as the Hortus Bulborum in Holland.

Double Early Group

Opinions on double flowers vary. Some people dismiss them all out of hand, while others like to try anything that is different. Some double flowers are beautiful—a rose is a classic example—but when it comes to tulips, I find it hard to see the attraction. The simple, elegant beauty of a tulip flower, opening wide to reveal its inner markings, is lost in double forms. The bunch of tepals appears tangled and distorted at the top of the stem, and this chaotic appearance just gets worse as the flower ages.

Double tulips are classified in two divisions, the Double Early Group

Tulipa 'Monte Carlo' (Double Early Group)

and the Double Late Group. The early doubles flower around the same time as the Single Early Group, but their flowers tend to last longer and show up better from a distance. For these reasons, doubles have their uses in bedding schemes, even if as individual flowers they lack the finesse of most other tulips. They grow around 30 cm (12 in.) tall. The yellow 'Monte Carlo' is considered typical of this group.

Triumph Group

Triumph tulips are among the most popular and numerous of the cultivar groups. They flower in April and are sometimes sold as mid-season tulips. They are similar to Single Early tulips, but the stems are slightly longer, nor-

Tulipa 'Prinses Irene' (Triumph Group)

mally 40 to 50 cm (16–20 in.) tall. These are robust, sturdy tulips, with a single, cup-shaped flower made up of rounded tepals.

More cultivars of Triumph tulips are available than of any other division. As well as the solid yellows, reds, pinks, and whites, there are bi-coloured and patterned flowers. For example, 'Shirley' has white flowers dusted with purple along the tepal edges, and 'Arabian Mystery' is the opposite, with purple flowers breaking into silvery white at the edges. 'Couleur Cardinal', dating from 1845, is a luxurious scarlet, brushed with plum on the outside, and 'Prinses Irene' is a sport from it, with orange flowers flamed with violet along the tepal midribs.

I am drawn to the Triumphs, as I am to the Single Early tulips, because of their compact, sturdy appearance and simple flower shape. However, if you are after huge flowers, you need to look at the Darwinhybrids.

Darwinhybrid Group

The Darwinhybrids flower in late April. Their strong stems are generally 50 to 60 cm (20–24 in.) tall and hold large flowers, with long tepals that open to an imposing goblet-shaped bloom, sometimes forming a shallow dish when fully opened in the sun. These bold, brash flowers certainly make an impact and are perfect for formal bedding and creating vibrant blocks of colour. The utilization of species like *Tulipa fosteriana* in their breeding prolongs their life in the garden when planted in a border.

Probably the most famous Darwinhybrid is the red-flowered 'Apeldoorn', raised by Lefeber and Company in 1951. Several sports from this cultivar are available, such as 'Apeldoorn's Elite', 'Golden Apeldoorn', 'Orange Apeldoorn', and 'Orange Queen'. All of these sports are variations on a red-and-

Tulipa 'Ivory Floradale' (Darwinhybrid Group)

yellow theme. Of course, there are many other flower colours in the Darwin-hybrids, from the subtle, creamy white 'Ivory Floradale' with its creamy yellow interior to the deep orange-pink 'Apricot Impression', a sport of the rose-pink 'Pink Impression'.

Single Late Group

Tall-stemmed, single-flowered tulips that bloom in late April and May belong to the Single Late Group, originally a combination of the old Darwin and Cottage tulips. They hold their flowers 60 cm (2 ft.) or more above the ground, which means they can be knocked around in windy weather. By the time they bloom, the weather should hopefully be calmer than it is when the Single Early tulips bloom.

As you would expect, the flowers of the Single Late Group come in the whole range of tulip colours, from plain whites, yellows, reds, and oranges to feathered and flamed sports. For example, 'Sorbet' has white flowers flamed with pinkish red, and 'Dordogne' has orange flowers subtly changing to rose-pink towards the centre of each tepal via a hint of red. 'Queen of Night' is a popular Single Late tulip with almost black flowers, which are in fact a very dark, velvety purple.

The Single Late Group contains tulips that are really too tall and regi-

Single Late tulips 'Halcro' (red) and 'Dordogne' mix together well in this formal bedding scheme.

mented to be grown in an informal setting unless grown through taller perennials, but they are the ultimate bedding tulips. Their towering stems, bright colours, and neat, rounded flowers are spring's final show before the summer perennials take the stage.

Lily-flowered Group

To me, the Lily-flowered cultivars are the most beautiful of the hybrid tulips. From a rounded base the tepals are drawn in, like a waist, before their pointed, elongated tips flare open, the whole flower giving the impression of an elegant vase or wineglass. This is as close as you can get to improving a wild tulip. The tulips in this group make great bedding plants, but unlike

Tulipa 'Ballade' (Lily-flowered Group)

many cultivars, an individual flower, seen on its own, is beautiful in its own right. Lily-flowered tulips were originally bred from the old Darwin and Cottage tulips, some of which already had more pointed, waisted flowers. The group was named in 1958.

Tulips in the Lily-flowered Group bloom in April or May so can be mixed with Triumphs, Darwinhybrids, or Single Lates. They range in height from 50 to 60 cm (20–24 in.) or more and are becoming increasingly popular as garden plants, especially grown in containers. The pure yellow 'West Point' is one of the most widely grown in this group, as is the pure white 'White Triumphator'. Some of the bi-coloured cultivars have sharply defined edges to the tepals, such as 'Ballade', with magenta tepals edged with white, and 'Synaeda King', which is red with yellow margins. More subtle in their patterning are the orange-and-red 'Ballerina' and the red-and-yellow 'Aladdin'.

Fringed Group

The truly beautiful Lily-flowered Group is far removed from the ugly Fringed Group. While the Lily-flowered tulips are the epitome of elegance and style, the Fringed tulips are just vulgar novelties. This relatively new group dates from 1981. Some people must like them, but to me they are a step too far in the quest for something different.

Tulipa 'Cummins' (Fringed Group)

The tepals of the tulips in this group look like they have been attacked by someone with a pair of scissors. Their margins, especially towards the tip, are cut into small triangular or crystal-shaped teeth that become more pronounced as the flower ages. They do not improve the flower but ruin what would otherwise be a simple, single-flowered tulip.

The Fringed Group can flower in April or May and typically grow from 40 to 60 cm (16–24 in.) tall. There are plain-coloured flowers as in 'Red Wing', 'Blue Heron', and the yellow 'Hamilton' or the lacerated tepal margins may be a paler colour, as in 'Cummins', which has lavender flowers with white frilly margins. Enough said.

Viridiflora Group

This group is so-called because the back of the tepals is washed with green. Otherwise, the flowers come in a range of colours. In some tulips the colour combination can be quite attractive, but in others it looks a little strange. 'Spring Green' is one of the most popular. Its fresh-looking, white flowers are flushed with green that rises from the base of each tepal and fades into greenish yellow. 'Groenland' (Greenland) is another popular cultivar in this group and has green-and-pink flowers. These two cultivars have rounded tepals but some of the Viridiflora tulips have more pointed tepals, including the salmon-pink and green 'Artist'.

The Viridiflora Group is late flowering, but its hybrids vary in height from 30 to 60 cm (12 to 24 in.). Some forms have variegated foliage and the leaves are edged with yellow or white. Although this group was only introduced in 1981, tulips that retain the green colouring on their tepals have been recorded for as long as tulips have been grown.

Rembrandt Group

This group was created to include the tulips infected with tulip breaking virus (TBV). They are derived from Darwin tulips. Their flowers are broken and patterned with flames and feathers, and some are extremely beautiful. Named after the Dutch painter, this group contains tulips that resemble the English florists' tulips, bred in the eighteenth and nineteenth centuries. Due to the possibility of the virus spreading to other tulips, Rembrandt tulips are not offered commercially. They are still grown and exchanged privately and can be seen in specialist or historical collections. In Britain, the English florists' tulips are exhibited by the Wakefield and North of England Tulip Society, the last remaining tulip society in the country.

Parrot Group

I used to feel the same way about the Parrot Group as I do about the Fringed Group. Their deformed and twisted flowers were not the reason I like tulips. That is until I grew 'Rococo'. This cultivar is a sport of 'Couleur Cardinal'

Tulipa 'Rococo' (Parrot Group)

and was raised in 1942. The red tepals are flushed with dusky purple at the centre and flecked with the occasional splash of yellow or green at the edge. Like all the tulips in this group, the petals are deeply slashed and contorted but the effect is fascinating when looked at closely.

Other cultivars in this group are not so interesting and some are just plain ugly. For example, 'Green Wave' is a sport of 'Groenland' and looks like a diseased version of it. Two of the more popular Parrot tulips are 'Black Parrot' and 'Blue Parrot', the latter probably being the closest you will get to a blue tulip, actually a shade of violet, tinged with bronze on the outside.

The Parrot Group takes its name from the shape of the flower in bud, which resembles a parrot's beak. They are sports or mutations of normal tulips and have been known since the mid-seventeenth century. They flower in April and May, and the stems range from 40 to 70 cm (16–28 in.) tall.

Double Late Group

Although I do not like double-flowered tulips, the Double Late Group contains some more acceptable cultivars than the Double Early Group. The taller stems of the Double Lates, reaching 40 to 60 cm (16–24 in.), are an improvement and in some hybrids the flowers are more compact and rounded. These include the purple 'Blue Diamond' and the pink 'Bonsoir'. Less tidy are cultivars like the maroon-red 'Uncle Tom' and the bi-coloured 'Wirosa', which has wine-red tepals edged with creamy white. 'Orange Princess' is a sport of 'Prinses Irene' and has a similar colour scheme, but spoilt by the extra tepals. This double has given rise to another sport, 'Red Princess', which is even worse.

Tulips in the Double Late Group are sometimes sold as peony-flowered tulips and have been grown since the early seventeenth century. They bloom in May, and the flowers can be very long-lived, making them useful as bedding plants.

Kaufmanniana Group

This group contains *Tulipa kaufmanniana* and the cultivars and hybrids associated with it. When large numbers of this species, along with *T. greigii* and *T. fosteriana*, were collected in central Asia and sent to Europe at the beginning of the twentieth century, they were crossed with each other to create a range of tough, colourful hybrids. The hybrids were placed in this and the following two divisions according to which of the original species they most closely resembled.

Tulips in the Kaufmanniana Group flower very early. Grown in pots in a glasshouse they can flower in February, and in the garden they can appear in March. They sometimes have dark spots or dashes on the leaves, due to the influence of *Tulipa greigii*. The flower stems are short, typically 20 cm (8 in.) tall, but the flowers are large. They are known as water-lily tulips because the flowers open very wide in the sun, displaying red spots or horizontal lines on the inside of the tepals. These marks surround the blotch, or the base of each tepal is the same colour as the rest of the flower. Most of the cultivars, such as 'Giuseppe Verdi' and 'Stressa', have yellow flowers but some, like 'Ancilla', are creamy white. The back of the outer tepals usually

Tulipa kaufmanniana 'Ancilla'

has a band of red running up the centre. 'Scarlet Baby' and 'Showwinner' are shades of red, with a yellow basal blotch inside the flower.

Fosteriana Group

The tulips in this group resemble *Tulipa fosteriana* and have broad leaves and large flowers held on stems 40 to 50 cm (16–20 in.) tall. The cultivar names often tell you the colour, such as 'Red Emperor' (syn. 'Madame Lefeber'), 'Orange Emperor', and 'Golden Emperor'. 'Purissima' (syn. 'White Emperor') is a popular white form and has given rise to 'Yellow Purissima' and 'Purissima King', which has red flowers flamed with yellow on the outside.

Tulipa fosteriana itself is a good garden plant, and the tulips in the Fosteriana Group will continue to grow outside for many years, as long as the soil is free-draining. These tulips flower in late March and early April.

Greigii Group

Tulipa greigii is a low-growing species with a distinctive flower shape and wide leaves marked with dark purplish brown dots and dashes. The hybrids with *T. fosteriana* and *T. kaufmanniana* that closely resemble this species are placed in the Greigii Group. They flower later than the Kaufmanniana Group, usually in late March and April, and their stems reach 20 to 30 cm (8–12 in.) tall. The leaves are held close to the ground and often have undulate margins.

Flower colour varies widely in the Greigii Group, but red predominates, with 'Red Riding Hood' being the classic example. Some cultivars are bicoloured, such as 'Pinocchio', with white flowers flamed with red up the centre of each tepal, and 'Quebec', which is creamy white flamed with reddish pink, and with a prominent pale yellow blotch inside. It is the single colours that are most dramatic.

The tulips in the Greigii Group make excellent bedding plants if you want to make an early impact.

Miscellaneous

This division incorporates all the tulips not included in the other fourteen divisions. It is where the cultivated species are placed along with their various named forms, such as the cultivars of *Tulipa clusiana*, *T. linifolia* Batalinii Group, and *T. humilis*. This division is what the rest of this book is about.

Tulipa clusiana 'Tinka'

Growing Hybrid Tulips

As I have previously said, hybrid tulips are produced for planting in regimented bedding schemes, forming blocks, strips, or rows of colour. They are then dug up in early summer to be replaced with new bulbs for the following spring. New bulbs of a particular cultivar will send up flowers of a uniform size, on stems of an even height. There are other ways of using them in a garden setting, but if you need proof that this is the use hybrid tulips are intended for, that they are bred with formality and uniformity in mind, then you only need to visit the Keukenhof garden in Holland.

Keukenhof, near Lisse, is only open for a couple of months in spring, from late March to late May. In the beds among the trees, over seven million bulbs are planted every year, and this is where the Dutch flower industry displays its products. Tulips are not the only bulbs grown here, but they are the mainstay, especially in mid-April. The borders are pristine, the flowers perfect, and the intensity of the colours is mind-blowing.

The Keukenhof garden demonstrates how the exporters of the bulbs expect them to be grown. They are planted in broad sweeps and curving bays, the blocks of colour competing with each other to dazzle you. Each bulb grower is allocated a plot, which is then filled in with old favourites and new

Tulipa greigii 'Ali Baba' with *Anemone* 'White Splendour'

hybrids. The growers are justifiably proud of their achievements. There are no informal borders here and it is worth noting that there are few species on display. This garden is a statement and it says that tulips are meant to be bold, bright, and upright.

In a formal garden, tulips are the ideal bedding plant. They can be grown in combination with other bulbs or winter- and spring-flowering perennials, and late tulips can follow early bulbs to prolong the season. Such a range of colours and forms is available that you can forever be experimenting with new cultivars, creating new effects every spring. However, once the flowers are over, you need to dig them up. In their second year the tulips will send up flowers of varying height and size. The bulb will have split and the smaller offsets will not flower immediately, so single-leaved, non-flowering shoots will appear. This is not such a problem in a less formal setting but unacceptable in a bedding scheme. Of course, this method of growing tulips is encouraged by bulb growers, who delight in selling you new bulbs every year.

It seems a terrible waste to throw the old bulbs away, but there are other options. One is to replant them in other parts of the garden. The climate in Britain is suitable for this and many hybrid tulips will flower for more than one year. In much of the United States and Australia, they are not so perennial and there is no choice but to replace them annually. In the right location, tulips in the Kaufmanniana, Fosteriana, and Greigii Groups, as well as some of the Darwinhybrids, will continue to flower for several years. Tulips that are close to their wild ancestors, like some of the single-coloured *Tulipa fosteriana* cultivars, keep flowering indefinitely, if left undisturbed, and the clump may gradually increase in size. If you plant them among herbaceous perennials, their leaves will be hidden as the perennials come into growth and the gaps they leave will be filled with summer flowers.

Tulipa fosteriana 'Golden Emperor'

Another option, if you have the space, is to plant them in rows, some-where out of the way. These will not be part of your garden display so the variable quality of the flowers is not a problem. You can choose the best flowering stems to cut. Tulips make wonderful cut flowers

Tulips are good mixers in a border. They can be replaced every year, allow-ing you to experiment with different effects and combinations. One of the greatest advocates of this style is Christopher Lloyd. In his garden at Great Dixter, England, he experiments with new planting schemes, and tulips are among his favourite flowers. Luckily, he is a prolific writer so if you cannot get to visit his garden, you can at least read about it. Anything that flowers at the same time as tulips should be experimented with, and attractive fo-liage, such as is found on lupins, can also provide a pleasing backdrop to the tulip's flowers.

If you are planting hybrid tulips for one season only, there is no need to dig deep. Plant them 5 cm (2 in.) beneath the surface and they will be fine. This depth also makes them easier to lift again. If the soil is liable to freeze, then plant them deeper, and if they are going to stay in the ground, then I would plant them at least 10 cm (4 in.) deep. Keep them 10 to 15 cm (4–6 in.) apart. They can be planted late, up until November is normally recom-mended, as long as the soil is not frozen or waterlogged, but you can get away with planting even later.

Once flowering is over and you need to make way for summer flowers, the tulips can be dug up before they have died down. Leave them in the soil as long as possible. Once out of the ground, keep them somewhere cool, dry, and well-ventilated, and the leaves will die back naturally. The dried-up leaves and stems can then be pulled away and the bulbs sorted.

Often two or three bulbs will appear where originally there was only one, so the smallest can be separated and grown on to flowering size. The larger bulbs can be replanted in an informal part of the garden or lined out for cut flowers. If you are planting them permanently, you should make sure the soil drains freely and the tulips are not crowded by other plants. Good air movement around the plants helps to keep fungal diseases away, especially tulip fire. The soil can be improved or even taken away and replaced with a new soil mix, something that was more common in the nineteenth century, when beds were often devoted to tulips. In the *Gardeners' Chronicle* of 2 October 1875, the following soil mix is recommended:

> Well-decayed turf from a pasture which affords a fine fibry loam. All
> wireworms should be carefully picked out of it. Add to this about one-
> third of leaf-mould, and some sharp sand or finely powdered charcoal,

the latter to be preferred. Let this be mixed together a month before being used, and well turned meanwhile. A free, porous soil, through which the water can readily percolate, is to be preferred to one that retains the moisture, and is of a soddened and cold nature in winter.

This soil would have been put in a bed raised about 15 cm (6 in.) above the surrounding ground, to improve drainage further, and the tulip bulbs then

Pots of tulips: *Tulipa greigii* 'Pinocchio' (left), 'Aladdin' (centre), and *T. clusiana* 'Tubergen's Gem' (right)

planted into it. Few people go to these lengths today, but the need for good drainage is still as important.

If the soil in your garden is not suitable for tulips, or if you want an ever-changing display near the house through the spring, plant tulips in containers. Any tulips can be grown in pots, tubs, or troughs; the only limiting factor is the size of the container. The pots can be overwintered in a glasshouse to bring on the flowers a little early and protect them from heavy rain or snow. When colour begins to show in the buds, bring the containers out. Pay attention to watering, as the containers will quickly dry out in mild, sunny weather, and this can cause the flower buds to abort.

As with bedding, tulips in pots are best replaced every year to maintain the quality of the display. They do not have to be planted very deep and you can cram as many bulbs into the pot as will fit. Plant a range of tulips in different pots to extend the flowering season, from Single Early tulips to Single Late, Lily-flowered, and Parrot. Bring them out when in flower, then take them away to be replaced with the next show of colour.

No other spring bulbs come in the variety of colours and forms found in tulips. Anyone can grow them, even if it means replacing them every year. But when you are planting your containers and borders, try and include a few of the species, just to remind yourself where tulips really come from.

CONVERSION TABLE

For readers who prefer inches to centimetres or millimetres, the following rough conversions will be of some help:

5 mm = 0.2 in.	10 cm = 4.0 in.
10 mm = 0.4 in.	11 cm = 4.4 in.
	12 cm = 4.8 in.
1.0 cm = 0.4 in.	13 cm = 5.2 in.
1.5 cm = 0.6 in.	14 cm = 5.6 in.
2.0 cm = 0.8 in.	15 cm = 6.0 in.
2.5 cm = 1.0 in.	16 cm = 6.4 in.
3.0 cm = 1.2 in.	17 cm = 6.8 in.
3.5 cm = 1.4 in.	18 cm = 7.2 in.
4.0 cm = 1.6 in.	19 cm = 7.6 in.
4.5 cm = 1.8 in.	20 cm = 8.0 in.
5.0 cm = 2.0 in.	25 cm = 10 in.
5.5 cm = 2.2 in.	30 cm = 12 in. (1 ft.)
6.0 cm = 2.4 in.	35 cm = 14 in.
6.5 cm = 2.6 in.	40 cm = 16 in.
7.0 cm = 2.8 in.	45 cm = 18 in.
8.0 cm = 3.2 in.	50 cm = 20 in.
9.0 cm = 3.6 in.	60 cm = 24 in. (2 ft.)

WHERE TO BUY TULIP SPECIES

The more commonly grown tulip species and their associated cultivars, such as the various forms of *Tulipa clusiana*, *T. linifolia* (including *T. batalinii*), and *T. praestans*, can be found almost anywhere that tulip bulbs are sold. The following firms have more extensive lists, and their catalogues and web pages are well worth browsing to find some of the less widely available tulip species.

CANADA

Pacific Rim Native Plant Nursery
P.O. Box 413
Chilliwack, V2P 6J7
British Columbia
www.hillkeep.ca

Thimble Farms
175 Arbutus Road
Salt Spring Island, V8K 1A3
British Columbia
www.thimblefarms.com

UNITED KINGDOM

Avon Bulbs
Burnt House Farm
Mid Lambrook
South Petherton
Somerset TA13 5HE
www.avonbulbs.com

Bloms Bulbs
Primrose Nurseries
Melchbourne
Bedfordshire MK44 1ZZ
www.blomsbulbs.com

Broadleigh Gardens
Bishops Hull
Taunton
Somerset TA4 1AE
www.broadleighbulbs.co.uk

Miniature Bulbs UK
9 Greengate Drive
Knaresborough
North Yorkshire HG5 9EN
www.miniaturebulbs.co.uk

Pottertons Nursery
Moortown Road
Nettleton
Caistor
Lincolnshire LN7 6HX
www.pottertons.co.uk

Rare Plants
(Paul Christian)
P.O. Box 468
Wrexham LL13 9XR
www.rareplants.co.uk

Van Tubergen UK
Thetford Road
Bressingham
Diss
Norfolk IP22 2AG
www.vantubergen.co.uk

UNITED STATES

Brent and Becky's Bulbs
7900 Daffodil Lane
Gloucester, Virginia 23061
www.brentandbeckysbulbs.com

Bulbmeister.COM
4407 Town Vu Road
Bentonville, Arkansas 72712
www.bulbmeister.com

Odyssey Bulbs
8984 Meadow Lane
Berrien Springs, Michigan 49103
www.odysseybulbs.com

GLOSSARY

Acuminate Gradually narrowing to a point.

Acute With a sharp point.

Anther The pollen-producing part of the stamen.

Apical At the tip or apex.

Arachnoid Fine, interlaced, web-like.

Axil The angle formed where a leaf joins the stem.

Bract A leaf-like organ associated with a flower or inflorescence.

Calyx The collective term for the sepals or outer perianth, which protect the other flower parts during their development.

Carinate Keeled.

Carpel The female parts of a flower, normally consisting of an ovary, style, and stigma.

Cilia Fine hairs, usually numerous.

Ciliate Fringed with fine hairs.

Ciliolate Fringed with minute hairs.

Claw Narrowed base of a petal.

Connective A continuation of the filament that joins on to the anther.

Contractile Able to shorten and pull, as in a contractile root.

Corolla The collective term for the petals or inner perianth.

Dehisce Splitting open at maturity.

Deltoid Triangular.

Dentate Toothed.

Ellipsoid Elliptical in outline.

Falcate Sickle-shaped.

Filament The stalk that holds the anther.

Free Separate, not joined or fused.

Glabrous Hairless.

Glaucescent Becoming glaucous.

Glaucous With a waxy, blue-grey bloom.

Inflorescence The arrangement of the flowering part of a plant.

Lanceolate Narrow and tapering, lance-shaped.

Linear Long and narrow, with parallel sides.

Nectar A sugary solution produced to attract pollinators.

Oblanceolate Lance-shaped but broadest towards the tip.

Oblong Rectangular with rounded end, when referring to leaves.

Obovate With an egg-shaped outline but broadest towards the tip.

Obtuse Blunt or rounded.

Ovary The part of the carpel that contains the ovules, which develop into seeds after fertilization.

Ovate With an egg-shaped outline.

Peduncle The stalk of an inflorescence.

Perianth The outer, non-reproductive parts of a flower, either consisting of two distinct whorls (the calyx and corolla) or two whorls that are not differentiated.

Perianth segment One part of the perianth, usually used when the two whorls of the perianth are not differentiated into petals and sepals.

Petal One segment of the corolla, often brightly coloured.

Petiole The stalk of a leaf.

Prostrate Lying flat.

Pubescent Covered with fine, short hairs.

Reflexed Bent back sharply.

Rhomboid Diamond-shaped.

Sepal One segment of the calyx.

Sessile Without a stalk.

Spathulate Spoon-shaped.

Stamen One of the male reproductive parts of a flower, usually comprising the anther, connective, and filament.

Stigma The receptive tip of the style, which receives pollen.

Stolon A long stem that bends down to the ground or grows underground and roots at a node.

Stoloniferous Bearing stolons.

Style The part of the carpel that bears the stigma.

Superior Referring to an ovary that is inserted above the other floral organs.

Tepals The segments of the perianth, when not differentiated into sepals and petals.

Terminal At the end.

Toothed With small, pointed projections along the margin.

Tunic The dry outer covering of a bulb or corm.

Undulate With a wavy edge or surface.

BIBLIOGRAPHY

Baker, J. G. 1874. Revision of the genera and species of *Tulipae*. *Journal of the Linnean Society* 14: 211–310.

Baker, J. G. 1875. *Tulipa greigii. Curtis's Botanical Magazine* 101: t. 6177.

Baker, J. G. 1879. *Tulipa schrenkii. Curtis's Botanical Magazine* 105: t. 6439.

Baker, J. G. 1883. The species of *Tulipa*—VI. *Gardeners' Chronicle*, ser. 2, 20: 71.

Baker, J. G. 1884. *Tulipa kesselringii. Curtis's Botanical Magazine* 110: t. 6754.

Baker, J. G. 1891. *Tulipa sintenisii. Curtis's Botanical Magazine* 117: t. 7193.

Baytop, T., and B. Mathew. 1984. *The Bulbous Plants of Turkey*. London: Batsford.

Boissier, E. 1842–1859. *Diagnoses Plantarum Orientalium Novarum*. 3 vols. Leipzig.

Boissier, E. 1882. *Flora Orientalis*. Vol. 5. Geneva. 191–201.

Botschantzeva, Z. P. 1982. *Tulips: Taxonomy, Morphology, Cytology, Phytogeography and Physiology*. Translated and edited by H. Q. Varekamp. Rotterdam: A. A. Balkema.

Briggs, M. 1990. First record of *Tulipa goulimyi* (Liliaceae) on Crete. *Annales Musei Goulandris* 8: 41–44.

Davis, P. H., ed. 1966–1985. *Flora of Turkey and the East Aegean Islands*. 9 vols. Edinburgh: Edinburgh University Press.

Davis, P. H., ed. 1988. *Flora of Turkey and the East Aegean Islands*. Vol. 10 (Supplement 1). Edinburgh: Edinburgh University Press.

Don, D. 1836. *Orithyia uniflora*. In R. Sweet. *The British Flower Garden*, ser. 2, 4: t. 336.

Dykes, W. R. 1925. Some wild species of tulip. *Journal of the Royal Horticultural Society* 50: 250–256.

Feinbrun-Dothan, N. 1986. *Flora Palaestina*. Vol. 4. Jerusalem: The Israel Academy of Sciences and Humanities. 39–43.

Gawler, J. B. 1805. *Tulipa suaveolens. Curtis's Botanical Magazine* 22: t. 839.

Grey-Wilson, C., and V. Matthews. 1980. *Tulipa* L. In Tutin et al. *Flora Europaea.* Vol. 5. Cambridge, England: Cambridge University Press. 28–31.

Güner, A., N. Özhatay, T. Ekim, K. Hüsnü, and C. Baser, eds. 2001. *Flora of Turkey and the East Aegean Islands.* Vol. 11 (Supplement 2). Edinburgh: Edinburgh University Press.

Hall, A. D. 1929. *The Book of the Tulip.* London: Martin Hopkinson.

Hall, A. D. 1940. *The Genus* Tulipa. London: Royal Horticultural Society.

Hall, A. D. 1943. *Tulipa whittallii. Curtis's Botanical Magazine* 164: t. 9649.

Hoog, J. 1902a. *Tulipa ingens*, spec. nova. *Gardeners' Chronicle,* ser. 3, 32: 14.

Hoog, J. 1902b. *Tulipa wilsoniana*, spec. nova. *Gardeners' Chronicle*, ser. 3, 32: 50.

Hoog, M. H. 1973. On the origin of *Tulipa. Lilies and Other Liliaceae.* 47–64.

Hooker, W. J. 1827. *Tulipa stellata. Curtis's Botanical Magazine* 54: t. 2762.

Jäger, E. J. 1973. Zur Verbreitung und Lebensgeschichte der Wildtulpe (*Tulipa sylvestris* L.) und Bemerkungen zur Chorologie der Gattung *Tulipa* L. *Hercynia* 10: 429–448.

Jonasson, I. 1999. Tulip spring. *Quarterly Bulletin of the Alpine Garden Society* 67 (3): 265–274.

Koch, C. 1849. Beitrage zu Ciner Flora des Orientes. *Linnaea* 22: 177–336.

Levier, E. 1884. Les Tulipes de l'Europe. *Bulletin de la Société des Sciences Naturelles de Neuchâtel* 14: 201–312.

Lindley, J. 1827. *Tulipa montana. Botanical Register* 13: t. 1106.

Maire, R. 1959. *Flora de l'Afrique du Nord.* Vol. 6. Paris: Éditions Paul Lechevalier. 102–105.

Marais, W. 1984. *Tulipa* L. In P. H. Davis, ed. *Flora of Turkey and the East Aegean Islands.* Vol. 8. Edinburgh: Edinburgh University Press. 302–311.

Matin, F., and M. Iranshahr. 1998. *Tulipa wendelboi. Iranian Journal of Botany* 7: 228.

Maunder, M., R. S. Cowan, P. Stranc, and M. F. Fay. 2001. The genetic status and conservation management of two cultivated bulb species extinct in the wild: *Tecophilaea cyanocrocus* (Chile) and *Tulipa sprengeri* (Turkey). *Conservation Genetics* 2: 193–201.

Meikle, R. D. 1985. *Flora of Cyprus* 2. Kew: Bentham-Moxon Trust. 1596–1599.

Pavord, A. 1999. *The Tulip.* London: Bloomsbury.

Phillips, R., and M. Rix. 1989. *Bulbs.* London: Pan Books.

Phillips, R., and M. Rix. 2002. *The Botanical Garden*. Vol. 2. London: Macmillan.

Prudhomme, J. 1996. Étude des Tulipes de France et de Suisse. *Bulletin Mensuel de la Société Linnéenne de Lyon* 65 (9): 284–295.

Raamsdonk, L. W. D. van, and T. de Vries. 1992. Biosystematic studies in *Tulipa* sect. *Eriostemones* (Liliaceae). *Plant Systematics and Evolution* 179: 27–41.

Raamsdonk, L. W. D. van, and T. de Vries. 1995. Species relationships and taxonomy in *Tulipa* subg. *Tulipa* (Liliaceae). *Plant Systematics and Evolution* 195: 13–44.

Reboul, E. de. 1847. Sulle divisione del genere *Tulipa* in sezioni naturali. *Giornale Botanico Italiano* 2: 57–61.

Rechinger, K. H., ed. 1990. *Flora Iranica*. Vol. 165. Graz, Austria: Akademische Druck. 76–102.

Regel, E. A. 1873. Enumeratio specierum hucusque cognitarum generis *Tulipae*. *Acta Horti Petropolitani* 2: 437–457.

Scheepen, J. van. 1996. *Classified List and International Register of Tulip Names*. The Netherlands: KAVB.

Sealy, J. R. 1948. *Tulipa clusiana* var. *chrysantha*. *Curtis's Botanical Magazine* 165: t. NS13.

Sealy, J. R. 1957. *Tulipa edulis*. *Curtis's Botanical Magazine* 171: t. 293.

Sealy, J. R. 1963. *Tulipa montana*. *Curtis's Botanical Magazine* 174: t. 433.

Sealy, J. R. 1970. *Tulipa humilis* forma. *Curtis's Botanical Magazine* 178: t. 571.

Smales, R. 2004. Darwin and Darwinhybrid tulips. *Daffodils with Snowdrops and Tulips* 2004–2005: 55–58.

Stapf, O. 1925. *Tulipa humilis*. *Curtis's Botanical Magazine* 151: t. 9048.

Stapf, O. 1928. *Tulipa lanata*. *Curtis's Botanical Magazine* 152: t. 9151.

Stapf, O. 1932. *Tulipa urumiensis*. *Curtis's Botanical Magazine* 155: t. 9288.

Stapf, O. 1933. *Tulipa tarda*. *Curtis's Botanical Magazine* 156: t. 9321.

Strid, A., and K. Tan, eds. 1991. *Mountain Flora of Greece*. Vol. 2. Edinburgh: Edinburgh University Press. 667–672.

Tubergen, C. G. van. 1947. *New Bulbous and Tuberous Rooted Plants Introduced into Cultivation by C. G. van Tubergen Ltd*. Haarlem, Holland: C. G. van Tubergen. 25–33.

Turrill, W. B. 1934a. *Tulipa cypria*. *Curtis's Botanical Magazine* 157: t. 9363.

Turrill, W. B. 1934b. *Tulipa kuschkensis*. *Curtis's Botanical Magazine* 157: t. 9370.

Turrill, W. B. 1934c. *Tulipa stapfii. Curtis's Botanical Magazine* 157: t. 9356.

Vvedensky, A. I. 1935. *Tulipa* L. In V. L. Komarov, ed. *Flora of the USSR*. Vol. 4. (English edition, 1968). Leningrad: Izdatel'stvo Akademii Nauk SSSR. 246–280.

Wallis, B. 1998. The bulb frame through the year. *Quarterly Bulletin of the Alpine Garden Society* 66 (3): 250–258.

Wendelbo, P. 1977. *Tulips and Irises of Iran and Their Relatives*. Tehran: Botanical Institute of Iran.

Wendelbo, P. 1985. *Tulipa* L. In C. C. Townsend and E. Guest, eds. *Flora of Iraq*. Vol. 8, *Monocotyledones (excluding Gramineae)*. Baghdad: Department of Agriculture and Agrarian Reform. 82–87.

INDEX

Page numbers in **bold type** indicate colour photographs.

Amana edulis, 173, **174**–175
Amana erythronioides, 174
Amana graminifolia, 173, 174
Amana latifolia, 174

horned tulip. See *Tulipa acuminata*

lady tulip. See *Tulipa clusiana*

Orithyia dasystemon. See *Tulipa dasystemon*
Orithyia edulis. See *Amana edulis*
Orithyia uniflora. See *Tulipa uniflora*
Ornithogalum uniflorum. See *Tulipa uniflora*

Tulipa acuminata, **74**–75, 145
Tulipa agenensis, 17, 18, 24, 54, 64, 75–76, 77, 78, 96, 97, 132, 138, 139
   subsp. *sharonensis*, 75–76
Tulipa aitchisonii, 60, 61, 68, 76, 92–94, 150
   subsp. *cashmeriana*, 93
   var. *clusianoides*, 76
Tulipa 'Aladdin', 186, **195**
Tulipa 'Alanya'. See *T. humilis* 'Alanya'
Tulipa albertii, 15, 55, 64, 76–77, 89, 169

Tulipa 'Albocaerulea Oculata'. See *T. humilis* 'Albocaerulea Oculata'
Tulipa aleppensis, 64, 77–78, 166
Tulipa 'Ali Baba'. See *T. greigii* 'Ali Baba'
Tulipa altaica, 16, 66, **78**–79, 102, 113, 114, 119, 158
   var. *ferganica*, 79, 102
Tulipa amabilis, 64, 79
Tulipa 'Ancilla'. See *T. kaufmanniana* 'Ancilla'
Tulipa anisophylla, 66, 79–80
Tulipa 'Apeldoorn', **178**, 182
Tulipa 'Apeldoorn's Elite', 182
Tulipa 'Apricot Beauty', 179
Tulipa 'Apricot Impression', 183
Tulipa 'Apricot Jewel'. See *T. linifolia* 'Apricot Jewel'
Tulipa 'Arabian Mystery', 182
Tulipa armena, 17, **28**, 63, **80**–81, 104, 146
   f. *galatica*, 80, 104
   var. *lycica*, 81
Tulipa 'Artist', 187
Tulipa aucheriana, 16, **56**, 70, 81–82, 95, 113
Tulipa australis, 18, 54, 69, 70, 82, 152, 168

Tulipa aximensis, **73**, 82

Tulipa bakeri, 18, **19**, 20, 25, 29, 70, 82–84, 95, 144
   'Lilac Wonder', **83**, 84, 144

Tulipa 'Ballade', **185**, 186

Tulipa 'Ballerina', **177**, 186

Tulipa batalinii, 68, 84, 125–126

Tulipa biebersteiniana, 17, 69, 84–85, 138, 154, 155, 168

Tulipa biflora, 16, 17, 28, 29, 51, **52**, 54, 58, **71**, 72, 85–86, 87, 138, 146, 147, 162, 163, 167

Tulipa bifloriformis, 15, 16, 29, 60, 71, 86–**87**, 135, 163
   'Starlight', 87

Tulipa binutans, 71, 87

Tulipa bithynica, 61

Tulipa 'Black Parrot', 188

Tulipa 'Blue Diamond', 188

Tulipa 'Blue Heron', 187

Tulipa 'Blue Parrot', 188

Tulipa boeotica. See *T. undulatifolia*

Tulipa 'Bonsoir', 188

Tulipa borszczowii, 15, 16, 64, 87–**88**

Tulipa breyniana, 54

Tulipa 'Bright Gem'. See *T. linifolia* 'Bright Gem'

Tulipa 'Bronze Charm'. See *T. linifolia* 'Bronze Charm'

Tulipa butkovii, 61, 64, 77, **89**, 169

Tulipa carinata, 64, 90

Tulipa cashmeriana. See *T. clusiana* f. *cashmeriana*

Tulipa celsiana, 18, **54**, 69, 90, 152, 153–154, 155

Tulipa chitralensis. See *T. clusiana*

Tulipa chrysantha, 68, 90, 93, 94, 131

Tulipa 'Cindy'. See *T. mauritiana* 'Cindy'

Tulipa cinnabarina, 17, 69, 70, 91

Tulipa clusiana, 16, 17, 18, 24, 26, 28, 37, 42, **43**, 54, 60, 61, 68, 69, 76, 90, 92, **93**–95, 119, 129, 131, 149, 150, 190
   f. *cashmeriana*, 93–95
   var. *chrysantha*, 93–94
   'Cynthia', **6**, 94
   f. *dinae*, 93–94
   'Honky Tonk', **95**
   'Lady Jane', **94**, 95
   'Sheila', 95
   f. *stellata*, 93–95, 150
   'Tinka', 95, **191**
   'Tubergen's Gem', 94, **195**

Tulipa confusa, 80

Tulipa cornuta. See *T. acuminata*

Tulipa 'Couleur Cardinal', 182, 187

Tulipa 'Cummins', **186**, 187

Tulipa cuspidata, 156

Tulipa cretica, 18, 20, 44, 57, 70, 95–**96**

Tulipa 'Cynthia'. See *T. clusiana* 'Cynthia'

Tulipa cypria, 18, 64, 76, 96–97

Tulipa dasystemon, 15, 67, 71, 97–**98**, 131, 132, 133, 158

Tulipa dasystemonoides, 15, 71, 98

Tulipa didieri, 73, 98, 104, 132, 137

Tulipa doerfleri, 18, 69, **99**

Tulipa 'Dordogne', 183, **184**

Tulipa dubia, 53, 64, 66, 99–100, 118

Tulipa 'Duc van Thol', 145, 150, 180

Tulipa 'Eastern Star'. See *T. humilis* 'Eastern Star'

Tulipa edulis, 173, 174
   var. *latifolia*, 173

Tulipa eichleri, 17, 24, 44, 58, 64, 100–**101**, 129, 166
   var. *micheliana*, 129

Tulipa erythronioides, 173, 174

Tulipa ferganica, 15, 44, 60, 66, 79, 101–102

Tulipa 'Flair', **180**

Tulipa 'Flava'. See *T. orphanidea* 'Flava'

Tulipa fosteriana, 15, 24, 26, 42, 58, 64, 90, 102–**103**, 106, 108, 109, 115, 123, 124, 177, 182, 189, 190, 193

  'Golden Emperor', 190, **193**

  'Madame Lefeber'. See 'Red Emperor'

  'Orange Emperor', 190

  'Purissima'. See 'White Emperor'

  'Purissima King', 190

  'Red Emperor', **58**, 103, 190

  'White Emperor', 190

  'Yellow Purissima', 190

Tulipa 'Fusilier'. See *T. praestans* 'Fusilier'

Tulipa galatica, **28**, 63, 80, 104

Tulipa 'Generaal de Wet', 179

Tulipa gesneriana, 54, 55, 63, 73, 104, 113, 142, 168

Tulipa 'Giuseppe Verdi'. See *T. kaufmanniana* 'Giuseppe Verdi'

Tulipa 'Golden Apeldoorn', 182

Tulipa 'Golden Emperor'. See *T. fosteriana* 'Golden Emperor'

Tulipa goulimyi, 18, **19**, 69, 105

Tulipa graminifolia, 173

Tulipa 'Green Wave', 188

Tulipa greigii, 15, 16, 24, 25, 53, 58, 64, **65**, 105, **106**, **107**, 108, 128, 177, 189, 190

  'Ali Baba', **192**

  'Pinocchio', 190, **195**

  'Quebec', 190

  'Red Riding Hood', **26**, 190

Tulipa grengiolensis, 24, 73, 108, 127

Tulipa grey-wilsonii, 61

Tulipa 'Groenland', 187, 188

Tulipa hageri, 18, 24, 61, 69, 99, 108, 133, 134, 149

  'Splendens', 108–**109**

Tulipa 'Halcro', **184**

Tulipa 'Hamilton', 187

Tulipa hellespontica. See *T. orphanidea*

Tulipa heteropetala, 16, 60, 67, 167

Tulipa heterophylla, 60, 67, 167

Tulipa heweri, 64, 140

Tulipa 'Honky Tonk'. See *T. clusiana* 'Honky Tonk'

Tulipa hoogiana, 16, **59**, 64, 79, 109, 123, 124, 161, 162

Tulipa humilis, 16, 17, 24, **34**, 35, 42, 60, 70, **71**, 81, 82, 91, 95, 96, 110, **111**–113, 121, 141, 169, 190

  'Alanya', **112**

  'Albocaerulea Oculata', 113

  'Eastern Star', 112

  'Liliput', 112

  'Odalisque', 112

  'Persian Pearl', 112

  'Violacea Black Base', 112

  Violacea Group, 112, 169

  'Violacea Yellow Base', 112

Tulipa hungarica, 63, 73, 104, 113, 168

  subsp. *rhodopea*, 113, 142

  var. *urumoffii*. See *T. urumoffii*

Tulipa iliensis, 15, **47**, 66, 79, 113–**114**

Tulipa ingens, 15, 25, 44, 59, 64, 109, 114, **115**, 116, 123

Tulipa 'Ivory Floradale', **183**

Tulipa julia, 17, 24, 59, 64, 76, 77, **116**–117, 164

Tulipa karabachensis, 80

Tulipa karamanica. See *T. cinnabarina*

Tulipa kaufmanniana, **8**, 15, 28, 37, 53, 55, 58, 59, 64, 89, 99, 100, 106, 107, 108, 117–**118**, 160, 177, 189, 190

  'Ancilla', 24, **189**

  'Giuseppe Verdi', **2**, 189

  'Scarlet Baby', 190

  'Showwinner', 190

  'Stressa', 189

Tulipa kesselringii. See *T. tetraphylla*

Tulipa kolpakowskiana, 15, 16, 24, 35, 37, 44, 58, **66**, 79, 80, 102, 113, 114, 119, 136, 137, 141, 158, 160

  coccinea. See *T. ostrowskiana*

  var. *humilis*. See *T. anisophylla*

Tulipa korolkowii, 16, 34, 66, **120**–121, 125

  'Bicolour', 121

Tulipa kurdica, 17, 70, 113, 121

Tulipa kuschkensis, 59, 64, 122

Tulipa 'Lady Jane'. See *T. clusiana* 'Lady Jane'

Tulipa lanata, 25, 64, 109, 115, 122, **123**, 124, 161

Tulipa latifolia, 173

Tulipa lehmanniana, 15, 16, 66, 120, 124, 171, 172

Tulipa 'Lilac Wonder'. See *T. bakeri* 'Lilac Wonder'

Tulipa 'Liliput'. See *T. humilis* 'Liliput'

Tulipa linifolia, 15, 24, 26, 37, 42, 58, 68, 84, 92, **125**–127, 128, 129

  'Apricot Jewel', 126

  Batalinii Group, 84, 126–127, 190

  'Bright Gem', **127**

  'Bronze Charm', 127

  var. *chrysantha*, 126

  'Red Gem', 127

  'Red Hunter', 127

  'Yellow Jewel', 127

Tulipa lownei, 111

Tulipa 'Madame Lefeber'. See *T. fosteriana* 'Red Emperor'

Tulipa maleolens, 73

Tulipa marjolletii, 73, 127

Tulipa mauritiana, 73, 128

  'Cindy', 128

Tulipa maximowiczii, 68, 125–126, 128

Tulipa micheliana, 59, 64, 128–129

Tulipa mogoltavica. See *T. greigii*

Tulipa montana, 16, 22, 24, 26, 58, **68**, 90, 92, 93, 94, 97, 125, 126, 129, **130**, 131, 171

  var. *chrysantha*, 131

Tulipa 'Monte Carlo', **181**

Tulipa 'Mount Zaghouan'. See *T. sylvestris* 'Mount Zaghouan'

Tulipa mucronata, 80

Tulipa neustruevae, 15, 71, 131–**132**

Tulipa oculus-solis, 55, 75–76, 78, 132

  var. *aleppica*. See *T. aleppensis*

Tulipa 'Odalisque'. See *T. humilis* 'Odalisque'

Tulipa 'Orange Apeldoorn', 182

Tulipa 'Orange Emperor'. See *T. fosteriana* 'Orange Emperor'

Tulipa 'Orange Princess', 188

Tulipa 'Orange Queen', 182

Tulipa oreophila, 61

Tulipa orithyioides, 15, 67, 71, 133

Tulipa orphanidea, 18, 42, **57**, 61, 69, 70, 91, 92, 99, 105, 108, 133, **134**, 135, 149, 160, 170, 171

  'Flava', **135**

  Whittallii Group, 171

Tulipa orthopoda, 71, 87, 135–**136**

Tulipa ostrowskiana, 15, 58, 66, 120, 136–**137**, 159

Tulipa paradasystemon. See *T. neustruevae*

Tulipa passeriniana, 73, 137

Tulipa patens, 16, 17, 69, 137–138, 154, 155

Tulipa 'Persian Pearl'. See *T. humilis* 'Persian Pearl'

Tulipa persica. See *T. celsiana*

  praecox. See *T. clusiana*

Tulipa 'Pink Impression', 183

Tulipa 'Pinocchio'. See *T. greigii* 'Pinocchio'

Tulipa planifolia, 73, 138, 143

Tulipa platystigma, 73, 138

Tulipa polychroma, 58, 71, 86, 138

Tulipa praecox, 18, 55, 64, 132, 138–139, 166

Tulipa praestans, 15, 37, 42, 55, 64, **139**–141, 150
  'Fusilier', **140**
  'Unicum', 140
  'Van Tubergen's Variety', 140
  'Zwanenburg Variety', 140

Tulipa primulina, 18, 69, 70, 141, 152, 155

Tulipa 'Prinses Irene', **182**, 188

Tulipa pulchella, 70, 110–112, 141
  violacea. See *T. humilis*

Tulipa 'Purissima'. See *T. fosteriana* 'White Emperor'

Tulipa 'Purissima King'. See *T. fosteriana* 'Purissima King'

Tulipa 'Quebec'. See *T. greigii* 'Quebec'

Tulipa 'Queen of Night', 183

Tulipa 'Red Emperor'. See *T. fosteriana* 'Red Emperor'

Tulipa 'Red Gem'. See *T. linifolia* 'Red Gem'

Tulipa 'Red Hunter'. See *T. linifolia* 'Red Hunter'

Tulipa 'Red Princess', 188

Tulipa 'Red Riding Hood'. See *T. greigii* 'Red Riding Hood'

Tulipa 'Red Wing', 187

Tulipa regelii, 34, 59, 72, 141–**142**

Tulipa rhodopea, 63, 73, 113, 142, 168

Tulipa 'Rococo', 187, **188**

Tulipa sarracenica, 73, 143

Tulipa saxatilis, **11**, 18, 20, 25, 29, 36, **43**, 44, 70, 82–84, 95, **143**–144
  Bakeri Group 'Lilac Wonder'. See *T. bakeri* 'Lilac Wonder'

Tulipa 'Scarlet Baby'. See *T. kaufmanniana* 'Scarlet Baby'

Tulipa schrenkii, 17, **63**, 104, 144–145, 150

Tulipa sharonensis. See *T. agenensis* subsp. *sharonensis*

Tulipa 'Sheila'. See *T. clusiana* 'Sheila'

Tulipa 'Shirley', 182

Tulipa 'Showwinner'. See *T. kaufmanniana* 'Showwinner'

Tulipa sinkiangensis, 67

Tulipa sintenisii, 17, 58, 63, 104, 145–**146**

Tulipa 'Snowstar', **178**

Tulipa sogdiana, 69, 71, 146–147

Tulipa 'Sorbet', 183

Tulipa sosnovskyi, 17, 64, 147

Tulipa 'Splendens'. See *T. hageri* 'Splendens'

Tulipa sprengeri, 22, 34, 37, 42, 45, 56, 69, 70, 146, 147, **148**, 149

Tulipa 'Spring Green', 187

Tulipa stapfii, 64, 149, 156–157

Tulipa 'Starlight'. See *T. bifloriformis* 'Starlight'

Tulipa stellata, 61, 68, 92–93, 149

Tulipa 'Stressa'. See *T. kaufmanniana* 'Stressa'

Tulipa suaveolens, 54, 55, 73, 140, 145, 150

Tulipa subpraestans, 24, **37**, 60, 64, 150–**151**

Tulipa sylvestris, 14, 16, 18, 24, 34, **41**, 42, 44, 54, 55, 69, 70, 82, 84–85, 90, 104, 133, 137, 138, 141, 151–**154**, 155, 156, 168
  subsp. *australis*, **70**, 82, 84, 90, 152–154
  subsp. *australis* var. *celsiana*, 155
  var. *biebersteiniana*, 85
  'Mount Zaghouan', **153**
  subsp. *primulina*, 155
  'Tabriz Variety', 152

Tulipa 'Synaeda King', 186

Tulipa systola, 16, 17, 26, **27**, 64, **65**, 76, 88, 149, 155, **156**, 157, 165

Tulipa 'Tabriz Variety'. See *T. sylvestris* 'Tabriz Variety'

Tulipa 'Tangerine Beauty'. See *T. vvedenskyi* 'Tangerine Beauty'

Tulipa tarda, 15, 25, 26, 29, 34, 37, 42, 45, 71, 97, 133, **157**–158

Tulipa tetraphylla, 15, 66, 137, 158–**159**

subsp. *ostrowskiana*, 137, 159

Tulipa theophrasti, 69, 160

Tulipa thracica. See *T. orphanidea*

Tulipa 'Tinka'. See *T. clusiana* 'Tinka'

Tulipa 'Tity's Star'. See *T. urumiensis* 'Tity's Star'

Tulipa tschimganica, 15, 53, **61**, 64, 66, 100, 118, 160

Tulipa tubergeniana, 59, 64, 109, 110, 115, 123, 124, 161–162

Tulipa 'Tubergen's Gem'. See *T. clusiana* 'Tubergen's Gem'

Tulipa turkestanica, 15, 22, 24, 27, 29, **30**, 35, 42, **45**, 71, 86, 87, 162–**163**

Tulipa ulophylla, 16, 64, **164**–165

Tulipa 'Uncle Tom', 188

Tulipa undulatifolia, 17, 18, 57, 64, 100, 101, 132, 165–**166**

Tulipa 'Unicum'. See *T. praestans* 'Unicum'

Tulipa uniflora, 16, 30, 54, 60, **67**, 166–167, 173

Tulipa urumiensis, 42, 58, 69, 167–168

'Tity's Star', 168

Tulipa urumoffii, 63, 73, 113, 142, 168

Tulipa 'Van Tubergens' Variety'. See *T. praestans* 'Van Tubergens' Variety'

Tulipa violacea, 70, 110, 112, 169

var. *pallida*, 111, 113

Tulipa vvedenskyi, 15, **29**, **49**, 61, 64, 77, 89, 169–170

'Tangerine Beauty', 24, **170**

Tulipa wendelboi, 64, 165

Tulipa 'West Point', 186

Tulipa 'White Emperor'. See *T. fosteriana* 'White Emperor'

Tulipa 'White Triumphator', 186

Tulipa whittallii, 18, 61, 69, 133, 135, 170–**171**

Tulipa wilsoniana, 58, 68, 131, 171

Tulipa 'Wirosa', 188

Tulipa 'Yellow Jewel'. See *T. linifolia* 'Yellow Jewel'

Tulipa 'Yellow Purissima'. See *T. fosteriana* 'Yellow Purissima'

Tulipa zenaidae, 61, 66, 171–172

Tulipa 'Zwanenburg Variety'. See *T. praestans* 'Zwanenburg Variety'

waterlily tulip. See *Tulipa kaufmanniana*